Aging and Skilled Performance
Advances in Theory and Applications

Aging and Skill Conference Participants. Photo by Kristen Gilbert. *First Row:* Beth Fraser Cabrera, Brian Cooper, Sherry Mead, Neff Walker. *Second Row:* Tom Hess, Mark Detweiler, Regina Colonia-Willner, Pam Tsang, Fredda Blanchard-Fields, Joyce Harris, Denise Park, Wendy Rogers, Katharina Echt, Peter Hancock. *Third Row:* Art Kramer, Phillip Ackerman, Don Fisher, Dan Fisk, Neil Charness, Sara Czaja, Catherine Kelley, David Kurzman, Chris Miller. *Fourth Row:* Gabe Rousseau, Chris Hertzog, Darin Ellis, Gus Craik, Dave Meyer, Rich Jagacinski, Susan Kemper, Brian Jamieson, Ken Watkins, Roger Morrell, Bob Widner-Caballero. *Not Pictured:* Kristen Gilbert and Fernando Gonzalez.

Aging and Skilled Performance
Advances in Theory and Applications

Edited by

Wendy A. Rogers
The University of Georgia

Arthur D. Fisk
Neff Walker
Georgia Institute of Technology

LEA LAWRENCE ERLBAUM ASSOCIATES, PUBLISHERS
1996 Mahwah, New Jersey

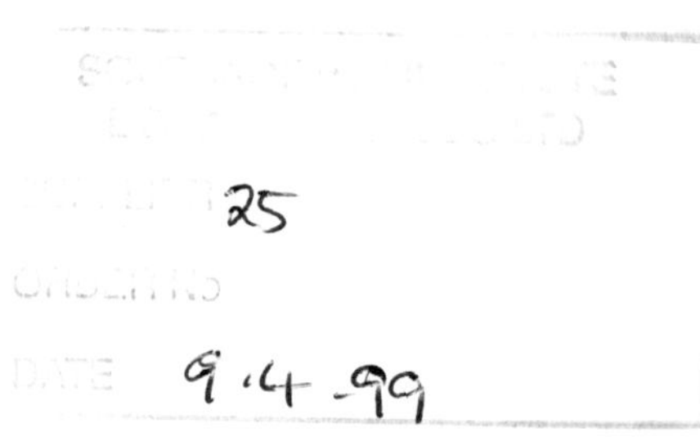

Lawrence Erlbaum Associates, Inc., Publishers
10 Industrial Avenue
Mahwah, New Jersey 07430

Library of Congress Cataloging-in-Publication Data

Aging and skilled performance : advances in theory and applications / edited by Wendy A. Rogers, Arthur D. Fisk, Neff Walker.
p. cm.
Papers originally presented at the Aging and Skill Conference sponsored by the Center for Applied Cognitive Research on Aging, Feb. 1995.
Includes bibliographical references and indexes.
ISBN 0-8058-1909-6 (cloth). — ISBN 0-8058-1910-X (paper)
1. Cognition in old age—Congresses. 2. Cognition—Age factors--Congresses. I. Rogers, Wendy A. II. Fisk, Arthur D. III. Walker, Neff. IV. Aging and Skill Conference (1995)
BF724.85.C64A38 1996
155.67—dc20 96-17205
CIP

Books published by Lawrence Erlbaum Associates are printed on acid-free paper, and their bindings are chosen for strength and durability.

Printed in the United States of America
10 9 8 7 6 5 4 3 2 1

To our parents

Carol and Jerry Rogers
Jackie Johnson and Art Fisk
Beth Walker and Pat Walker

Contents

Preface

The term *skill* encompasses an array of topics and issues. For example, individuals are skilled in a variety of domains (chess, typing, air traffic control, knitting); researchers study skill in a variety of ways (speed of acquisition, accuracy of performance, retention over time), and there are a variety of approaches to the study of skill (computer modeling, experimental analysis). Contributing to the understanding of whether, how, when, and why skills may decline as a function of age is the goal of this volume.

Fisk and Kirlik, in chapter 1, set the stage by explicating the criticality of practically relevant research. The authors argue that research that addresses issues derived from real, practical problems must also be theoretically relevant. Fisher, in chapter 2, provides an elegant example of how mathematical models may be used to understand, and to predict, age-related differences in learning. His research has important implications for the development of training schedules for young and older adults.

Movement control skills are discussed in chapter 3, by Walker, Philbin, and Spruell, as well as in chapter 4 by Jagacinski. Many skills have movement control components; thus, it is crucial to understand basic age-related changes in movement control. Walker et al. investigate how individuals adjust and optimize performance to meet the restrictions of their perceptual-motor system and the task constraints. Jagacinski uses control theory to examine the stability of behaviors and suggests that an understanding of stability may provide insight for compensatory strategies.

The next three chapters illustrate the breadth of areas in which aging and skill have been studied. In the attention domain, Kramer and Larish (chapter 5) investigate age-related differences in dual task performance. They provide evidence that variable priority training strategies can improve acquisition rate and ultimate mastery of a skill. In chapter 6, Craik and Jacoby tie together an established approach to the study of memory (process dissociation procedure) with an established theory of age-related changes (environmental support). They suggest that to fully understand age-related differences in memory it is crucial to separately assess consciously controlled processes from automatic processes. Ackerman's chapter on the study of intelligence for adults (chapter 7) applies a unique approach to understanding the nature of intellectual development across the lifespan. He suggests that knowledge structures (i.e., what an individual knows) become an increasingly important determinant of intellectual life as individuals grow older.

Detweiler, Hess, and Ellis provide a detailed analysis in chapter 8 of skill acquisition on a visual-spatial task. They demonstrate that spatial support can help participants keep track of information but also that older adults are more susceptible to interference due to intervening events. Rogers' discussion in chapter 9 provides a review of the extant literature on the long-term retention of skills for older adults. She points to a number of issues and variables that are not well understood from the perspective of skill-retention across extended periods.

The last three chapters have the unifying theme of technology use by older adults. Czaja, in chapter 10, provides a general review of the impact of technology on the lives of older adults. She also discusses the cognitive skills necessary for successful interactions with technology. Charness, Kelley, Bosman, and Mottram focus in chapter 11 on training individuals to use word processors. They provide suggestions for future research to improve prediction of age-related differences in performance. In chapter 12, Morrell and Echt describe how basic cognitive theory may be used to develop training materials for computer use by older adults. They also suggest that a multidisciplinary approach drawing on education, instructional technology, human factors, and cognitive psychology may be the best way to optimize training materials and training methods.

This book is based on the Aging and Skill Conference (February, 1995) sponsored by the Center for Applied Cognitive Research on Aging (one of the Edward R. Roybal Centers for Research on Applied Gerontology sponsored by the National Institute on Aging). In addition to the speakers, other members of the research community participated in the discussion periods. The conference attendees are pictured on p. ii.

ACKNOWLEDGMENTS

We would like to thank the presenters as well as the other participants in the conference for helping us to make the conference a success. We would also like to acknowledge the many individuals who assisted in various aspects of the conference. Denise Park and Roger Morrell were very helpful during the planning stages of the conference. Chris Miller, the Program Coordinator for the Center, was instrumental in the success of the conference from start to finish. Also, many thanks to the students who helped us with a myriad of details before and during the conference: Beth Fraser Cabrera, Brian Cooper, Kristen Gilbert, Brian Jamieson, Sherry Mead, and Gabe Rousseau.

The editorial staff at Lawrence Erlbaum Associates has been very supportive throughout the process of bringing this book to fruition, and we especially thank Judi Amsel, Kathy Dolan, and Debbie Ruel. We also thank the individuals who assisted in the review process: Richard Abrams, Phillip Allen, Deborah Boehm-Davis, Susan Bovair, Alan Hartley, Christopher Hertzog, Darlene Howard, Richard Jagacinski, David Madden, and Richard Marsh.

Finally, we thank each of the contributors for their dedication to the goal of understanding aging and skill. Each author was asked to discuss the cognitive theory relevant to their topic, discuss how such theory informs the field about aging, discuss where gaps exist among general cognitive theory in this area and theories of aging, and demonstrate the practical relevance of the theory to enhancing or enabling activities of daily living (for work, home, or leisure) for older adults. We believe that they have succeeded admirably.

CHAPTER 1

Practical Relevance and Age-Related Research: Can Theory Advance Without Application?

Arthur D. Fisk
Alex Kirlik
Georgia Institute of Technology

Progress in a scientific field can be measured in a variety of ways. Certainly, theoretical maturity and advancement is one such measure. The ability of a scientific field to motivate and inform solutions of practical importance seems also to be a key measure. As researchers, the authors are often called upon by our students or colleagues to explain the relevance of our work to one theory or another, to defend the theoretical positions we hold, or to simply explain the theoretical advances we hope to make as we embark on a new set of experiments. Generally, such requests provide us little reason for pause. However, when we leave our academic offices we sometimes encounter less than rewarding experiences. More often than not, we feel awkward when discussing our field, say, with acquaintances at parties or during visits from our relatives. We can discuss how our research has been directly applied to the design of training systems to support skill refinement of American football quarterbacks (''Inside the South,'' 1994); yet, when discussing cognition and aging, the examples are not as forthcoming.

Sometimes we are asked how our work in aging can be used to solve a specific problem such as designing a plan to make use of public transportation easier (from a navigation perspective), designing an effective interface and training program to make use of an on-line card catalog system easy and effective, or documenting the best way to ensure that older adults can use various types of new technology currently existing only in the minds of some design team. Such encounters sometimes constrain our otherwise high enthusiasm about the true progress of our theoretical advances.

Psychological research, especially within the field of skill acquisition, should be able to answer the questions mentioned earlier. Our goal for this chapter is to explore the need for an expansion of both domains of study and research techniques to afford the opportunity for more ease in answering questions of a practical nature. We also have set out to discuss details of a set of criteria that would allow such expansion to be productive as well as to discuss the process to achieve such a goal. We highlight evidence in the literature from psychology and other fields that suggests that such a research approach will not only improve the applicability of research findings but also will result in theoretical advances that cannot be gained otherwise. To summarize, our plan for this chapter is to: (a) discuss our definition of research that has practical relevance, (b) outline the characteristics of practically relevant research, (c) present and attempt to dispel some common misconceptions about this class of research, and (d) discuss why such work is important.

WHAT WE DO NOT DEBATE

As a beginning point we wish to emphasize what this chapter is *not* concerned with: This is not a debate about the merits of so called "basic" versus "applied" research. Such an ill-founded debate has been ongoing for far too many years. In such a confrontation one often hears from one side that too few results from the laboratory can be applied because "academic" researchers study meaningless problems and on the other side one can hear that "applied" research has no generality and is conducted by individuals who are not talented enough to do "real science." These are simply inflammatory comments that miss the important issues that should be discussed. The discussion should concern how we solve important scientific and practical problems and why we should decide upon and make use of research techniques that can be most appropriate to address a specified research issue.

DEFINITION OF RESEARCH THAT HAS PRACTICAL RELEVANCE

The concept of practically relevant research is certainly not new. Indeed, the discussion of the need for research with practical relevance has survived the lifetimes of many psychologists. To have practical relevance, research should derive from real, practical problems with the intent to solve those problems, but the work also should be designed to incorporate, build on, and advance theory. It should be clear that every single study conducted will not necessarily solve a real-world problem, just as a single study may not necessarily resolve a complex theoretical issue. Hence, practical relevance must be thought of more broadly in regard to a research program.

Many examples of practically relevant research programs come to mind, for example, Broadbent's early work on attention was driven by the need to solve practical problems encountered by air traffic controllers. Communication theory originated from efforts to deal with the problem of maximizing information transmission over the telephone line. Speech research at the Haskins laboratories began with the problem of building a reading machine for the blind. The ecological approach to perception emerged, in part, from the issue of landing an aircraft.

Adams (1972) pointed out that in the modal case many years pass before the results of research on human abilities have a meaningful impact on technology or in dealing with real-world problems. Yet, attention to real, practical problems when undertaking research can provide valuable tools for delimiting a problem and selecting the most fruitful course for the investigation. In addition, such efforts can speed the recognition of the value of a body of research from a given area and more quickly allow useful application.

CHARACTERISTICS OF PRACTICALLY RELEVANT RESEARCH

This type of research transcends many domains and approaches used to address psychological research issues. Fisher (1993), when discussing the concept of ''Optimal Performance Engineering,'' cogently argued that the well-known trio of empirical, theoretical, and analytical studies are candidates for what we have refered to as practically relevant research. It is not the class of research technique but rather the characteristics of the approach that determine the practical relevance of the work. One useful approach, and an important characteristic, is to design the tasks to be studied in the spirit of Brunswik's concept of representative design (see Hammond, 1966).

Representative design encourages the researcher to give the same care and attention to the issue of sampling task environments as is currently given, say, to the issue of sampling subject populations. The generalizability of research is constrained by the validity of induction from a subject sample to the relevant subject population, as well as by the validity of induction from a sampled task to the population of relevant tasks. Currently, the dimensions of subject variability are perhaps better understood than the dimensions of task variability, and, thus, subject sampling is a more mature enterprise than task sampling. To improve this situation, the theory and logic underlying the selection of an experimental task must be made explicit so that the class of tasks to which findings should generalize can be identified. Thus, the validity of the task sampling theory can be treated empirically and therefore subject to refinement or falsification.

Such an approach requires the use and thorough understanding of task analysis. Task analysis is a concept of complete familiarity to the human factors engineer (Drury, Paramore, Van Cott, Grey, & Corlett, 1987), yet it is a remarkably foreign concept in most psychology laboratories. Use of a task analytic method is important when designing research because it forces one to attend closely to the important factors of the task, environment, subject and subject population, and choice of dependent variables.

The Task

How can such a focus help the research enterprise? Consider first an analysis of the task. There are numerous definitions of what constitutes a *task*. However, there can at least be consensus that a task is a set of activities—for our purposes, mental activities that contribute to a specific functional objective. Drury et al. (1987) outlined the characteristics of a task: Actions are grouped together by their objective and their temporal nature. These actions include perceptions, discriminations, decisions, control actions, and communications. Every task involves some combination of cognitive and physical action. Each task has a stimulus or cue that identifies its starting point. A task also has a stopping point that is identified by some related information or feedback. Tasks usually are defined as units of action performed by a single individual (but see, e.g., issues in team training, Swezey & Salas, 1992).

To perform a proper task analysis one must be able to describe the task, understand the task requirements, and analyze and interpret the task requirements in terms of knowledge and theory about human characteristics. For our purposes, major attention should be directed at understanding cognitive processes and their interaction with the targeted task. Assume we were interested in the issue of age-related time-sharing during multitask performance. One strategy might be to design a dual-task test where two tasks must be performed simultaneously. It is fair to say that most laboratory experiments examining multi-tasking performance allow (or require) the two tasks to be integrated to the point that successful performance could depend more on the effectiveness of task integration than on the effectiveness of true task time-sharing (e.g., Korteling, 1993). Such research may well inform us about aging and task integration; however, an analysis of activities encountered in daily living suggests that to achieve the overarching goals required for successful performance of most complex tasks there is a requirement for coordination of cognitive processing associated with the task activities. Such analysis would make salient the idea that independent actions must be planned and coordinated at different times, different amounts of resources must be applied to the components at different times, and some components must be put on hold while others are emphasized at a given point in time. Such observations have been the basis of formal models that optimally describe time-sharing performance (Schneider & Detweiler, 1988) and lead to experimental design drastically different than the traditional dual-task experiment.

Other examples of the usefulness of this type of approach can be found in various areas. For example, the skills-analysis based training movement in the United Kingdom made substantive use of task analytic methodologies to translate issues related to perceptual and motor difficulties of industrial skills learning to research questions (e.g., Crossman, 1956; Seymour, 1968). Schneider, Vidulich, and Yeh (1982), Eggemeier and Fisk (1992), and more recently Kirlik, Walker, and Fisk (in press), made use of extensive task analysis to translate real-world training problems involving complex perceptual rule-based learning into complex, but well controlled laboratory research questions.

Gibson (1965) stated well the need for task analysis when she emphasized the need to understand the important elements of stimuli for research on learning to read:

> Some alphabetic writing systems have nearly perfect single-letter-to-sound correspondence, but some like English, have far more complex correspondence between spelling patterns and speech patterns. Whatever the nature of the correspondence, it is vital to a proper analysis of the reading task that they be understood. . . . It would be useful to know just what the distinctive feature of letters are. What dimensions of difference must a child learn to detect in order to perceive each letter as unique? (pp. 1067–1068)

From the analysis she performed, Gibson was able to create relevant stimuli and experimental tasks to bring the research questions under conditions of control while maintaining close connection with the real-world problem of interest.

The Environment

Now consider the environment. Numerous authors noted the failure of psychology to meaningfully contribute to understanding how to solve practical problems to some degree because of a lack of appreciation of the context within which cognition and behavior occurs (but see Chapanis, 1988; Fisher, 1993; Kirlik, in press, for a review and a rebuttal). If these suggestions, that the products of a basic science do not provide effective resources for application, are even only partially true then such realization can provide important lessons for basic science itself. Such ''lessons learned'' point to the need to understand the context in which cognitive activity occurs.

The endeavor of understanding the environment in which cognitive activity will take place may be as important as understanding the overarching task in which the cognitive activity of interest is embedded. Thus, one must focus on determining under what environmental conditions various cognitive activities will be activated, and required, for effective task performance. The issue is not only to understand cognitive processes such as problem solving, working memory, or skill acquisition but also to determine in what context problems must be solved, when decisions must be made and what factors affect their outcome, what task characteristics lead to working memory demands, or what skills must be acquired given various environmental constraints.

An example provided by Kirlik (in press) may better make the point. Kirlik pointed out that one of the earliest attempts to model human–machine interaction concerned manual control behavior, such as steering a car or flying an aircraft. Engineers familiar with the design of electromechanical feedback control systems turned their attention to modeling the human as a feedback control system in order to assess human capabilities and limits so that vehicles could be designed so that control demands were within these limits. Control theory has a well-specified language for environmental modeling. The thing being controlled can be described in terms of a transfer function that relates system inputs (steering adjustments) to system outputs (headings). The goal of this endeavor was to discover the human transfer function, that is, a description of the function relating stimuli to responses during manual control behavior.

As Kirlik (in press) stated, the engineers were in for a rude awakening. The empirical results indicated that there was no single human transfer function. Rather, the human transfer function appeared to adjust to changes in the dynamics of the controlled system. Birmingham and Taylor (1954) noted that the ability of the human to adjust to the environmental transfer function was so great that the control system designer was doomed to failure. Subsequent modeling attempts (McRuer & Jex, 1967) were successful only once the search for invariance in behavior shifted to the level of the human–machine system rather than in human behavior alone.

Given this finding concerning human perceptual–motor behavior, why should we expect cognitive-level behavior to be any less adaptive to environmental structure than is perceptual–motor behavior? Much modern psychology research, especially in cognitive aging, paints a rather dismal picture of human cognitive abilities and limitations, leaving us to wonder how it can ever be possible for human cognition to allow our subjects even to find their way into the laboratory. But rarely does the cognitive system operate in isolation from external environmental aids.

How often have we discovered the cleverness of participants of our experiments who are able to confound our studies of complex cognitive activity by cueing off what we might think of as extraneous aberrations? Often our response is to bring tighter and tighter control to the experiment by producing more and more sterile environments. But as Kirlik (in press) stated in regards to understanding skilled behavior, we should cease "to be surprised and frustrated by such cleverness, and [begin] to view the tendency toward such selective use of environmental stimuli as a fundamental aspect of skilled behavior. There is no doubt that empirical research is needed to clarify this issue." The need to understand the environmental contribution to cognition and behavior may be especially critical for understanding age-related differences. Empirical evidence suggests that age differences are often decreased when environmental support, in the form of encoding, retrieval, or other contextually appropriate cues, are available (e.g., Craik & McDowd, 1987; Shaw & Craik, 1989; Sharps & Gollin, 1988). Many everyday tasks are performed in the presence of environmental support (e.g., checkbooks, calendars, maps). If the exploitation of environmental support in practical contexts is indeed pervasive, then additional research on the interaction of cognition and environment is necessary to paint a faithful picture of the actual limitations faced by older adults in their natural contexts. However, the necessary experiments must provide rich enough environmental conditions and enough practice time so that participants have the opportunity to reap the potential benefits of environmental support.

Hence, one must examine environmentally meaningful situations in which the behavior of interest will occur. Such an approach requires careful analysis. Adoption of such an approach does not imply a commitment to only studying behavior in natural environments. Ecological psychologists argue for using environmental conditions as the basis of scientific study that are representative of the conditions in which the target behavior of interest occurs. At some level we must be sympathetic to and should not argue with such a goal. However, we must take care in deciding what is or is not a representation of a "natural" environment. For better or worse, an aircraft cockpit, a nuclear control room, or even the driver's side of an automobile looks much more like a laboratory than it does the natural terrestrial environment. The important point is that the environment in which a study is conducted should not artificially restrict the scientific theory. This we all know. Careful attention and analysis to environmental factors can go a long way toward ensuring practical relevance of the enterprise of psychological science.

Subject Population

Next consider the subject or subject population. At some level, individuals studying aging carefully consider the population of participants under study, at least implicitly. Certainly if one is interested in the effects of normal aging without the influence of health-related problems, then care is taken in the selection of the participant population. Yet, other considerations may be just as important, but often overlooked. Consider the question of task familiarization. Many research studies give subjects no more than a few minutes to familiarize themselves with the task before measurements are begun. A task analysis can make salient the need for, and the type of, preparation and training subjects should receive before data collection for the main investigation begins.

Choice of Dependent Variables

Choice of dependent variables can also be assisted by task analysis of real-world correlates on which the scientific investigation rests. Sometimes dependent variables are chosen because they are easy to measure, because instrumentation is available, because they are "tradition," or because they are "sensitive" (statistical significance is easy to get). These are not reasons to reject use of a dependent variable; however, through task analysis one should be able to determine which dependent variables will have the greatest likelihood of transfer to the practical issue which has motivated the scientific question.

SOME POTENTIAL MISCONCEPTIONS

There are possibly a large number of misconceptions about the need for research we have labeled as having practical relevance. We address just a few of these next.

1. Applied research is, by definition, practically relevant. Many individuals argued that research conducted within the field of human factors and ergonomics, clearly an applied field, has been inconsequential and isolated from the so-called real world. In fact Admiral Rickover in the 1970s expressed his dissatisfaction with the generalizability of human factors research efforts when asked about a proposal involving a major human factors program in the research and development program of Navy ships by stating that it is about as useful as teaching your grandmother how to suck an egg. Indeed, the human factors and ergonomics community has dealt with and continues to deal with this important issue of relevance; ultimately, the reasons for concern must be embraced by researchers interested in cognitive aging. The main point is that the fact that a research effort is applied does not necessarily afford that effort practical relevance. The problem with, and limitation of, much applied research seems to rest on its piecemeal approach and the fact that such research is often driven primarily by technology. Hence, the integration of some bodies of applied research is quite difficult, as is the generalizability of that research beyond the specific targeted problem. A concern for practical relevance as outlined above can do much to overcome this problem.

2. The critical basic science is conducted and only then are applications made. This is untrue for many reasons. Basic and applied science must live a symbiotic relationship. Certainly attempts at application can bring to light quickly the inadequacy of an elegant theory. Also, application brings to the forefront issues that may never arise in any other context. A statement that applied issues must follow issues of basic science also seems to assume that "basic" and "applied" research are ends of a continuum. Basic research does not avoid examining a research space in which applied interests lie but encompasses that space in its problem definition and research design.

3. Such an approach does not allow proper control. We hope that it is obvious that the concern for practical relevance does not imply that research be done in a sloppy fashion (see Cook & Campbell, 1979). Scientific journals are replete with examples of numerous individuals who have demonstrated that they are quite capable of designing and carrying out rather complex research designs. The effort is often large but so is the potential payoff.

4. Ecologically valid tasks weaken generalization. Some researchers motivate their selection of spartan conditions by the assumption that because such experiments abstract away environmental context, they measure fundamental cognitive abilities that underlie behavior in a wide range of environmental conditions. In this view, research using complex, realistic environmental conditions is less likely to yield generalizable results since few other situations will posses the same constellation of environmental conditions. In some sense, it must be true that some cognitive mechanisms are context-independent. However, the last 25 years of research on higher cognitive activities such as reasoning, judgment, and decision making suggest that context-independent mechanisms can be extremely difficult to find. In case after case, findings from reasoning tasks have failed to generalize to contextualized versions of these tasks. Gigerenzer et al. (1989) highlighted this issue well by stating that currently "the bulk of experimental evidence available today, both on probabilistic and deductive reasoning, suggests that the judgment of children and adults is not so much conditioned by the structure of the problem—as the various normative views would have it—but by the content, context, and presentation of information—which should be irrelevant to most normative models" (p. 232).

Merely stripping a task of its context of course does not assure that a context-independent activity is being engaged through the performance of that task. Rather, and especially to the extent that such tasks are found to be more difficult than contextualized tasks, it is possible that what is being observed is how a cognitive system, which evolved in the presence of a rich environmental context, can contort itself to solve problems that lie possibly quite outside its natural "design specifications." Perhaps some of the fundamental aspects of cognition involve how cognition identifies and exploits environmental information. If so, studies of cognition and aging in a wide range of environmental contexts are likely to be the only route toward identifying the fundamental activities underlying behavior in practically relevant situations.

5. Ecologically valid tasks hinder identification of age differences. Some researchers motivate their selection of novel laboratory tasks with the assumption that because such experiments equate the experience of both young and old participants, they are measuring fundamental cognitive abilities that are independent of task-relevant experience. In this view, research that uses familiar, everyday tasks is less likely to identify fundamental differences between the cognitive systems of young and old participants, because such studies would involve a confound of "true" age effects with experiential knowledge

relevant to the task. Indeed, it must be the case that some cognitive abilities do not rely upon declarative or procedural knowledge gained through experience. However, the degree to which such abilities play a large role in the production of realistically complex behavior is open to question. Modern cognitive research suggests that much responsibility for the selection of behavior in complex tasks lies in the effective storage, retrieval, and manipulation of experiential information (e.g., Anderson, 1982; Ericsson, Krampe, & Tesch-Römer, 1993; Logan, 1988; Morrell & Park, 1993; Morrow, Leirer, & Altieri, 1992). It is unclear whether the cognitive activities that are independent of experiential information are any more fundamental than those activities associated with how a person uses knowledge of the world. Studies of how both young and old adults approach tasks when experiential information is both unavailable and available are necessary to understand the actual age-related differences in how the cognitive system operates in practically relevant situations.

6. As a basic scientist I am not interested in the real world. We cannot address this except to say that it appears to us that the brain and human behavior exist in the real world.

WHY IS SUCH RESEARCH IMPORTANT?

There are perhaps numerous reasons why research grounded in practical relevance is important. We mention three.

Communication

By thoroughly understanding how laboratory research is related to real-world activities and tasks, it is much easier to communicate the reason that such research is being conducted and of interest to those outside the specific research area. The fact that Admiral Rickover thought that human factors research was equated with "egg sucking" may be reason enough to wish to communicate well with those outside the immediate research area. If this is not sufficient motivation, consider a comment that was part of the dedication of the American Psychological Association's headquarters building in 1965:

> Despite the fact that behavioral sciences affect every aspect of our lives and interact with every function of government, I believe we would all agree that they have not been applied to government problems in the same systematic way as the natural sciences. . . . I confess that I was surprised to learn that you are one of the largest publishers of technical

journals in the world. Naturally . . . one wonders what happens to all of the ideas and facts they contain. (Hornig, 1965, cited in Mackie, 1984)

Solutions to Immediate Problems

Because concern with the practical relevance of research requires a closer attention to real-world human behavior and environments, the opportunity exists to provide answers to real, immediate problems. Assume we were interested in learning how perceptual factors come to enhance declarative, rule-based learning. Also assume that we observed that such learning is the foundation for many real-world activities, such as driving, being a football quarterback, and performing as a police officer in a shoot–don't shoot situation. Studying abstractions of where such learning occurs allows us at least a closer first approximation to solutions to questions such as ''How do I train a police officer who is under stress not to shoot innocent people?'' than might otherwise be possible.

Generalization

If one understands the range of environments, subjects, and task constraints within which behavior or cognitive processes occur, then it can be argued that the ensuing results of experiments used to develop a given theory would be general. If a theory were put forward concerning some aspect of age-related skill acquisition, and that theory's predictions replicate *only* under a limited set of circumstances, then obviously most scientists would be concerned about the generality of that theory. Concern with the issue of practical relevance enhances our opportunity for generality of theory. At the very least, knowing that findings do not replicate across certain groups of individuals, certain aspects of tasks, or certain environments, is itself a generalization and should lead naturally to the beginnings of research to expand and enhance theory.

In addition, concern with practical relevance allows us the opportunity to develop, not a good, not a better, but a best solution to our research question. We can learn from engineering history. Fisher (1993) described how most fields of engineering have developed. He pointed out that engineering fields progress in a three-step process. Fisher pointed out that in the first step, a solution is proposed to an applied problem without an attempt fully to document the advantages of the solution. Because only one solution has been prepared, the most that can be said of it is that it is a *good* solution. In the second step, several solutions are both proposed and tested. Data are gathered and the necessary experimental controls are introduced. The favored solution is documented as the *better* one. Finally, in the third step a very large . . . number of solutions are generated and [based on both theory and applied considerations] the most promising ones are tested. The [winning] solution is identified as the *optimal* or the best one. Fisher documented a valuable lesson for us. Without concern for design of practically relevant research it seems that we may find a good or even a better solution to the scientific problem of interest, but we run the risk of missing the chance of discovering the best solution.

SUMMARY AND CONCLUDING COMMENTS

We argue that practically relevant research, research that advances both theory and practice, is important for continued progress in the field of cognitive aging. The answer to the question posed in the title of this chapter seems to be that, in isolation, purely applied research as well as basic research that severely sterilizes the cognitive experience could critically restrict progress in the field. We argue that there is a need for an expansion of the domains of study. To that end we focus on the details of a set of criteria that would allow such expansion to be productive as well as discussed the process to achieve such a goal. The central premise of our discussion can be summarized as follows: Practically relevant cognitive aging research is most likely to emerge when (a) the actual psychological activities underlying a particular behavior or class of behaviors are understood (via task analysis); (b) it is appreciated that in most, if not all, practical situations these psychological activities exploit, or benefit from, environmental support for cognition; and therefore (c) laboratory research should investigate performance on tasks that engage the psychological activities manifested in practical situations and should provide the environmental support normally available in these situations (representative design). Most important, we claim that evidence in the literature from psychology and other fields suggests that such a research approach will not only improve the applicability of research findings but also will result in theoretical advances that cannot be gained otherwise. The context of our discussion and research on aging is those factors that affect skill acquisition. Certainly within the field of skill acquisition, the relevance of research should be measured in terms of the ability of findings to inform the change of some aspect of either the individual (e.g., through training), the trainee pool (e.g., through selection), or the environment (e.g., through design). Although our views are presented in this context, we clearly hope that they extend to the study of psychological activities other than skill acquisition and to interventions beyond training, selection, and design.

It also seems appropriate to emphasize what is at least obvious to us. Our focus is on the need to reduce the potential for restrictiveness of phenomena and findings, not on the claim that any current research conducted outside the realm considered practically relevant provides "false" answers or is irrelevant. Current theories may not necessarily be "wrong;" rather, they may be overly limited. Surely it may be true that practically relevant research is less likely, at least initially, to result in the same surface level elegant and "clean" experimental designs that are characteristic of the more traditional approach. However, we are convinced that such research is necessary to expand and supplement our current knowledge of skill and aging in particular and cognitive aging phenomena in general.

REFERENCES

Adams, J. A. (1972). Research and the future of engineering psychology. *American Psychologist, 27*, 615–622.

Anderson, J. R. (1982). Acquisition of cognitive skill. *Psychological Review, 89*, 369–406.

Birmingham, H. P., & Taylor, F. V. (1954). A design philosophy for man-machine control systems. *Proceedings of the I.R.E., 42(12)*, 1748–1758.

Chapanis, A. (1988). Some generalizations about generalization. *Human Factors, 30*, 253–267.

Cook, T. D., & Campbell, D. T. (1979) *Quasi-experimentation: Design and analysis issues for field settings*. Boston: Houghton Mifflin.

Craik, F. I. M., & McDowd, J. (1987). Age differences in recall and recognition. *Journal of Experimental Psychology: Learning, Memory, and Cognition, 13*, 474–479.

Crossman, E. R. (1956). Perceptual activity in manual work. *Research, 9*, 42–49.

Drury, C. G., Paramore, B., Van Cott, H. P., Grey, S. M., & Corlett, E. N. (1987). Task analysis. In G. Salvendy (Ed.), *Handbook of human factors* (pp. 370–401). New York: Wiley.

Eggemeier, F. T., & Fisk, A. D. (1992). *Automatic information processing and high performance skills*. (AL-TR-1992-0134). Wright-Patterson AFB, OH: Armstrong Laboratory, Logistics Research Division.

Ericsson, K. A., Krampe, R. T., & Tesch-Römer, C. (1993). The role of deliberate practice in the acquisition of expert performance. *Psychological Review, 100*, 363–406.

Fisher, D. L. (1993). Optimal performance engineering: Good, better, best. *Human Factors, 35*, 115–139.

Gibson, E. J. (1965). Learning to read. *Science, 148*, 1066–1072.

Gigerenzer, G., Swijtink, Z., Porter, T., Datson, L., Beatty, J., & Kruger, L. (1989). *The empire of chance*. Cambridge, England: Cambridge University Press.

Hammond, K. R. (1966). *The psychology of Egon Brunswik*. New York: Holt, Rinehart & Wilson.

Inside the south. (1994, September 12). *Sports Illustrated*, 58.

Kirlik, A. (1995). Requirements for psychological models to support design: Toward ecological task analysis. In J. M. Flach, P. A. Hancock, J. Caird, & K. J., Vincente (Eds.), *Global Perspectives on the ecology of human-machine systems* (Vol. 1, pp. 68–120). Hillsdale, NJ: Lawrence Erlbaum Associates.

Kirlik, A., Walker, N., & Fisk, A. D. (in press). Supporting perception in the service of dynamic decision making. *Human Factors*.

Korteling, J. E. (1993). Effects of age and task similarity on dual-task performance. *Human Factors, 35*, 99–113.

Logan, G. D. (1988). Toward an instance theory of automatization. *Psychological Review, 95*, 492–527.

Mackie, R. R. (1984). Research relevance and the information glut. In F. A. Muckler (Ed.), *Human factors review* (pp. 1–11). Santa Monica, CA.: Human Factors and Ergonomics Society.

McRuer, M. D., & Jex, H. R. (1967). A review of quasi-linear pilot models. *IEEE Transactions on the Human Factors in Electronics, HFE-8.3*, 231–249.

Morrell, R. W., & Park, D. C. (1993). The effects of age, illustrations, and task variables on the performance of procedural assembly tasks. *Psychology and Aging, 8*, 389–399.

Morrow, D. G., Leirer, V. O., & Altieri, P. A. (1992). Aging expertise, and narrative processing. *Psychology and Aging, 7*, 376–388.

Schneider, W., & Detweiler, M. (1988). The role of practice in dual-task performance: Toward workload modeling in a connectionist/control architecture. *Human Factors, 30*, 539–566.

Schneider, W., Vidulich, M. A., & Yeh, Y. (1982). Training spatial skills for air traffic control. *Proceedings of the Human Factors Society 26th Annual Meeting* (pp. 10–14). Santa Monica, CA: Human Factors and Ergonomics Society.

Seymour, W. D. (1968). *Skills analysis training*. London: Isaac Pitman.

Sharps, M., & Gollin, E. S. (1988). Aging and free recall for objects located in space. *Journal of Gerontology: Psychological Sciences, 43*, P8–P11.

Shaw, R. J., & Craik, F. I. M. (1989). Age differences in predictions and performance on a cued recall task. *Psychology and Aging, 4*, 131–135.

Swezey, R. W., & Salas, E. (1992). *Teams: Their training and performance*. Norwood, NJ: Ablex Publishing Corporation.

CHAPTER 2

State Models of Paired Associate Learning: The General Acquisition, Decrement, and Training Hypotheses

Donald L. Fisher
University of Massachusetts

Older adults learn more slowly than younger adults on almost all tasks. Perhaps this is most evident when one considers the learning required to master the ever changing new technologies. Older adults frequently struggle to learn these new technologies. Even the most simple interaction sometimes proves frightening. For example, older adults by and large still choose to ignore interactions with automated teller machines (ATMs) whenever possible. Anything that can be done to reduce the time that it takes older adults to learn how to use the new technologies is not only a gain in efficiency; it may well be the difference between older adults' taking advantage of and not taking advantage of all that the new technologies have to offer. In many cases, the learning required of older adults in order successfully to interact with the new technologies is identical to the learning required in order to master more pedestrian paired associate tasks (Kausler, 1992). Thus, if one could reduce the time that it took older adults to master these latter paired associate tasks, in principle, one could reduce the time that it took older adults to master the former more practical tasks.

Three general conclusions follow from the work reported in this chapter. First, and primarily of theoretical importance, I find that one and the same formal model characterizes the performance of younger and older adults on paired associate tasks. Of course, the values of the parameters in the model are influenced by the age of the subject (older adults do learn more slowly than younger adults), not only the structure of the model. Second, and of more substantive importance, I find that a detailed analysis of the effect of aging on the component learning processes indicates that this effect is not a monolithic one. For example, when there exists even a moderate association between the elements of a paired associate (the stimulus and the response), both younger and older adults are equally good at storing the paired associate in long term memory. Only when there exists no (or very little) association is it the case that younger adults are more successful than older adults at storing the paired associate. Third, and primarily of practical importance, I find that in principle it is possible to reduce significantly the time that it takes older adults to learn a list of paired associates. The key to this reduction lies in the proper selection of training schedules (Fisher, Wisher, & Ranney, 1996). In fact, if the optimal schedule is selected it should be possible completely to eliminate the effects of aging on the learning process. By this, I mean that the time that it takes older adults to learn a list of paired associates when these older adults are trained optimally should differ imperceptibly from the time it takes younger adults to learn the same list of paired associates when these younger adults are trained using standard procedures.

In order to address the question of how the time it takes older adults to acquire information in paired associate tasks can be reduced, I need to travel back in time almost 50 years. I want to unearth the very simple models of paired associate learning that were first described by Estes (1950; also see Bush & Mosteller, 1951) in the early 1950s. These models make it possible to construct detailed tests of hypotheses about the step by step process by which both younger and older adults acquire new information in a paired associate task. Although many such tests have been run using younger adults as subjects, few, if any, such tests have been conducted using older adults as subjects. Thus, when recently I dusted off these models, I really had no idea what they might tell me about the aging process. However, I hoped that they would let me examine at least three separate hypotheses about this process.

First, I wanted to identify the basic assumptions that are necessary for the construction of a model which can describe the step by step learning of older adults. In particular, I wanted to know whether the models that have been used so successfully to describe the performance of younger adults could also be used just as successfully to describe the performance of older adults (the general acquisition hypothesis). Second, assuming that the same formal models can be used to describe the performance of younger and older adults, I wanted to determine for each process in the model the size of the decrement observed for that process in the older adult population. In particular, I wanted to know whether a decrement was observed in all tasks and for all processes used to model the performance of older adults (the general decrement hypothesis; Kausler, 1992) or instead was observed for only certain of the processes, certain of the tasks, or certain of the combinations of tasks and processes. Finally, assuming again that a formal model can be identified that describes the performance of older adults in paired associate tasks, I wanted to construct a training algorithm that would minimize the time it took older adults to achieve some criterion level of learning. In particular, I wanted to determine whether the algorithm that optimized the training of older adults is identical to the existing set of algorithms that can be used to optimize the training of younger adults (the general training hypothesis), or whether, in fact, separate algorithms need to be designed for training younger and older adults.

THE GENERAL ACQUISITION HYPOTHESIS

To begin, I describe the basic paired associate task and the simple state models that have been used to capture behavior in this task. Most readers are presumably familiar with the laboratory examples of paired associate learning to which the state models have been applied. Each paired associate consists of a stimulus element, s, and a response element, r. Typically, words, nonsense syllables, or digits serve as the elements of the paired associate. A list of *n* paired associates is then constructed. Subjects must learn this list. The exact details of the training vary from one experiment to another. In many experiments, a stimulus s is presented by itself during the *test* interval. Subjects must supply the response r. After doing such, the stimulus and response are presented together for some brief period of time during the *study* interval. A new stimulus is then tested followed by a study interval, and so on. A number of dependent variables can be derived from such a paradigm. The most common dependent variable is the proportion of subjects responding correctly on each trial *i*. Another common dependent variable is the number of trials on average that it takes subjects to reach some criterion percentage of correct responses in a given block of trials.

State Models of Paired Associate Learning

Although most readers are presumably familiar with the paired associate task, not all readers are necessarily familiar with the models of paired associate learning that have been developed over the years. I want to begin by describing one of the simplest such models (Bower, 1961, 1962). Briefly, three assumptions are made. First, it is assumed that a stimulus is in either one of two states on each trial, state *L*, the conditioned or learned state, or state *U*, the unconditioned or unlearned state (Table 2.1). Second, it is assumed that the response a

TABLE 2.1
Two-State Model of Paired Associate Learning

State: Trial *i*	*State: Trial i + 1* L	U	P(Correct) Trial *i*
L	1	0	1
U	c	1 − c	g

subject gives to a stimulus depends on the state of the stimulus. If on trial *i* a stimulus is learned, then a subject gives the correct response to that stimulus with probability 1. If on trial *i* a stimulus is unlearned, then a subject gives the correct response with probability g and an incorrect response with probability 1 − g. Finally, it is assumed that the state of a stimulus on the next trial depends only on the state of the stimulus on the current trial. Specifically, if on trial *i* a stimulus is learned, then on trial *i* + 1 the stimulus remains learned with probability 1. If on trial *i* a stimulus has not been learned, then on trial *i* + 1 it becomes learned with probability c and remains unlearned with probability 1 − c. Together, these assumptions constitute what I will refer to as the formal model of paired associate learning.

When these models were first proposed, little if any thought was given to the mental or cognitive processes whose outcome they might reflect. In fact, cognitive processes were generally suspect in the early 1960s when behaviorism was still the reigning paradigm in experimental psychology. However, much changed during the 1960s, and just one decade later it had become common to talk about the states in a model as reflecting different types of memory and the transition between states as reflecting the success of various retrieval or storage processes. I will adopt here the more contemporary cognitive framework in which the paired associate task has been cast. In this light, the transition probability c represents the likelihood that a subjects stores successfully a paired associate in long term memory. Thus, analysis of this parameter can indicate whether one of the processes involved in learning paired associates, the storage process, is equally efficient for younger and older adults. Similar remarks apply to the guessing parameter.

The Acquisition Curve: Younger and Older Adults

It is now a simple matter to predict the first of the two dependent variables I mentioned previously, in particular, the probability that a subject responds correctly on a given trial *i*. To begin, it is generally assumed that subjects do not know the paired associates before beginning the experiment. Thus, the probability that a subject responds correctly on the first trial is simply the probability g of guessing. The probability that a subject responds correctly on the second trial is equal to the probability that the subject learned the stimulus on the first trial or, having failed to learn the stimulus on the first trial, guesses correctly on the second trial. More generally, the probability that a subject responds correctly on trial i is equal to the probability of the complement of the event that the subject has failed to learn the stimulus on the preceding $i - 1$ trials and then guesses incorrectly on the ith trial:

$$P(\text{Correct Trial } i) = 1 - (1 - g)(1 - c)^{i-1}. \qquad (1)$$

We can now compare the predictions of the model with our observations. For example, we can use the model to predict the percentage of correct responses at each successive trial. I have done so for selected values of the conditioning and guessing parameters (Fig. 2.1, dashed lines). On the first trial, it is predicted that subjects will never respond correctly. On the last or twelfth trial it is predicted that subjects will respond correctly almost always. I have also graphed the results from an actual experiment (Cieutat, Stockwell, & Noble, 1958) in which 80 younger subjects (mean age = 20.7) were asked to learn lists of 10 paired associates (Fig. 2.1, solid lines). Both the stimulus and response

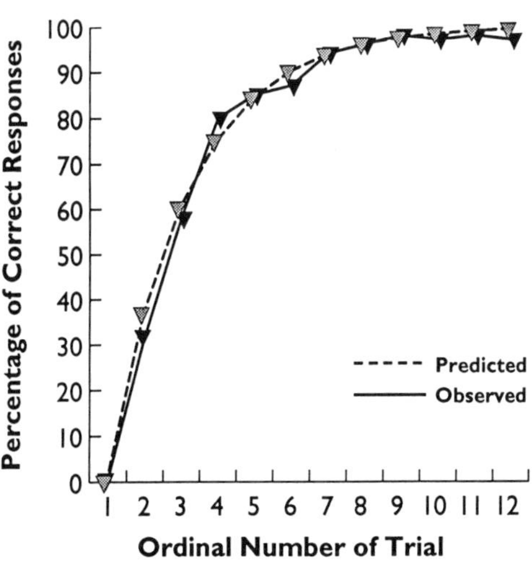

FIG. 2.1 Younger adults' acquisition curves: predicted (dashed lines) and observed (solid lines). (Predicted points from Equation 2: $c = .37$, $g = 0$. Observed points from Cieutat, Stockwell, & Noble, 1958.)

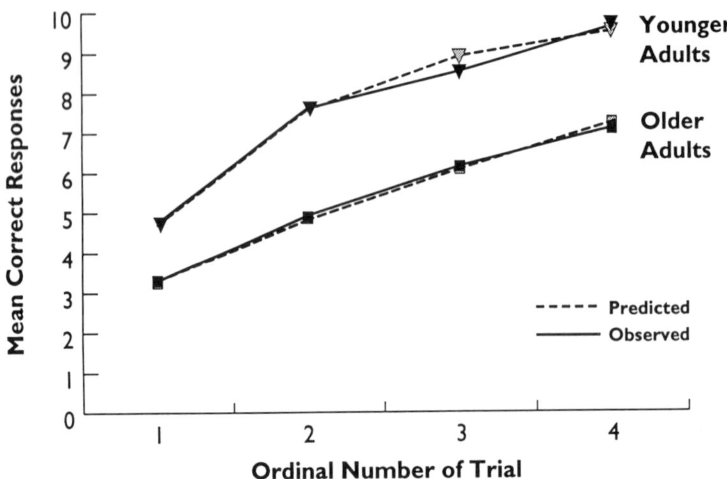

FIG. 2.2 Younger and older adults' acquisition curves: predicted (dashed lines) and observed (solid lines). (Predicted points from Equation 2; parameters from Table 2.2. Observed points from Kausler & Puckett, 1980.)

elements were words. Each stimulus was tested 12 times. Clearly the theoretical and empirical curves are qualitatively very similar to one another.

The question at this point is whether the simple two-state model does equally well predicting the performance of older adults on successive training trials. To determine this, we need to consider a study where both older and younger adults were used as subjects. In Fig. 2.2 I plotted the results from a study reported by Kausler and Puckett (1980). They trained 16 younger (mean age = 21.3 years, range 18.25–26.25 years) and 16 older (mean age 70.6 years, range 60.25–83 years) subjects for 4 trials on a list containing 10 paired associates. Both the stimulus and response elements were nouns and were unrelated to one another. It is clear that the older adults (squares, solid lines) performed more poorly across trials than the younger adults did (triangles, solid lines). For example, at the start of training younger adults responded correctly on average 4.75 times out of 10 whereas older adults responded correctly on average only 3.3 times out of 10.

I then fit the two-state model separately to the results of both the younger and older adults and selected values of the parameters which minimized chi-square. Specifically, let f_i equal the observed number of correct responses on trial i. And let t equal the number of times a stimulus is trained (assuming all stimuli are trained equally often). Then, chi-square was computed as follows:

$$\chi^2 = \sum_{i=1}^{t} \frac{\{f_i - n[1 - (1 - g)(1 - c)^{i-1}]\}^2}{n[1 - (1 - g)(1 - c)^{i-1}]} + \sum_{i=1}^{t} \frac{\{f_i - n[1 - (1 - g)(1 - c)^{i-1}]\}^2}{n - n[1 - (1 - g)(1 - c)^{i-1}]} \quad (2)$$

The values of the conditioning and guessing parameters which minimize the preceding sum were then identified. In Fig. 2.2, I have overlaid the predictions (dashed lines; based on values of parameters which minimized chi-square) and the observations (solid lines). Visually, the fit looks quite good. Indeed, the two-state model could not be rejected, for either the younger [$\chi^2(2) = 2.35$, $p = 0.30$)] or older [$\chi^2(2) = 0.27$, $p = 0.88$] adults.

At this point, it appears that the simple two state-model, which predicts so successfully for younger adults the probability of a correct response on a given trial i, predicts equally well for older adults this same probability. Thus, at least when acquisition is the sole variable of interest, aging does not appear to influence greatly the formal model needed to describe performance. In short, support exists for the general acquisition hypothesis (also see following). Of course, aging must influence the values of the parameters. Otherwise, the older and younger adults' performance would be indistinguishable.

THE GENERAL DECREMENT HYPOTHESIS

For many years, it has been argued that the decrement observed in older adults' paired associate learning is a general one. A decrement is a general one in this context if, in every paired associate, task the influence of aging on each of the individual processes is negative (Kausler, 1992). For our purposes, we can assume that there are two critical processes in the paired associate task. The first process corresponds to the attempt to store a paired associate in long term memory when the stimulus is not conditioned. Thus the conditioning parameter c reflects the likelihood that this process succeeds on any given trial. The second process corresponds to the generation of a response when the stimulus is not conditioned. Sometimes this process is guided by only chance factors, as might be the case when each stimulus was randomly paired with either one of two digits. At other times, this process reflects both an individual subject's world knowledge and problem solving-skills, as might be the case when the stimuli and responses are words highly related to one another. In either case, the guessing process g indicates the likelihood that this process succeeds on any given trial.

Once values of the conditioning and guessing parameters have been estimated, these estimates can then be used to test the general decrement hypothesis. Specifically, estimates of the conditioning and guessing parameters obtained from younger and older adults would be consistent with the general decrement hypothesis if across all tasks $c_{young} > c_{old}$ (the conditioning parameter for the younger adults is greater than the conditioning parameter for the older adults) and $g_{young} \geq g_{old}$. (Note that the second inequality is not a strict one because in some tasks there is no possibility of predicting the correct response; for example, words might be randomly paired with the digits 1 or 2.) The general decrement hypothesis has since been challenged by Hasher and Zacks (1979), among others. They have argued that automatic processes are not compromised. Only effortful processes show a decrement. It would not appear unreasonable to assume that the two critical processes that are identified here, the guessing and storage processes, are effortful processes. Thus, estimates of the parameters must satisfy the same set of inequalities in order to be consistent with the more limited decrement hypothesis proposed by Hasher and Zacks.

Evidence Consistent With General Decrement Hypothesis: Study I

Somewhat surprisingly, no one has actually attempted to identify the size of the decrement associated with each of the putative effortful processes. An analysis of the parameters that govern the performance of younger and older adults in paired associate tasks is a straightforward enough task. Consider two experiments. The first we have already discussed. Specifically, consider the results reported by Kausler and Puckett (1980). If the models of the younger and older adults are fit separately, it is seen that younger adults are better at guessing the correct response and more likely to learn the response on any given trial. In particular, the probability that the younger adults guess the correct response is .47, whereas this probability for older adults is .33 (see Table 2.2A). Similarly, the probability that the younger adults learn a response on a given trial is .52, whereas this same probability for older adults is only .24. Thus, at first glance the results from Kausler and Puckett are consistent with the general decrement hypothesis insofar as both the guessing and conditioning processes are compromised. Furthermore, as we have seen, the differences between the observations and predictions for both the younger and older adults are not significant (Fig. 2.2).

TABLE 2.2
Parameter Estimates Based on Kausler and Puckett (1980) Data

	A. Separate Markov Models	
	Guessing	*Conditioning*
Young	.47	.52
Old	.33	.24
	B. Common Guessing Model	
	Guessing	*Conditioning*
Young	.39	.55
Old	.39	.22
	C. Common Conditioning Model	
	Guessing	*Conditioning*
Young	.60	.31
Old	.28	.31

Unfortunately, the different parameter estimates could be the result of chance variation alone. Perhaps had we held one parameter constant and allowed the other to vary, the difference between the observations and predictions would have been no more than was expected on the basis of chance alone. So, I first fit a model that held the guessing parameter for the younger and older adults constant (Table 2.2B). The model with a common guessing parameter could be rejected, $\chi^2(5) = 22.59$, $p < 0.005$. Similarly, I fit a model that held the conditioning parameter constant (Table 2.2C). This model also could be rejected, $\chi^2(5) = 61.04$, $p < 0.005$. Thus, the general decrement hypothesis, at least for this particular task, appears to be unshakable.

Evidence Not Consistent With General Decrement Hypothesis: Study II

The question we now have to ask ourselves is whether this general decrement will be observed across changes in the task. Consider then a different paired associate task run by Korchin and Basowitz (1957). The stimuli and responses were words that were low associates of one another. This differs from the study run by Kausler and Puckett (1980) that we just discussed. There, the stimuli and responses were unrelated to one another. This change in meaningfulness has a profound effect on the conditioning parameter. Specifically, there is now an identity of the conditioning parameter when separate models are fit to younger and older adults (Table 2.3A). The two-state model could not be rejected when fit either to the younger, $\chi^2(4) = 1.75$, $p > .10$ or older, $\chi^2(4) = 2.40$, $p > .10$, adults.

TABLE 2.3
Parameters Estimates Based on Korchin and Basowitz (1957) Data

	A. Separate Markov Models	
	Guessing	*Conditioning*
Young	.62	.13
Old	.33	.13
	B. Common Conditioning Model	
	Guessing	Conditioning
Young	.62	.13
Old	.33	.13

We now want to test a model with a common conditioning and different guessing parameters to determine whether the general decrement hypothesis can be rejected (Table 2.3B). Not too surprisingly, one cannot reject a model with a common conditioning parameter, $\chi^2(9) = 8.30$, $p = .60$. Thus, the hypothesis that all processes show some decrement is not supported by the results from the Korchin and Basowitz (1957) study. In fact, it appears that when words are even moderately associated with each other, as they were in the Korchin and Basowitz study, older and younger adults are equally likely to learn the response to a stimulus on any given trial.

In summary, I have argued that one and the same formal model can be used to capture the trial by trial performance of both younger and older adults. Because older adults almost always perform more poorly than younger adults, if it is not the formal model of performance that is influenced by aging, it is the specific values of the parameters in the more formal model. Indeed, we have seen that older adults are both less likely to guess correctly and, in some (but not all) tasks, less likely to learn the response on any given trial. Thus, at least for the studies reanalyzed in this chapter there is little support for the general decrement hypothesis.

GENERAL TRAINING HYPOTHESIS

I now want to ask the following question. Specifically, can we use our knowledge of the way that learning operates in the two state model to construct an algorithm that minimizes the time on average that it takes younger and older adults to learn a list? Or, instead, must we construct separate algorithms for younger and older adults? I had thought when first I asked this question that I would find a number of different studies bearing on the answer. In fact, there exists no empirical or formal work using older adults as subjects and very little in the way of empirical or formal work using younger adults as subjects (Atkinson & Paulson, 1972; Dear, Silberman, Estavan, & Atkinson, 1967; Karush & Dear, 1966).

Optimal Training Algorithms: Two-State Model

I want to describe here one of the two attempts to identify formally the optimal training schedule. This attempt was first reported by Karush and Dear (1966). Briefly, they proved that when the conditioning probabilities were identical across paired associates, the probability that all stimuli were jointly conditioned in a fixed number n of trials could be maximized if one used a simple rule to identify the stimulus that was to be selected as the next one to train. In particular, all stimuli are trained once at the outset in any order. After each stimulus has been trained once, a running count of the number of correct responses since the last error is kept for each stimulus. Specifically, after the first block of trials, the count starts at zero for each stimulus, regardless of the response to the stimulus in the first block. On each new trial, the stimulus with the smallest count is selected for training. When several stimuli tie for the smallest count, the stimulus to be trained next is selected randomly from among the stimuli tied for the smallest count.

Intuitively, the algorithm described previously operates as one might expect. If subjects are truly guessing at the outset, then the character of a response (correct or incorrect) the first time a stimulus is presented indicates only the influence of chance factors. Thus, the response can be ignored. However, such is not the case on remaining trials. Then, the history of the responses does indicate something about the likelihood that a stimulus is in a given state. Specifically, note that if a stimulus has been learned, its count will increase by one every time it is trained. If a stimulus has not been learned, then its count will be set back to zero every time the subject guesses incorrectly. Thus, the stimuli with the smallest counts should be those most in need of practice.

An example can make clear what needs to happen. Specifically, consider the example in Table 2.4. Under each training trial, I have listed the stimulus being trained ($s_1, \ldots, s_4$), the response (0 if incorrect; 1 if correct) and the values of the counters ($r_1, \ldots, r_4$) at the beginning of each trial. Until each stimulus has been trained once, the value of the counters is of no consequence, and I have indicated this by placing a dash in the relevant column. On the first four training trials, the first four stimuli can be trained in any order. Correct responses

TABLE 2.4
Training Algorithm Based on Karush and Dear (1966) Data

Trial	*Stimulus*	*Response*	*Counter*			
			r_1	r_2	r_3	r_4
1	s_1	1	—	—	—	—
2	s_2	0	—	—	—	—
3	s_3	0	—	—	—	—
4	s_4	1	—	—	—	—
5	s_1	1	0	0	0	0
6	s_2	1	1	0	0	0
7	s_3	0	1	1	0	0
8	s_4	0	1	1	0	0
9	s_3	1	1	1	0	0
10	s_3	1	1	1	1	0

were made to stimuli s_1 and s_4 (Trials 1 and 4) whereas incorrect responses were made to the remaining two stimuli (Trials 2 and 3). The counter for each stimulus is set to zero after the first block of (four) trials is complete, regardless of the response in the first block. In this case, because all counts are zero, we can randomly select from among the four stimuli. Suppose we select stimulus s_1 and the response is correct. Then at the beginning of the next trial counter r_1 will be one and the counters of the remaining three stimuli are still at zero. Thus, we randomly select the next stimulus to train from among that set. Suppose that we select stimulus s_2 and that the response to it is correct. Then at the beginning of the next trial counters r_1 and r_2 will be set to 1 and the remaining two counters will still be zero. Thus, we can randomly select to train next either s_3 or s_4, and so on.

The effect of using an optimal schedule on the time it takes older adults to reach criterion with the above list of four paired associates can now easily be explored. In order to get started, we need to select values for the conditioning and guessing parameters. I will arbitrarily assume that $c = .20$ and that $g = .5$. We also need to select a criterion value. I will assume here that the criterion is reached when the probability that a subject responds correctly to all four stimuli is .99. To begin, assume that older adults are trained using the standard *blocked schedule* (i.e., each stimulus is trained an equal number of times). Then, using Equation 2 to predict their performance, it should take older adults a total of 100 trials (25 trials per stimulus) to reach criterion. Instead, assume that older adults are trained using the optimal schedule. Then using a simulation to predict their performance, it should take on average 60 trials to reach criterion. Thus, the optimal schedule in this case decreases the time to reach criterion by 40%, a significant decrease by any standard.

There is another, perhaps more informative way to evaluate the effect of using an optimal schedule on the time it takes older adults to reach criterion. In particular, one can compare the time it takes older adults to reach criterion using an optimal schedule with the time it takes younger adults to reach criterion using a standard schedule, assuming (of course) that younger adults are significantly more likely to learn the response to a stimulus on any given trial than older adults. For example, assume that the probability that younger adults are conditioned is .35 whereas the probability that older adults are conditioned is .20. Then, as we just saw, using an optimal schedule it takes older adults 60 trials to reach criterion. Interestingly, it can be shown that this is exactly the same number of trials using a standard blocked schedule that it takes younger adults to reach criterion, even though younger adults are fully 75% more likely to learn the response to a stimulus on any given trial. Thus, the optimal schedule in this example has the effect of entirely mitigating the effect of aging.

In summary, simply by rearranging the order in which the paired associates are trained, we can potentially achieve a large reduction in the number of trials that it takes older adults to learn a list of paired associates. Moreover, older adults trained using an optimal schedule can learn to criterion a list of paired associates in the same time it takes younger adults using a standard blocked schedule to learn the list. Finally, the training algorithm does not vary as a function of age. Thus, because the algorithm applies equally well to younger and older adults, support exists for the general training hypothesis.

LAG SENSITIVE MODEL

The effort required to implement the optimal training schedule using the Karush and Dear (1966) algorithm is a practitioner's dream. No parameters need to be estimated beforehand. We do not need to know the guessing probability. We do not need to know the conditioning probability. A running count simply has to be kept of the number of correct responses to each stimulus since the last error. Of course, the training schedule is optimal only if the assumptions of the two-state model are met. These assumptions deserve more scrutiny. One way to do such is to derive predictions from these assumptions and then test the predictions.

Predictions of Two-State Model

Two predictions stand out as requiring a more rigorous test. First, it is easy to show that the assumptions of the two-state model imply that the number of trials that intervene between successive presentations of the same paired associate does not influence the likelihood that a stimulus will be conditioned. Second, it is easy to show that the assumptions of the two-state model imply that there should be a monotonic relation between performance as measured during acquisition and performance as measured on a later test of retention.

Lag Invariance. To begin, consider the relation between performance and the number of items that intervene between successive presentations of the same paired associate (i.e., the lag). According to the two-state model, the likelihood that the subject responds correctly on the second presentation of a stimulus is equal to $c + g(1 - c)$ for any lag size (Equation 2, $i = 2$). This lag invariance prediction holds for any trial i, not just $i = 2$. The prediction is a critical one to test because the lag between successive presentations is exactly what is being varied (indirectly) in the optimal training schedule suggested by Karush and Dear (1966).

A study run by Peterson and his colleagues (Peterson, Wampler, Kirkpatrick, & Saltzman, 1963) using younger adults as subjects can provide us with a test of the lag invariance assumption. Specifically, Peterson et al. used a continuous paired associate training paradigm instead of the blocked paradigm discussed to date to study the influence that the number of items intervening between successive presentations of the same pair had on performance. Words were used as the stimulus elements, digits as the responses. The word–digit pairs were presented twice with either 0, 1, 2, 4, 8, or 16 other pairs between successive presentations. Several (eight) filler items followed the second presentation and then the word was shown alone for test. All pairs were presented at a 2-second rate. The results are displayed in the Fig. 2.3. It is clear from the figure that performance is poorest when the presentation is massed, that is, when the lag is 0. Performance then improves as the lag increases up to 8–16 intervening items. At that point it appears that performance declines. Of course, one study is too few to conclude that performance is maximized at a lag of 8–16 items and decreases on either side. However, we do not have to rely on this study only. Other studies find an inverted U-shaped function too, with a maximum in the neighborhood of 8 intervening items (Young, 1966). In short, the lag invariance assumption must be rejected and, by implication, the two-state model.

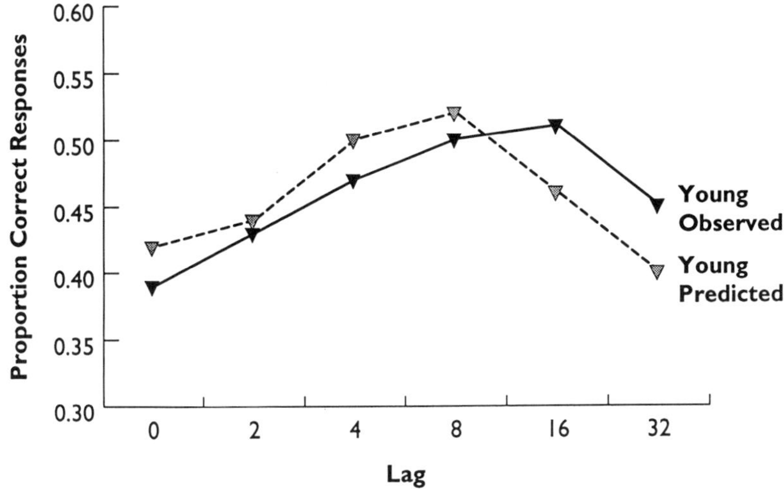

FIG. 2.3 Effect of lag on younger adults' acquisition: predicted (dashed lines) and observed (solid lines). (Predicted points from lag sensitive model. Observed points from Peterson, Wampler, Kirkpatrick, & Saltzman, 1963.)

Massed and Spaced Training: Acquisition and Retention. I began by stating that there were two predictions of the two-state model which clearly needed to be tested. Now I shall discuss this second prediction. In particular, the two-state model predicts that the likelihood that a subject is conditioned on some trial i is a monotonically increasing function of the probability that a subject responds correctly on the trial. This assumption, like the lag invariance assumption, is a particularly critical one to test. In this case, we want to use a schedule that minimizes the number of trials it takes subjects to reach some criterion level of responding during training only if this also maximizes retention.

In a recent review of training research, Schmidt and Bjork (1992) described a number of experiments that bear on the preceding prediction. For example, in an experiment by Landauer and Bjork (1978), subjects were given three training trials. The trials were either massed together or spaced out. The probability of a correct response was measured on the third trial. Subjects responded correctly almost 100% of the time when the trials were massed and only 40% of the time when the trials were spaced. However, in a test of retention given 30 minutes later there was a radical shift in these probabilities. In particular, subjects responded correctly more often if they had been trained in a spaced condition than if they had been trained in a massed condition. Thus, the probability that a subject responds correctly during training, as given on the third trial, is not monotonically related to the probability that the subject is conditioned, as given by the final retention test.

Lag Sensitive Model

The finding that performance is a function of the lag between successive presentations of an item clearly requires a modification to the simple two state model. The finding that the level of spacing interacts with the time of the test also requires a modification to the two-state model. I now want to describe such a model, one I refer to as the lag sensitive model.

To begin, consider the changes that are required in order to predict the sensitivity of training to the size of the lag. Intuitively, an inverted U would come about if two factors jointly determined performance where the influence of one factor was such that it greatly depressed performance at the shorter lags, the influence of the second factor was such that it greatly depressed performance at the longer lags, and the joint influence of the two factors was such that they increased performance at the intermediate lags. What might the first factor be, the factor that decreases disproportionately the likelihood that a stimulus is learned as the lag becomes very small? Note that with short lags, the correct response may still reside in short term memory. Thus, retrieval from long term memory is not required for a correct response. It is well known that the act of retrieval from long term memory is itself important to the strengthening of the paired associate bond. Therefore, as the lag decreases, the likelihood that the response is retrieved from long rather than short term memory decreases as well and learning should degrade accordingly. What might the second factor be, the factor that decreases disproportionately the likelihood that a stimulus is learned as the lag becomes very large? Imagine here that a stimulus initially stored in long term memory is fragile and can decay. I label the state of such a stimulus as critical because it must be trained relatively soon after entering this state in order to be stored permanently in long term memory. As the lag increases, the likelihood increases that the stimulus will decay from this critical state, and performance should suffer accordingly. Finally, note that the influence of the first lag potentiating factor (lag potentiating because the factor acts to increase performance as the lag increases) and the second lag diminishing factor will jointly raise performance at intermediate lags, thus producing (at least in theory) the observed inverted U.

The existence of the first lag potentiating factor and second lag diminishing factor require three extensions to the simple two-state model. First, I need to expand the model from two to four states. I have labeled the states as follows: *L* for long term memory, *C* for the critical learning state, *S* for short term memory, and *U* for unlearned (Table 2.5). Second, I need to separate training and nontraining matrices. The training matrix *M* describes the transitions among states in the test and

TABLE 2.5
Lag Sensitive Model

Trial *i*	State: Trial *i* + 1			
	L	C	S	U
L	1			
C	c	(1 − c)d	(1 − c)(1 − d)	
S		s	(1 − s)	
U			u	1 − u

A. Training Matrix

Trial *i*	State: Trial *i* + 1			
	L	C	S	U
L	1			
C		c′	(1 − c′)d′	(1 − c′)(1 − d′)
S		t_i'	s_i'	t_i'
U				1

B. Nontraining Matrix

Note. $s_i' = \exp(-f'/8)$, f': number of nontraining trials since last training trial.
$t_i' = (1 - s_i')/2$

study phase. The nontraining matrix N describes the transitions among states when other items are being trained. Finally, I need to make the likelihood that an item is lost from short term memory during a nontraining trial, given that it is in short term memory, increase as the number of consecutive nontraining trials increases. Specifically, the probability s_i' that an item is lost from short term memory after f' nontraining trials will be set equal to $e^{-f'/8}$. (So, for example, if a stimulus in state S at the beginning of trial *i* was trained in the previous trial, but is not being trained in the current trial *i*, then $f' = 0$ and $s_i' = 1$.) The negative exponential function creates a much steeper drop in the probability that an item remains in short term memory than is typically observed in studies of short term memory retention time (e.g., Peterson & Peterson, 1959). It was found that without such a drop, the lag sensitive model predicted the increase in recall that was observed when the lag increased from 0 to 8 intervening items. However, the model failed to predict the decrease in recall that was observed when the lag increased beyond 8 items. Note that the steep drop is justified in the current context because there exists in the paired associate task, but not the Peterson and Peterson task, the real possibility that the learning of new paired associates will push out of short term memory paired associates from previous trials which still are in residence.

Qualitatively, it is clear that the prior model captures both the lag potentiating and lag diminishing factors. The question at this point is whether the lag sensitive model can actually predict the observed variation in performance as the level of the lag changes when particular probabilities are assigned to the parameters. To determine this, I need to introduce several terms. In particular, let l equal the lag between the first and second presentation of a target item. Let r equal the number of filler items between the second presentation of the target item and the test of retention. Then, the probability that a subject responds correctly during a test of retention is simply equal to the probability that the target stimulus at test is in one of states L, C, or S plus the probability that the subject guesses correctly if the target stimulus at test is in state U. More formally,

$$P(\mathit{Correct\ at\ Test}) = e_1' M N^l M^r e_2 + g \bullet e_1' M N^l M N^r e_3, \qquad (3)$$

$$e_1' = (0,0,0,1), \quad e_2' = (1,1,1,0), \quad e_3' = (0,0,0,1).$$

It is now a simple matter to compute the preceding probability across changes in the lag l. And, indeed, for appropriate choices of the parameters, the lag sensitive model does predict an inverted U shaped function much like what has been observed, peaking somewhere in the neighborhood of eight intervening items (Fig. 2.3).

Second, consider the interaction between spacing and the time of the test. To begin, consider the test of acquisition. Note that an item in short term memory is very likely to stay there if there is no lag between successive presentations of the items. Thus, it is highly probable that a subject will respond correctly when the lag is very short. However, as the lag increases the probability that the item remains in short term memory decreases. Thus, the subject may well forget the appropriate response and performance will be compromised. Next, consider the test of retention that occurs after some appreciable number of non-training trials. Items that were trained using a massed schedule were likely to remain in short term memory throughout training and thus never enter the critical learning state. However, items that were trained using a spaced schedule were likely during the nontraining trials to enter the critical learning state and then pass on to long term memory. Qualitatively, then, the lag sensitive model predicts the interaction between spacing and time of test. What about quantitatively? As Fig. 2.4 indicates, the model just described nicely predicts the observed interaction.

Sometime after I had completed work on this chapter, I came across a model—the immediate-delayed (I–D) model—related to the lag sensitive model that was originally described almost 30 years ago by Young (1966, 1970). Young showed that the I–D model can predict the first of the above two findings (the finding that performance is an

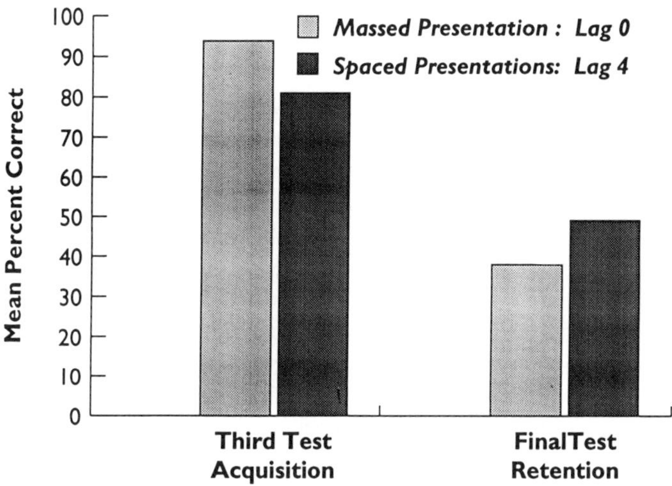

FIG. 2.4 Predicted interaction between spacing and time of test. (Predicted points from lag sensitive model.)

inverted U-shaped function of the lag between successive presentations of an item). Although Young did not show that the I–D model can predict the second of the above two findings (the finding that the level of spacing interacts with the time of test), it would appear that the I–D model can easily do so because if an item is repeatedly trained it never enters long term memory, whereas if several trials intervene between the training of the same item, the item can enter long term memory. Although both models make the same two predictions, they differ in at least three important respects. First, the models have different numbers of states. Specifically, the I–D model has five states (three short term memory states, one long term memory state, and one unlearned state), whereas the lag sensitive model has four states (two long term memory states, one short term memory state, and one unlearned state). Second, the assumptions about the learning process are quite different, at least on the surface. For example, suppose that an unlearned item that is in short term memory (immediate short term memory in Young's model) is retrained. Then, in the I–D model it is assumed that learning is unlikely because the code used for retrieval from long term memory remains inadequate after retraining, whereas in the lag sensitive model it is assumed that learning is unlikely because retrieval occurs from short rather than long term memory. Third, and not surprisingly given the foregoing (and other) qualitative differences, the models make different assumptions about which transitions are allowable and which are not. Thus, the models appear to differ substantially from one another. However, it remains to be determined whether the models are indeed identifiably different (Greeno & Steiner, 1964). Work on this determination is now underway.

General Acquisition, Decrement and Training Hypotheses

The lag sensitive model can predict the desired features of paired associate learning and therefore appears worthy of further investigation. At this point, it would be nice to be able to report that the lag sensitive model had been used just as the two-state model to test the general acquisition, decrement and training hypotheses. Unfortunately, a great deal more information is required to use the lag sensitive model to test these hypotheses than is available in published reports. For example, in order to use the lag sensitive model to test the general acquisition hypothesis, it is necessary to know for each subject the particular lag between successive presentations of the same paired associate, because learning is tied critically to this lag. This lag varies randomly from one presentation to the next and, thus, is never reported. However, once this lag is known it is easy enough to fit the lag sensitive model. To see this, let l_1 be the lag between the first and second presentations of an item, l_2 be the lag between the second and third presentations of an item, and so on. Then, the probability that a subject responds correctly on trial i can be computed as follows:

$$P(\mathit{Correct\ Trial}\ 1) = g,$$

$$P(\mathit{Correct\ Trial}\ i) = e_1\left[\prod_{k=1}^{i-1} MN^{l_k}\right]e_2 + g \cdot e_1\left[\prod_{k=1}^{i-1} MN^{l_k}\right]e_3,\ i > 1. \tag{4}$$

Values of the parameters are selected that minimize chi-square (the sum across trials of two quantities: the ratio of the square of the difference between the observed and predicted number of correct responses to the predicted number of correct responses and the ratio of the square of the difference between the observed and predicted number of incorrect responses to the predicted number of incorrect responses). The values of the parameters can be selected by a simple grid search or by more sophisticated optimization algorithms. We have now run an experiment which will provide the detailed information required to test the above three hypotheses. We are in the process of analyzing the results.

The preliminary analyses that were undertaken indicate that, again, the results are consistent with the general acquisition hypothesis but not the general decrement hypothesis. If this is the case, then we can go on to speculate about the general training hypothesis. It is this speculation which I want to advance now since, ultimately, from the standpoint of the older adults (which eventually and thankfully includes most of us), interest is focused primarily on the practical improvements that can be gleaned from a study of paired associate learning. Briefly, the Karush and Dear (1966) algorithm no longer applies categorically, because the assumptions behind the model of paired associate learning are not satisfied. However, a modification to the Karush and Dear algorithm follows naturally from the conceptual analysis that led to the lag sensitive model.

The modification relies on the observation that paired associates trained too closely together will reside in short term memory and thus not be stored in long term memory on a more permanent basis. Thus, it is not advantageous to train an item that was just trained on the previous trial. Similarly, paired associates trained too far apart will have decayed from both short term memory (state S) and labile long term memory (state C). Thus, it is not advantageous to train an item that was been trained quite some time ago. Rather, it makes sense to select next for training a paired associate with the smallest number of successive correct responses subject to the constraint that a lag greater than some minimum and less than some maximum separates the current and most recent training trials of the relevant paired associate. So, for example, if the count of one stimulus were 0 and it had been trained on the immediately preceding trial and the count of a second stimulus were 1 and it had last been trained several trials earlier, the second stimulus would be chosen over the first, because the lag is greater than 0.

A simulation was run to compare performance using a standard blocked training schedule with both the Karush and Dear (1966) algorithm and the modification to the Karush and Dear algorithm described previously. Specifically, in the modified Karush and Dear algorithm a count is kept of the number of correct responses. A paired associated is trained next if it has the smallest count among those paired associates with a lag of at least 4 (no maximum was used in the simulation). If no stimuli with a lag of at least 4 existed (possible at the end of training), then a paired associate was trained next if it had the smallest count among those paired associates with a lag of at least 3. And so on. We assumed that $g = 0$, that the number of stimuli was equal to 20, and that each stimulus was trained 41 times in the blocked condition. When simulating performance with the Karush and Dear and modified Karush and Dear algorithms, a total of 820 trials were run, where the exact number of trials each paired associate was trained depended on the sequence of responses. We found that the probability that a paired associate was in long term memory was equal to .15 using the blocked schedule, .23 using the Karush and Dear algorithm, and

.48 using the modified Karush and Dear algorithm. Thus, by implication, the modified Karush and Dear algorithm may well greatly reduce the time it takes older adults to reach criterion.

DISCUSSION

In the 1950s, models of learning in simple paired associate tasks were proposed that proved to predict a great many of the most significant results. However, these models have since been all but ignored. I argue that we need to revisit these models, both for what they can tell us about the effects of aging on the learning process and for what they can tell us about the effects of different training schedules on the time it takes older adults to acquire new information. I now want to summarize and extend this discussion.

Theory

To begin, I want to talk about the current state of our theoretical understanding of paired associate learning in older and younger adults. Then I want to look more finely at one particular hypothesis, the general decrement hypothesis, and discuss how it relates to an hypothesis at a similar level of detail, the general slowing hypothesis.

Hypotheses. At the start of the chapter I identified three hypotheses with clear theoretical import, the general acquisition, decrement, and training hypotheses. It is evident from the above analysis that the two state model predicts well the acquisition performance of both younger and older adults. This is consistent with the general acquisition hypothesis. It is also clear that the decrements observed in the processes implicit in the two state model are not identical across tasks since decrements were observed in some tasks but not in others. This is not consistent with the general decrement hypothesis. Finally, it is clear that the algorithm used to minimize the number of trials it takes an individual to reach some criterion percentage correct does not depend on the age of the subject. This is consistent with the general training hypothesis.

The story would end neatly at this point if it were not for the fact that the two-state model cannot predict two critical features of the results. First, it does not predict the finding that performance varies as a function of the lag between successive presentations of the same paired associate. And second it does not predict the finding of an interaction between the size of the spacing and the time of test. As we saw, a model can be constructed that makes these predictions (also see Young, 1970). This model, what I have called the lag sensitive model, needs to be tested more fully. Once such is done, then it can be used to determine the status of the general acquisition, decrement, and training hypotheses.

General Slowing. As noted previously, based on preliminary analyses of the lag sensitive model, it would appear very likely that the general acquisition hypothesis will continue to receive support. And it would appear likely that the general decrement hypothesis will fail again. Thus, as was discussed, one and the same formal model will explain both younger and older adults' paired associate performance, but not all processes will be affected identically across tasks. The question I ask at this point is whether a failure of the general decrement hypothesis also implies a failure of the general slowing hypothesis (Cerella, Poon, & Williams, 1980; although see Fisk, Fisher, & Rogers, 1992; Fisk & Fisher, 1994; Fisher, Fisk, & Duffy, 1995). At first glance it may seem that the general slowing and general decrement hypotheses are unrelated to one another. However, Salthouse (1980; Salthouse & Kail, 1983) argued that older adults may have difficulty storing material in long term memory in a fixed interval of time because they process this material more slowly and, therefore, in theory, engage in a shallower or less elaborate encoding of the material. This argument is consistent with the finding that older adults are less likely on any given trial to learn a paired associate in the Kausler and Puckett (1980) study. However, it is not consistent with the finding that older and younger adults are equally likely on a given trial to learn a paired associate in the Korchin and Basowitz (1957) study. Rather, because time was limited in the latter study interval and because, hypothetically, older adults engage in a more shallow encoding, the likelihood that the older adults stored material in long term memory on any given trial should have been less than this same likelihood for younger adults. Although the work reported in this chapter is too preliminary to draw any final conclusions, it can be said at this point that the modeling approach advocated herein offers the first real chance to explore in much more detail relations between the general slowing and general decrement hypotheses.

Application

Ultimately, one would like to know whether the advances in theory translate into advances in practice. In this case, it would appear that the two are intimately connected, and, perhaps more important, an advance in theory can be translated more or less immediately into an advance in practice. Here, I discuss very briefly the relation between theory and practice when the theory is less than fully formed. I also speak directly to the issue of the relevance of paired associate learning to older adults' daily lives.

Training Algorithms. In principle, the Karush and Dear (1966) algorithm can decrease greatly the number of trials required to reach criterion, even when the assumptions underlying the model on which the algorithm is based are not satisfied. The modified Karush and Dear algorithm can decrease even more the number of trials required to reach criterion. In fact, we saw that it is possible to speed older adults' learning using an optimal schedule to the point at which they acquire paired associates at the same rate as younger adults using a standard schedule (and, in particular, the blocked schedule). Thus, the effects of aging on the learning of paired associates can be reduced to zero.

The foregoing synopsis of the advances in the development of optimal training algorithms contains an important and often missed point. Specifically, the success of a given design (training schedule in this case) does not necessarily require a perfect understanding of the underlying phenomenon which governs performance. Thus, in this case the original Karush and Dear (1966) algorithm improves performance, even though it does not predict every aspect of performance. Of course, it could have happened otherwise, which is why one always wants to determine whether alternative designs selected by a model are indeed better than existing designs. And, of course, the closer one gets to understanding the underlying phenomena, the better able one is to propose the best design. However, engineering is filled with examples of models that are only approximations to the underlying phenomena, models which predict well the performance of various systems and structures. These models are tested in the real world and modified accordingly, learning much in the process. Similarly, it may well be the case that cognitive psychology has become mature enough to base good design recommendations on the underlying models of processing even though these models, as always, could be improved.

Paired Associate Learning in Daily Functioning. I have argued that decreases in the time that it takes older adults to learn a list of paired associates could make accessible to older adults many of the new technologies from which currently they shy away: ATMs, voice mail, word processing programs, and so on. In particular, I have argued that if it were possible to speed the learning of these new technologies sufficiently, then older adults may be more willing to give them a try. The reader may well ask what relation exists between a simple laboratory task, such as learning a list of paired associates, and a complex real-world task, such as learning a word processing program. The answer depends on the application. Next, I discuss three applications in more detail.

To begin, consider the application just mentioned, the learning of a new word processing program. All word processing programs require the user to activate a sequence of icons or keystrokes in order to execute a given function. The stimulus in this case is the function that the user wants to execute. The response is the sequence of icons or keystrokes. The identical analysis quickly convinces me, and I hope the reader, that ATMs, voice mail, and other related applications are in large part just paired associate tasks. Second, consider the myriad of continuing education courses in which older adults enthusiastically enroll. Much of the material that is learned is factual: parts of the anatomy (the stimuli) must be linked to their names (the responses), works of art (the stimuli) must be joined to particular artists (the responses), and so on. Finally, consider the actual retraining of older adults in the workplace for new jobs. Again, much new remains to be learned and this new material typically requires long hours of memorization.

In all of the preceding cases, the time it takes older adults to learn the material could be reduced, sometimes by upwards of 50%, if the analyses reported here generalize beyond the laboratory. Such reductions may open a world of opportunity to older adults. The studies that need to be undertaken in order to realize this opportunity follow clearly from the material discussed in this chapter. Conferences like the one from which this chapter evolved will prove to be an important stimulus to such studies.

ACKNOWLEDGMENTS

The research was supported in part by a grant from the National Institutes of Health (NIA No. R01AG12461) to the author.

REFERENCES

Atkinson, R. C., & Paulson, J. A. (1972). An approach to the psychology of instruction. *Psychological Bulletin, 78,* 49–61.

Bower, G. H. (1961). Application of a model to paired-associate earning. *Psychometrika, 26,* 255–280.

Bower, G. H. (1962). A model for response and training variables in paired-associate learning. *Psychological Review, 69,* 34–53.

Bush, R. R., & Mosteller, F. A. (1951). A mathematical model of simple learning. *Psychological Review, 58*, 313–323.

Cerella, J., Poon, L. W., & Williams, D. M. (1980). Age and the complexity hypothesis. In L. W. Poon (Ed.), *Aging in the 1980s* (pp. 332–340). Washington, DC: American Psychological Association.

Cieutat, V. J., Stockwell, F. E., & Noble, C. E. (1958). The interaction of ability and amount of practice with stimulus and response meaningfulness (*m,m'*) in paired-associate learning. *Journal of Experimental Psychology, 56*, 193–202.

Dear, R. E., Silberman, H,. F., Estavan, D. P., & Atkinson, R. C. (1967). An optimal strategy for the presentation of paired-associate items. *Behavioral Science, 12*, 1–13.

Estes, W. K. (1950). Toward a statistical theory of learning. *Psychological Review, 57*, 94–107.

Fisher, D. L., Fisk, A. D., & Duffy, S. A. (1995). Why latent models are needed to test hypotheses about the slowing of word and language processes in older adults? In P. Allen and T. Bashore, *Advances in Psychology: Age differences in word and language processing* (pp. 1–29). New York: North-Holland.

Fisher, D. L., Wisher, R. A., & Ranney, T. (1996). Static and dynamic training strategies: A framework for optimizing training strategies. *Journal of Mathematical Psychology, 40*, 30–47.

Fisk, A. D., & Fisher, D. L. (1994). Brinley plots and theories of aging: The explicit, implicit and muddled debates. *Journal of Gerontology, 49*, P81–P89.

Fisk, A. D., Fisher, D. L., & Rogers, W. A. (1992). General slowing alone cannot explain age-related search effects: A reply to Cerella. *Journal of Experimental Psychology: General, 121*, 73–78.

Greeno, J. G., & Steiner, T. E. (1964). Markovian processes with identifiable states: General considerations and application to all-or-none learning. *Psychometrika, 29*, 309–333.

Hasher, L., & Zacks, R. T. (1979). Automatic and effortful processes in memory. *Journal of Experimental Psychology: General, 108*, 356–388.

Karush, W., & Dear, R. E. (1966). Optimal stimulus presentation strategy for a stimulus sampling model of learning. *Journal of Mathematical Psychology, 3*, 19–47.

Kausler, D. H. (1992). Comments on aging memory and its everyday operations. In L. W. Poon, D. C. Rubin, & B. W. Wilson (Eds.), *Everyday cognition in adulthood and late life* (pp. 483–495). Cambridge, England: Cambridge University Press.

Kausler, D. H., & Puckett, J. M. (1980). Frequency judgments and correlated cognitive abilities in young and elderly adults. *Journal of Gerontology, 35*, 376–382.

Korchin, S. J., & Basowitz, H. (1957). Age differences in verbal learning. *Journal of Abnormal and Social Psychology, 54*, 64–69.

Landauer, T. K., & Bjork, R. A. (1978). Optimum rehearsal patterns and name learning. In M. M. Gruneberg, P. E. Morris, & R. N. Sykes (Eds.), *Practical aspects of memory* (pp. 625–632). London: Academic Press.

Peterson, L. R., & Peterson, M. J. (1959). Short-term retention of individual items. *Journal of Experimental Psychology, 58*, 193–198.

Peterson, L. R., Wampler, R., Kirkpatrick, M., & Saltzman, D. (1963). Effect of spacing presentations on retention of a paired associate over short intervals. *Journal of Experimental Psychology, 66*, 206–209.

Salthouse, T. A. (1980). Age and memory: Strategies for localizing the loss. In L. W. Poon, J. L. Fozard, L. Cermak, D. Arenberg, & L. W. Thompson (Eds.), *New directions in memory and aging* (pp. 47–65). Hillsdale, NJ: Lawrence Erlbaum Associates.

Salthouse, T. A., & Kail, R. (1983). Memory development throughout the lifespan: The role of processing rate. In P. B. Baltes & O. G. Bring (Eds.), *Life-span development and behavior* (Vol. 5, pp. 89–116). New York: Academic Press.

Schmidt, R. A., & Bjork, R. A. (1992). New conceptualizations of practice: Common principles in three paradigms suggest new concepts for training. *Psychological Science, 3,* 207–217.

Young, J. L. (1966). *Effects of intervals between reinforcements and test trials in paired-associate learning* (Tech. Rep. No. 101). Stanford: Stanford University, Institute for Mathematical Studies).

Young, J. L. (1970). Reinforcement-test intervals in paired-associate learning. *Journal of Mathematical Psychology, 8,* 58–81.

CHAPTER 3

The Use of Signal Detection Theory in Research on Age-Related Differences in Movement Control

Neff Walker
David A. Philbin
Christopher Spruell
Georgia Institute of Technology

One truism about the effects of aging on performance is that physical movement skills decline from middle age onwards. A passing knowledge of professional sports makes clear that few people can function at the same high level of performance after age 35, and those that do tend to rely on "guile" to compensate for their "lost physical abilities."

Though we know that age-related differences in movement performance exist, the exact nature of the differences, much less their cause, is far from clear. One explanation for lower performance is based on loss of strength or muscle mass as one ages. An extensive body of research exists showing that for average adults muscle mass and strength drop off after age 40 (Aniansson, Sperling, Rundgren, & Lehnberg, 1983; Fisher & Birren, 1947; Norris & Shock, 1960). For many movement skills, this loss in strength could explain performance differences, but this explanation is far from complete. Research has also shown that even though loss of strength is normal with aging, this loss can be reduced or even stopped with increased exercise. Research shows, however, that even with increased exercise, performance seems to suffer as age increases (Frontera, Meredith, O'Reilly, Knuttgen, & Evans, 1988; Moritani & deVries, 1980).

Movement performance decrements also occur for tasks in which strength does not seem to be a limiting factor. In golf, for example, even though strength plays some role in determining performance, the age-related drop in performance is more often ascribed to nonstrength decrements. The execution of "Yips" in putting (a task related more to fine motor control than to strength) rather than of "driving" the shorter distance off the tee (a task more related to strength) appears to be more affected by the age-related decline in performance.

So what does research in the area of movement control have to say about the causes of these changes in performance? In this chapter we are going to review research on age-related differences in movement control and try to outline what we believe to be a critical failing of some of this work. In this review we focus on movement tasks that are not affected by—or at least we identify where performance level is not primarily determined by—differences in strength.

To this end, we first briefly summarize the major theoretical explanations for age-related differences in movement control. Second, we review the experimental evidence about the exact nature of these age-related differences in performance, emphasizing the inconsistencies in the findings. Third, we suggest that age-related differences in the speed–accuracy tradeoff have contributed to this lack of consistency. Fourth, we present a study in which the speed–accuracy tradeoff function was manipulated and signal detection theory was used to test this argument.

EXPLANATIONS FOR AGE-RELATED DIFFERENCES IN MOVEMENT CONTROL

Explanations of overall slower movement times among older adults can be divided into four major categories: first, that older adults are more conservative, producing slower movements in an effort to reduce error; second, that there is an increase in motor noise as one ages, and older adults must slow down movements to reduce error caused by this increase in noise; third, that older adults have more perceptual noise in the system and this excess slows down performance; and fourth, that older adults have a generalized slowing in their perceptual motor system that produces the slower movements. These explanations are not necessarily mutually exclusive; two or more of these factors could be contributing to the overall slower movement of older adults. Next we review the general claims made by each of these explanations.

More Conservative

This explanation for slower movement times among older adults suggests that older adults plan slower movements because they are more "error averse" or "conservative" than younger adults (Goggin & Stelmach, 1990). In all movement tasks, a person must deal with a speed–accuracy tradeoff. As the force or resulting speed of a movement increases, the probability of the movement ending at the planned location decreases. For each movement task, a person must decide how to optimize performance on speed and accuracy. Whether one decides to have faster but less accurate movements or slower but more accurate movements depends on an individual's strategy given the nature of the task constraints. For many experimental tasks, the speed–accuracy tradeoff is manipulated by rewards being placed differentially on speed and accuracy of movement. This speed–accuracy tradeoff holds for all ages, but, according to this explanation, older adults choose a higher accuracy level than do younger adults when placed under the same movement conditions.

Increased Motor Noise

Almost all current theories of movement control are based on a set of related assumptions. First, there is noise in the motor system. That is, even if one plans and programs a correct set of muscle forces for a movement, error will occur due to noise that is inherent in the system (Fitts, 1954). Second, noise increases with the amplitude of the force. In other words, if one plans a rapid movement that requires the application of greater muscle force, the amount of noise or error will increase with that force (Schmidt, Zelasnik, Hawkins, Frank, & Quinn, 1979).

Noise-related explanations for movement slowing (Welford, 1981) suggest that the noise-to-force ratio increases with age. This means that when an older adult produces a force of a set amount, the noise associated with the resulting movement is greater than when a younger adult produces the same movement with the same force. Given this assumption, older adults produce slower movements than younger adults because they must move more slowly in order to maintain the same level of movement accuracy as younger adults.

Increased Perceptual Noise

Research has also suggested that older adults have more noise in their visual processing system than do younger adults (Cremer & Zeef, 1987; Verrillo & Verrillo, 1985). This perceptual impairment leads to poorer movement performance by impeding the visually guided feedback mechanism involved in most movements. This is a source of age-related differences in movement control that results in longer deceleration (homing) phase of movement, because in this phase corrective adjustments based on visual and kinesthetic feedback are made.

General Slowing

The fourth explanation is that age-related differences in movement control may be due to a generalized slowing of cognitive, motor, and perceptual processes (see Salthouse, 1985, 1991 for overviews of this position). For a broad range of tasks, if the task is made harder for younger adults, the difficulty also increases proportionally for older adults. The central idea behind this explanation is that all underlying processes (cognitive, perceptual, and motor) become less efficient or slower with age, resulting in slower performance. This explanation would predict roughly equal proportional differences for all stages of a movement task.

As noted previously, few theorists believe that all age-related differences in movement performance are due to only one of these factors. Instead, two or more of these factors probably cause the performance differences. The key research issue should be to determine the relative importance of each of these factors in performance.

AGE-RELATED DIFFERENCES IN MOVEMENT PERFORMANCE

Research on simpler ballistic movements has found age-related differences in movement (Welford, 1981). In general, there are two consistent findings. First, movement times increase with age. Older adults are slower when making the same movements as younger adults (Bennett & Castiello, 1994; Welford, 1981).

Second, older adults spend more of their movement time in the second, homing phase of movement (Bennett & Castiello, 1994; Warabi, Noda, & Kato, 1986). This is often defined as the amount of movement time after peak velocity has been reached, or deceleration.

AGE-RELATED DIFFERENCES IN THE SPEED–ACCURACY TRADEOFF

One well-documented phenomenon that has often been studied within the context of aging is the speed–accuracy tradeoff. As the requirement for rapid completion of a reaction time task increases, the accuracy associated with the task decreases, and vice versa. Simply put, increases in speed yield decreases in accuracy, whereas increases in accuracy yield decreases in speed of performance.

Evidence exists that suggests a relationship between the speed–accuracy tradeoff and age. In several different experiments, older adults performed significantly slower than younger adults in most cases (Salthouse, 1979; Welford, 1981). The cause of this slowing has been disputed, although Welford (1981) suggests that a combination of the first and second theoretical explanations (increased desire for accuracy and increased motor noise) are to blame.

Despite finding the predicted slowing as age increased, Salthouse (1979) discovered that when the level of speed is fixed, accuracy shows no age difference, and vice versa. In the same article, Salthouse found that the young subjects were considerably more accurate than the older subjects, particularly when reaction times were slow to medium in speed. These findings indicate that the increased time that older adults required to complete reaction time tasks is not entirely explained by the older subjects placing more emphasis on accuracy.

INCONSISTENCIES IN THE RESEARCH

Few absolute consistencies exist in findings about age-related differences in movement performance. Whereas most studies report that older adults take longer to make a movement, this finding is not always reproduced (Cooke, Brown, & Cunningham, 1989; Murrell & Entwhistle, 1960). Second, whereas many recent studies find an increased proportion of movement time spent by older adults in the homing or deceleration phase of movement, there are counterexamples (Welford, Norris, & Shock, 1969; Murrell & Entwhistle, 1960). Given the normally robust nature of movement control findings—there are laws, not theories—it is surprising that so many inconsistencies in defining the age-related differences in movement performance have been found. This, of course, still begs the question of why these differences, if they exist, occur.

So why is it that work on age-related differences in movement control seems to lag so far behind the "mainstream" movement control work? We are going to propose two explanations. First, we argue that one reason that work in movement control has been able to establish well specified, lawful relationships between a movement task and movement performance is that the research has largely ignored individual differences. Second, we argue that the inconsistency of findings regarding age-related differences in movement control, and the resulting theoretical ambiguity, are party due to a confounding of differences attributable to differences in the speed–accuracy tradeoff and differences in movement control processes.

THE AGGREGATION PROBLEM

One aspect of research on movement control that hinders our understanding of age-related differences is the focus on average performance and the prediction of movement difficulty. Of course, one could argue that this focus on average performance is what most of psychology is about, so why does research on movement control pose a particularly difficult problem? Our argument is that beginning with Fitts' Law, the focus was on describing how physical constraints on movement (e.g., the distance of the movement, the size of the target) determine performance. Toward this end, much research had as its goal the development of a descriptive equation of performance. Arguments have centered on which function best described movement performance in terms of an index of difficulty of movement (e.g., $\log_2$ (2D/W), Fitts, 1954; $\log_2$ (D/W) + 0.5, Welford, 1960; square root (D/W), Meyer, Abrams, Kornblum, Wright, & Smith, 1988). While this research has not ignored the theoretical explanations for why the specific tradeoff function occurs, the research has largely ignored individual differences in the theoretical and empirical work.

How can we claim that individual differences were ignored, when there is a large body of research on special populations (Welford, Norris & Shock, 1969; Wade, Newell, & Wallace, 1978; Wallace, Newell, & Wade, 1978)? The key to this assertion relates to the way the best descriptive tradeoff function is determined. In all of the research we have seen, the regression equations are based on mean performance data for each level of the predictive equation. For example, whereas a study may include 16 subjects, who make 10 movements at each of 20 different distance by target width values, the regression equation is based on mean movement times for the 20 (or fewer) unique values of the predictor function being tested.

By using mean values based on collapsing across trials and subjects, this form of analysis eliminates any effects related to individual differences. Although we will not make a case for the drawbacks of this approach here (but see Walker & Catrambone, 1993, for a discussion of the problems associated with aggregation), we do believe that this focus has resulted in standard research methods and procedures that are less sensitive to the role that individual differences may play in determining performance.

THE CONFOUNDING-OF-VARIABLES PROBLEM

One of the real problems in delineating the different theoretical explanations is the lack of clear predictions that distinguish among them. An especially troublesome problem relates to the possibility that there are age-related differences in strategy. Why is this especially troublesome?

All of the theoretical explanations make the prediction that older adults will have slower movements. A primary goal of research is to determine the relative contribution of each possible explanation for age-related differences in movement performance. To do this, one must use experimental techniques that isolate each specific factor (e.g., Jagacinski, Liao, & Fayyad, 1995). For example, to determine the relative importance of visual processing on movement performance, a standard technique is to have one condition for which no visual feedback is allowed. By comparing age-related differences on a task that permits visual feedback to the same task with no visual feedback, one can determine the importance of that process in producing age-related differences in movement performance.

The problem with this approach to research has been that we have not developed ways to separate out strategy differences in how subjects adjust to the speed–accuracy task constraints from differences due to fundamental limitations. One option would be to ignore these strategy differences as a possible explanation. That approach is not very satisfying for at least two reasons. First, as we reviewed previously, there is evidence to suggest that older adults differ in how they approach problems that involve the speed–accuracy tradeoff (e.g., Salthouse, 1979; Welford, 1981). Second, most theories of movement performance have built-in assumptions about the strategic component of adjusting to relative speed–accuracy tradeoff functions (e.g., Meyer et al., 1988). Unfortunately, this is also the aspect of the models that is least developed, as the standard procedure is to ignore both individual differences in performance and to use a single point on the speed–accuracy tradeoff function.

SIGNAL DETECTION

Signal detection theory may be a way to isolate the effect of age-related strategy differences from age-related differences in physiological processes. Signal detection theory is an approach to understanding human performance when there are two discrete states between which one must discriminate. For example, a physician looking at a lung x-ray can either discover a dark spot that represents a tumor or not detect a dark spot. Given these two possible states, the person then has two resulting responses: Yes, there is a signal (a dark spot representing a tumor); or No, there is not a signal (no dark spot). According to signal detection theory (e.g., Green & Swets, 1988), there are distinct stages of processing that a person goes through in making such a judgment. First, sensory information is gathered about the presence or absence of the signal. Second, a decision is made about whether the sensory evidence constitutes a signal.

Given the two possible states of the world and two response types, there are four possible outcomes in a judgment tasks. First, a *hit* is when there is a signal in the environment and the person decides yes, there is a signal. A *miss* is when there is a signal in the environment but the person decides that there is no signal. A *false* alarm is when there is no signal in the environment but the person decided there is. Finally, a *correct rejection* occurs when there is no signal in the environment and the person decides that no signal is present (see Table 3.1).

A key point about signal detection theory is that it makes a distinction between the effects of sensory sensitivity (e.g., visual acuity) and response bias (the person's tendency to say "yes" or "no") in making a decision. Returning to our example of the physician reading an x-ray, sensory sensitivity refers to the ability to discriminate between an x-ray with and without a dark spot. Even though in some x-rays it is easy to discriminate between the presence and absence of the signal, in others it is not. Sensitivity depends on the strength of the signal (how dark and large is the spot) and the surrounding noise (the occurrence of other dark areas or the background). Therefore, a person's sensory sensitivity is one determinant of correctly sorting x-rays into those that show the presence of a tumor and those that do not.

The second factor that affects this ability to discriminate correctly between the two states is the response bias that the person has when making the decision. Returning to our medical example, one's decision of whether or not there is evidence of a tumor in the x-ray can be altered by prior events or predilections that the person brings to the task. If the physician reading the x-ray has just gone through a course on the early signs of lung cancer, the probability of deciding that the x-ray shows a

TABLE 3.1
Classification Scheme for the Signal Detect Analysis

	Decision	
Signal	*Yes (Don't Move)*	*No (Move)*
Present (In the box)	Hit	Miss
Absent (Out of the Box)	False Alarm	Correct Reject

spot could increase. Or the physician may have just had a case in which he or she decided to operate and then discovered that the lump was benign. In both of these cases, a person's response bias or decision criteria can be altered. Therefore, decision criteria is the second factor that determines performance.

Signal detection theory uses the characterization of decisions into these four categories to calculate measures of sensitivity (usually d′) and response bias (usually β) by which to judge a person's performance (e.g., Gescheider, 1985). In this study we use signal detection as a means of measuring both subject sensitivity to the state of being in the target box and the response criteria used to make this decision.

To do this we must define the signal and what constitutes a hit and a false alarm when one makes a movement in our experimental task. First, a person plans a movement toward the center of the target. Next the movement is initiated, and the subject then begins to determine whether the movement endpoint is in the target region or not (primarily through visual cues but also through kinesthetic cues). At the end of each submovement, a decision must be made. The possible outcomes of a submovement are that the movement either ended in the target (signal present) or it did not (signal absent). A person must then decide whether or not to make an additional corrective submovement. In terms of signal detection theory, when a movement ends in the target region and no additional submovement is made, the movement is classified as a *hit*. If the submovement ends in the target region and an additional submovement is made, it is classified as a *miss*. Submovements that do not end in the target region and are followed by an additional submovement are classified as a correct rejection. Submovements that end out of the target region with no additional submovement being made are classified as *false alarms*. Based on the classification of submovements into one of these four categories, we can calculate a measure of sensitivity and decision criteria.

By using signal detection theory, we can generate a measure of decision criterion that should be independent of physiological differences between the two age groups. With this measure we can then separate the effects of strategy differences and fundamental limitations on age-related movement performance.

In order to test this, we re-analyze a set of data (from Walker, Philbin, & Fisk, 1996) in which we (a) use signal detection to calculate a measure of decision criteria; and (b) re-analyze some of the primary dependent variables, but controlling for differences in decision criteria. In order to do this, we present a brief review of the methods and results of this previous work (for a full report of that study, see Walker, Philbin, & Fisk, 1996) along with the new analyses.

EXPERIMENTAL TASK

In this experiment older and younger adults were compared on their ability to position a cursor with an electromechanical mouse in a task that simulated common cursor positioning tasks required to use a computer. In the experiment, distance of the movement, size of the target, and relative emphasis on the speed or accuracy of the movement were manipulated. The study was designed to evaluate the effects of increased motor noise, increased perceptual noise, strategy differences, and generalized slowing as explanations for age-related differences in movement control.

Subjects

Two groups of 16 subjects participated in this experiment. One group consisted of older adults between the ages of 65–75 (mean = 70.2), and younger who ranged in age from 18–28 (mean = 21.9).

Design

The experiment used a mixed factorial design. The grouping variable was age, either young or old. The within-subjects variables were target distance (D = 100, 200, 300, 400, or 500 pixels), target width (W = 4, 8, 16, or 32 pixels), and penalty (P = −4, −8, −16, or −32 points).

Subjects were tested for one session per day for eight days. In the first session, ability tests were administered. In the next session the experimental task was demonstrated, the nature of the speed–accuracy tradeoff was explained, and the grading of performance on both speed and accuracy was discussed. This and the next two sessions were practice; the subjects performed 8 blocks of 20 practice trials in session two and 12 blocks of 20 in each of sessions three and four. For these training sessions, subjects were told to make movements as quickly as possible and try to eliminate any errors. A baseline of performance was established for each subject based on these trials, as described under Feedback Procedure. These baseline data were used later to establish mean movement times for each movement distance by target width condition for each subject. The point and penalty system was introduced in the last half of the third practice session. For the remainder of the sessions, subjects were given feedback on their performance in terms of points earned on a trial.

The fifth through eighth sessions were the experimental sessions. Each had 12 blocks of 20 trials at one of the four levels of penalty. The order of penalty was counterbalanced between subjects using a Latin squares design.

Feedback Procedure

During the last four blocks in the third session during the cursor positioning practice before the point and penalty system was introduced, the mean times for each subject at each of the 20 *D* by *W* conditions (5 *D*s × 4 *W*s) were calculated. These times were set as the baseline times against which each subject would compete for points. If a trial ended outside of the target box, subjects received a penalty according to the current penalty level (i.e., either −4, −8, −16, or −32 points), but if the trial ended within the target box, points were calculated based on the total positioning time, and the subject's baseline (mean) time for that *D* and *W* value target. Each point was based on a 5% deviation from the baseline time. If one performed 50% faster than one's mean, then one would earn 10 points; likewise, if one performed 50% slower than one's mean, then one would earn −10 points. This meant that a slow correct trial could result in more negative points than a fast trial that ended in an error if the penalty condition was low. The purpose of this manipulation was to force people to adjust their movement strategies. When penalty condition was low, optimal performance would be yielded by faster movements, even if more errors occurred. When the penalty condition was high, the optimal strategy would be to slow down the movements and avoid making errors.

Procedure

At the beginning of each day the subject was informed of that day's penalty value. At the beginning of each block a text box appeared saying "click here to begin next block." Using the computer mouse, the subject positioned the cursor within the box and pressed the mouse button. This initiated the block of trials. At the beginning of each trial the home box appeared on the left edge of the screen, and the target box, of *W* height and width, appeared with its center horizontally displaced *D* pixels away from the center of the home box.

Recording of the mouse position and time began when the subject initiated a trial. This was done by positioning the cursor within the home box and pressing and holding the mouse button. The trial ended when the subject released the mouse button. The computer then displayed a message reporting the results of the subject's movement. This report consisted of two pieces of information: whether upon the release of the mouse button the cursor was positioned within the target box (e.g., "Right" or "Wrong"), and the number of points the subject gained or lost in that particular trial. On the early trials for which no points were calculated, the feedback was simply time in ms. If the cursor was not in the target box at the end of the trial, the trial was randomized back in with the remaining trials to be performed for that block; otherwise the trial was considered completed. The home box and target box for the next trial then replaced the current screen. The subject repeated these steps until all the trials for that block had been completed.

At the end of each block, the subject was presented with a summary report of his or her results for that block of trials. This report included information on the number of correct trial points earned during that block, the number of incorrect trial points lost that block, and the total number of points for the subject that session. If all of the blocks in the session had not been performed, a text box indicating the beginning of a new block appeared. If all blocks had been completed the computer presented the subject with the total number of points that he or she had earned for the session.

Movement Parsing

The movement data were categorized using a movement parsing algorithm. The algorithm was based on our previous work (Walker, Meyer, & Smelcer, 1993), which was based on the work of Meyer et al. (1988) and Jagacinski, Repperger, Moran, Ward, and Glass (1980). As in Walker et al. (1993), the parsing algorithm decomposed overall movements into submovements based on distance, velocity and acceleration profiles. An initial movement of at least 75 pixels/sec lasting at least 20 ms was considered to begin the first submovement. The submovement was considered to end either when the velocity reached zero or when the acceleration changed signs after a relative minimum in velocity.

Signal Detection Analysis

Specifically, in this study we used the classification of individual submovements into hits, misses, false alarms, and correct rejects as specified in Fig. 3.1. Based on this classification, we then calculated measures of sensitivity and decision criteria for each subject for each penalty condition.

The nonparametric signal detection measures A' and B'' were employed in this experiment instead of their normally distributed counterparts, d′ and β. There were two main rationale for this substitution. First, the data did not conform well to any simple statistical distribution, and in particular it did not conform to the normal distribution. Since an assumption of normality and constant variance are required for the use of *d*′ and β, they had to be discounted as possible measures of sensitivity and response bias. Secondly, *A*′ and *B*″ are defined when hit rates are 1.0 or false alarm rates are 0.0; also, these nonparametric measures do not yield extremely large response bias values when hit rates and false alarm rates are very close to their respective extremes, as they are in our data set.

The measures *A*′ and *B*″ were initially derived from analyses of ROC graph characteristics. In the case of the sensitivity measure A′, Pollack and Norman (1964) demonstrated how a subject's hit probability and false alarm probability could be plotted on a unit square, then connected to the upper right-hand corner and lower left-hand corner of the graph by two respective lines. This divided the graph into four regions. If another data point fell into the upper left region, it was considered superior to the initial condition, whereas if it fell into the lower right region, it was considered inferior. The other two regions were regions of ambiguity, in which data points could not be considered significantly different from the initial condition. Hodos (1970) extended this graphical theory by adding a nonparametric response bias measure, B″. Grier (1971) quantified these geometric interpretations into algebraic formulas that were easier to understand and calculate as follows:

$$A' = 1 - \left(\tfrac{1}{4}\right)\left[\frac{P(F)}{P(H)} - \frac{(1 - P(H)}{(1 - P(F)}\right]$$

$$B'' = \frac{P(H)[1 - P(H)] - P(F)[1 - P(F)]}{P(H)[1 - P(H)] + P(F)[1 - P(F)]}$$

where P(F) is the probability of a false alarm and P(H) is the probability of a hit. For the derivation and analysis of these two measures, see Grier (1971), Frey and Colliver (1973), and Craig (1979).

RESULTS OF RE-ANALYSIS

After extracting the signal detection measures from our data, a penalty by age analysis of variance was performed on both A′ and B″. For *A*′ there was a significant main effect of age, $F(1,30) = 12.21$, $MS_E = 0.00111$, $p < .05$, a significant main effect of penalty condition, $F(3,90) = 5.11$, $MS_E = 0.00010$, $p < .01$, and a significant interaction,

$F(3,90) = 2.80$, $MS_E = 0.00010$, $p < .05$. Although a primary function of these analyses was not to look for differences in sensitivy, these results do show that there are age-related differences in sensitivity. More interesting (and possibly troubling) was the effect of penalty condition on A′. In most signal detection tasks, one assumes that A′ will be unaffected by penalty.

To understand the cause of the effect of penalty on A′ one must consider how this application of signal detection analysis differs from most applications. In this experiment, the degree of perceptual distinctiveness from the two states (in the box, not in the box) is not set by the experiment. The average distance from the target box is a result of the movements made by the subjects. As we assumed that penalty condition would result in different patterns of submovements, it may have been that penalty affected the types of discriminations that subjects had to make. That is, there may have been a systematic bias of the number of easy discriminations (when the cursor was a further distance from the target box). To investigate this, we calculated mean distance from the edge of the target box for each of the penalty conditions. This revealed that for both age groups, the mean distance (and standard deviations) from the edge of the target box increased with penalty condition. Although we do not discuss this issue further in this chapter, it does suggest that any interpretation of age-related differences in A′ must be made with caution. However, we do not believe that this invalidates the use of signal detection analyses.

The analysis on B″ yielded a significant main effect of age, $F(1,30) = 16.20$, $MS_E = 0.06887$, $p < .001$, a significant main effect of penalty condition, $F(3,90) = 11.44$, $MS_E = 0.01256$, $p < .0001$, and a significant interaction, $F(3,90) = 7.18$, $MS_E = 0.01256$, $p < .001$. As can be seen in Fig. 3.1, while older adults continued to maintain a higher decision criteria, as the penalty increased the discrepancy between B″ for younger and older adults diminished. Follow-up analyses showed the highest penalty condition the age-related difference in B″ is not significant, but at the lower penalty conditions the difference is significant.

It seems quite apparent that even after attempting to equate subjects' performance on the speed–accuracy tradeoff by using each subject's own performance as the experimental baseline, there are still changes in B″ across the experimental conditions. If the differences in B″ are responsible for inconsistencies in experimental findings, we would expect to be able to find differences in effects between conditions where B″ is similar and dissimilar. In order to investigate this we chose two subsets of the data to re-analyze: first the condition where the penalty was −32 and B″s were similar for the two age groups; and second, the condition where the penalty was −4 and B″s were

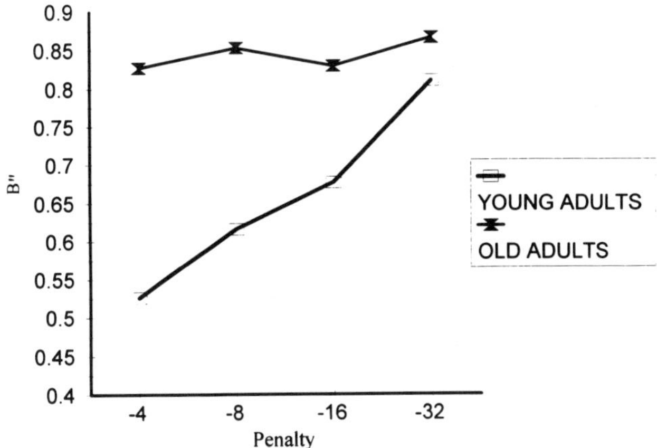

FIG. 3.1 Changes in B'' for old and young across penalty values.

different for the two age groups. Next we performed our analyses on each of these data sets and compared the results.

Even though not all of the age-related effect sizes decreased as B″ became more similar (in fact, a small number actually increased), many of them did. Perhaps the most impressive changes occurred in two of the dependent variables that are intimately related to the movement production, namely errors and maximum acceleration. When B'' was different, the proportion of correct trials as a function of age was significant, $F(1,30) = 12.66$, $p < .02$; yet when the data from the same subjects was chosen to reflect the condition where B'' was similar between old and young the main effect of age on proportion of correct trials dropped quite dramatically to statistical nonsignificance, $F(1,30) = 0.001$, $p > .96$. This change is illustrated graphically in Fig. 3.2.

Maximum acceleration also changed in significance between the similar and different B'' data sets. Although there was a similar trend of age in both data sets, as can be seen in Fig. 3.3, the difference between young and older subjects decreased as B″ became more similar. The analysis on maximum acceleration when B″ was different yielded a significant main effect of age, $F(1,30) = 6.91$, $p < .01$, whereas in the similar B'' the main effect of age was not significant, $F(1,30) = 2.71$, $p > .10$.

This same set of analyses was performed on all of the major dependent variables reported by Walker et al. (1996). Although the effects of analyses done separately for similar and different B'' did not always yield changes from significant to nonsignificant effects of age, there were changes in many of the analyses. These changes sometimes shifted the main effect of age, other times made age by distance or age

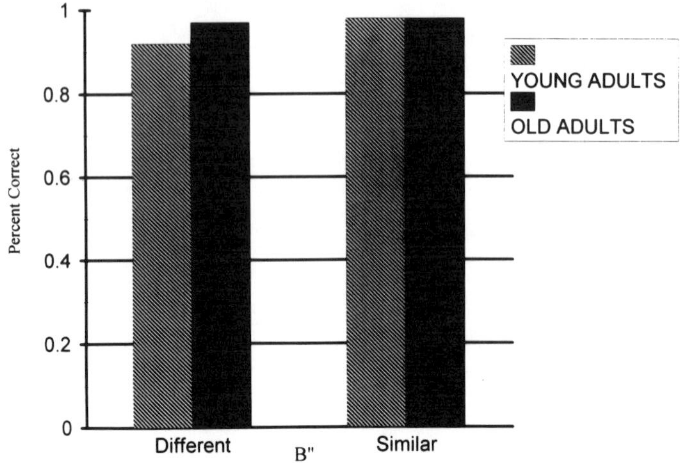

FIG. 3.2 Error rates by age and *B″*.

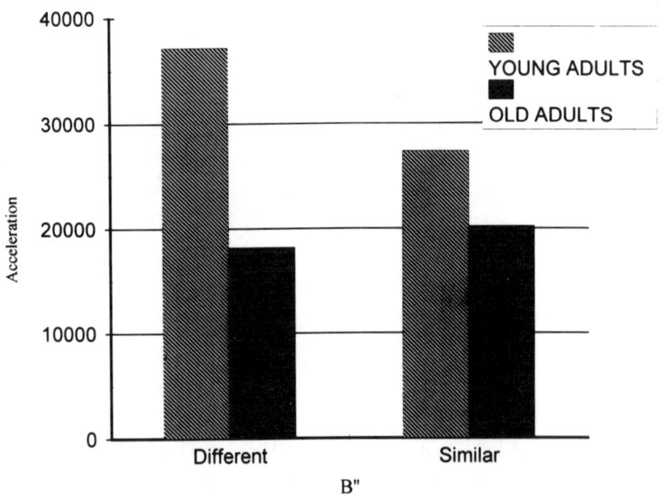

FIG. 3.3 Maximum acceleration (pixel/ms^2) by age and *B″*.

by width interactions no longer significant. The key point to note is that if one used only the analyses from when B″ was similar, one pattern of results appears. If one only had the analyses in which the B″ was different, another pattern of results is found.

CONCLUSIONS

The first conclusion to draw from this re-analysis is that previous work may have confounded decision criteria or strategy differences with physiological differences in explaining age-related differences in movement control. In our study we varied penalty condition as a way to adjust each subject's speed–accuracy tradeoff function. What is clear from the analysis of the B'' measure is that older adults do not adjust their decision criteria in the same way as do younger adults. They used a significantly different decision criteria at three of the four levels of penalty. Based on this, we suggest that previous work which did not vary penalty or measure B'' may well have been comparing younger adults at one point on the speed–accuracy continuum to older adults who are at a different location on that continuum. This confound would then preclude drawing firm conclusions about physiological differences causing age-related differences in movement performance.

The re-analysis also showed that when we looked for age-related differences in the cases where B'' differences were largest and smallest, we did find differences in the pattern of results. Equating for the level of B'' did not eliminate most or all of the age-related differences. Yet it did change the pattern of results. This finding may be important in understanding the lack of consistency in the literature on age-related differences in movement performance. It may well be that the failure to replicate results across experiments is due to age-related differences in speed–accuracy tradeoff functions between the two experiments.

This is not to say that researchers have ignored the speed–accuracy tradeoff in their work. Rather, it may be that using gross measures or controls (e.g., all subjects must have an accuracy rate of 90%; "Move as quickly as you can but try to eliminate errors.") may not have resulted in setting similar criteria among the subjects of the two age groups. In the data reported here, the error rates were always less than 10%, yet we still found large differences in B''. Therefore, simply setting a criterion based on an accuracy rate of above 90% will not equate older and younger adults on their decision criteria.

In the study we reported, the feedback mechanism for speed and accuracy was quite explicit (points awarded on each trial), and it was based on an individual's mean asymptotic performance. This type of control should have reduced age-related differences in the decision criterion. In fact, only at the highest penalty condition were the B'' values similar for the two age groups. This suggests that other studies which do not use such a stringent feedback condition may have even greater age-related differences in decision criteria.

In the beginning of this chapter, we outlined two major problems facing researchers investigating age-related differences in movement control. First, the effects of physiological and strategic processes are confounded, causing inconsistencies in the findings about age-related differences in movement control. Second, major theories of movement control do not adequately account for the effects of individual differences. The work reported here suggests that signal detection theory can provide useful techniques for separating the effects of strategic processes from physiological processes. Although our work has not gone that far, it seems plausible that with the development of an adequate body of research, these tools could result in an empirically tractable account of strategic effects on movement control. Also, the use of a decision criteria measure would provide a basis for the comparison of results across studies. Once research is able to isolate the effects of the physiological and strategic processes, then the work on developing models of movement control that incorporate individual differences can begin in earnest.

PRACTICAL IMPLICATIONS

So what does this methodological argument about how to approach understanding the causes of age-related differences in movement control have to say about real world problems faced by older adults? Obviously, there are many everyday situations where poorer movement control skills can have significant impact on performance. Two examples are driving a car and using a computer. In both cases, older adults must compensate for declining abilities to maintain acceptable (and in driving, safe) performance. In both of these cases, either training or redesign interventions could be used to improve performance. Yet for the interventions to be most effective, one must understand the causes of declining performance. If a primary cause of poorer performance is related to increased perceptual noise, augmenting feedback could improve performance. If increased motor noise is a primary cause of the age-related difference in performance, one could use changes in the gain ratio of the control system to compensate. The key is that one must understand the causes of age-related declines in performance before optimal design or training solutions can be developed.

REFERENCES

Aniansson, A., Sperling, L., Rundgren, A., & Lehnberg, E. (1983). Muscle function in 75-year-old men and women, a longitudinal study. *Scandinavian Journal of Rehabilitation Medicine, 193*(Suppl.) 92–102.

Bennett, K. M. B., & Castiello, U. (1994). Reach to grasp: Changes with age. *Journal of Gerontology: Psychological Sciences, 49,* 1–7.

Cooke, J. D., Brown, S. H., & Cummingham, B. A. (1989). Kinematics of arm movements in elderly humans. *Neurobiology of Aging, 10,* 159–165.

Craig, A. (1979). Nonparametric measures of sensory efficiency for sustained monitoring tasks. *Human Factors, 21*, 69–77.

Cremer, R., & Zeef, E. J. (1987). What kind of noise increases with age? *Journal of Gerontology, 42*, 515–518.

Fisher, M. B., & Birren, J. E. (1947). Age and strength. *Journal of Applied Psychology, 31*, 490–497.

Fitts, P. M. (1954). The information capacity of the human motor system in controlling the amplitude of movement. *Journal of Experimental Psychology, 47*, 381–391.

Frontera, W. R., Meredith, C. N., O'Reilly, K. P., Knuttgen, H. G., & Evans, W. J. (1988). Strength conditioning in older men: Skeletal muscle hypertrophy and improved function. *Journal of Applied Psychology, 64*, 1038–1044.

Frey, P. W., & Colliver, J. A. (1973). Sensitivity and responsivity measures for discrimination learning. *Learning and Motivation, 4*, 327–342.

Gescheider, G. A. (1985). *Psychophysics: Method, theory, and application* (2nd ed.). Hillsdale, NJ: Lawrence Erlbaum Associates.

Goggin, N. L., & Stelmach, G. E. (1990). Age-related differences in a kinematic analysis of pre-cued movements. *Canadian Journal on Aging, 9*, 371–385.

Green, E. M., & Swets, J. A. (1988). *Signal detection theory and psychophysics*. New York: Wiley.

Grier, J. B. (1971). Nonparametric indexes for sensitivity and bias: Computing formulas. *Psychological Bulletin, 75*, 424–429.

Hodos, W. (1970). A non-parametric index of response bias for use in detection and recognition experiments. *Psychological Bulletin, 74*, 351–354.

Jagacinski, R. J., Liao, M. J., & Fayyad, E. A. (1995). Generalized slowing in sinusodial tracking by older adutls. *Psychology and Aging, 10*, 8–19.

Jagacinski, R. J., Repperger, D. W., Moran, M. S., Ward, S. L., & Glass, B. (1980). The microstructure of rapid discrete movements. *Journal of Experimental Psychology: Human Perception and Performance, 6*, 309–320.

Meyer, D. E., Abrams, R. A., Kornblum, S., Wright, C. E., & Smith, J. E. K. (1988). Optimality in human motor performance: Ideal control of rapid aimed movements. *Psychological Review, 95*, 340–370.

Moritani, T., & deVries, H. A. (1980). Potential for gross muscle hypertrophy in older men. *Journal of Gerontology, 35*, 672–682.

Murrell, K. F. H., & Entwhistle, D. G. (1960). Age differences in movement pattern. *Nature, 185*, 948–949.

Norris, A. H., & Shock, N. W. (1960). Exercise in the adult years—with special reference to the advanced years. In W. R. Johnson & E. R. Buskirk (Eds.), *Science and medicine of exercise and sports* (pp. 466–492). New York: Harper.

Pollack, I., & Norman, D. A. (1964). A non-parametric analysis of recognition experiments. *Psychonomic Science, 1*, 125–126.

Salthouse, T. A. (1979). Adult age and the speed–accuracy trade-off. *Ergonomics, 22*, 811–821.

Salthouse, T. A. (1985). Speed of behavior and its implications for cognition. In J. E. Birren & K. W. Schaie (Eds.), *Handbook of the psychology of aging* (pp. 400–426). New York: Van Nostrand Reinhold.

Salthouse, T. A. (1991). *Theoretical perspectives on cognitive aging*. Hillsdale, NJ: Lawrence Erlbaum Associates.

Schmidt, R. A., Zelasnik, H., Hawkins, B., Frank, J. S., Quinn, J. T. (1979). Motor output variability: A theory for the accuracy of rapid motor acts. *Psychological Review, 86*, 86, 415–451.

Verrillo, R. T., & Verrillo, V. (1985). Sensory and perceptual performance. In N. Charness (Ed.), *Aging and human performance* (pp. 1–46). Chicester, England:

Wiley.

Wade, M. G., Newell, K. M., & Wallace, S. A. (1978). Decision time and movement time as a function of response complexity in retarded persons. *American Journal of Mental Deficiency, 83,* 135–144.

Wallace, S. A., Newell, K. M., & Wade, M. G. (1978). Decision and response time as a function of movement difficulty in preschool children. *Child Development, 49,* 509–512.

Walker, N. & Catrambone, R. (1993). Aggregation bias and the use of regression analysis in evaluating model of human performance. *Human Factors, 35,* 397–411.

Walker, N., Meyer, D. E., & Smelcer, J. B. (1993). Spatial and temporal characteristics of rapid mouse movements in human–computer interaction. *Human Factors, 35,* 431–458.

Walker, N., Philbin, D. A., & Fisk, A. D. (1996). *Age-related differences in movement control: Adjusting submovement structure to optimize performance.* (Manuscript under review)

Warabi, T., Noda, H., & Kato, T. (1986). Effect of aging on sensorimotor function of eye and hand movements. *Experimental Neurology, 92,* 686–697.

Welford, A. T. (1960). The measurement of sensory-motor performance: Survey and reappraisal of twelve years' progress. *Ergonomics, 3,* 189–230.

Welford, A. T. (1977). Motor performance. In J. E. Birren & K. W. Schaie (Eds.), *Handbook of the psychology of aging* (pp. 450–496). New York: Van Norstrand Reinhold Co.

Welford, A. T., Norris, A. H., & Shock, N. W. (1969). Speed and accuracy of movement and their changes with age. *Acta Psychologica, 30,* 3–15.

CHAPTER 4

Control Theoretic Approaches to Age-Related Differences in Skilled Performance

Richard J. Jagacinski
Ohio State University

THE STABILITY OF BEHAVIOR

Many tasks studied by cognitive psychologists involve a series of relatively independent stimulus patterns. Experimental participants view, listen to, or feel some stimulus pattern for a short period of time and respond by pressing one of several buttons or by writing or saying one of several limited response messages. After a short pause, another stimulus pattern is presented, and the procedure is repeated. Typically, the presentation of the next stimulus pattern is independent of the preceding response.

The tasks that are studied in control theoretic approaches to skilled performance differ from this prototypical structure in several ways (e.g., Flach, 1990). The response is extended over time, and it interacts with at least part of the stimulus pattern, which also varies over some extended time period. The response consists of a stream of behavior, and similarly the stimulus consists of a stream of patterns over time. The interactive coupling of the response stream to the stimulus stream and of the stimulus stream to the response stream creates a loop structure, which may or may not be stable (e.g., Milsum, 1966; Pew, 1974). For example, vehicular control tasks such as driving a car or piloting an aircraft involve interactive streams of stimuli and responses. One only has to lose control of a car on icy pavement or induce oscillations in a cloud enshrouded aircraft to appreciate that stability is an important property of these loop structures. Like many other things in life, we appreciate stability only when we are about to lose it (anon).

Most of the time, however, people's driving or flying performance is stable. They stay on the road despite perturbations due to irregularities in the roadway, wind gusts, random variations in their steering, or momentary losses of view due to fog or glare. Whether one regards this result as a remarkable achievement or simply an incidental property of behavior can have a very strong influence on the way one models human performance. Many models implicitly assume that behavior is stable. In contrast, control theoretic approaches explicitly describe the stability of a behavior as an emergent property of dynamic couplings.

Is stability only of concern for vehicular control, or is it an important property of other behaviors as well? Holding an egg without crushing or dropping it, pounding a nail without bending it, following the flight of a hummingbird without losing sight of it, walking without falling, walking through a building without getting lost, telling a story without losing one's train of thought, diagnosing a problem without becoming confused, dealing with frustrations without losing one's temper—all of these are behaviors that extend over significant amounts of time, and all of them can result in a loss of stability. *Stability* is used very generally here to mean convergence toward a specific behavioral goal despite the influences of various perturbations.

If one considers the performance of these behaviors by older adults, a major concern is whether, as adults age, it becomes more difficult for them to maintain stable performance. As people age, the sensory information on which they act and the motor system they control undergo changes that can impair performance (e.g., Verrillo & Verrillo, 1985; Welford, 1982). Additionally, information processing capability becomes slower (e.g., Birren, 1974; Myerson, Hale, Wagstaff, Poon, & Smith, 1990; Salthouse, 1985). Important issues are how these changes affect the stability of behavior and how well people can compensate for these changes.

MEASURING STABILITY

If stability is an important property of behavior, then how does one go about measuring it? There are at least two general approaches, one based on holistic measurement and one based on combining mathematical representations of different parts of the overall system. The holistic approach is to look at global convergence properties of the person–environment interaction in the presence of various types of perturbations and as a function of variations in the structure of the environment. The second approach is to use these same experimental manipulations to derive explicit expressions for parts of the system, for example, the coupling from stimulus stream to response stream and from response stream to stimulus stream. The stability of the overall system can then be explicitly represented as a property emerging from these mutually interactive couplings. The latter approach requires more elaborate behavioral measurement, but it has the potential to permit greater analytic insight into the nature of behavioral stability.

Consider an example of vehicular control. A car driver uses certain aspects of the perceived visual flow field, vestibular perception, and tactual perception to generate steering wheel, accelerator, and braking motions. An explicit model of how these perceptual patterns are coupled to the motions of the driver might be termed a *control law*. It is a model of the driver that specifies which aspects of the very rich perceptual environment are selected, combined, and dynamically transformed into motion patterns. Similarly, there is a complementary model of the car, which specifies how the motions of the driver are transformed by the steering, engine, transmission, suspension, and braking systems to influence the motions of the car. Finally, there is a model of the ambient environment that specifies how the motion of the car influences the stimulus patterns available to the driver (e.g., Allen, McRuer, & Thompson, 1989). Thus, at a finer level of detail there are three couplings—from stimulus stream to driver motions, from driver motions to vehicle motion, and from vehicle motion to stimulus stream. The driver, the car, and the environment are portrayed as dynamic couplings in a stream of perceptions and motions.

At what level of detail should these couplings be measured in order to adequately account for the stability of the driver-car-environment system? As simulation capabilities become more and more powerful, there has been a trend toward increasing amounts of fidelity in models of both the car and the environmental flow field. Rather than reviewing the details of such models, this chapter discusses some elementary laboratory examples of person–environment interaction in the hope of illustrating experimental approaches that will be applicable in the domains of higher fidelity simulation and modeling as well.

An elementary laboratory task that probes the stability of behavior is the critical tracking task (Jex, McDonnell, & Phatak, 1966). A person manipulates a control stick to keep a moving dot of light as close as possible to a stationary center marker on a video display. The "vehicle" that the person is controlling in this task is inherently unstable. If the person does not actively manipulate the control stick, any small perturbation in the system will be increasingly amplified until the moving dot of light runs off the video display.

How well a person can perform this task is dependent on how quickly the unstable vehicle tries to run away and how quickly the person can respond. Several dynamic couplings need to be considered. First, the dynamic coupling between the motions of the control stick and the position of the unstable vehicle can be quantified in terms of the vehicle's time constant, the time it takes to amplify deviations from a null input by some percentage. The time constant is known from an electromechanical analysis of the laboratory simulation. Secondly, the coupling from the position of the unstable vehicle to the position of the moving dot of light on the video display is simply that one is proportional to the other.

The third coupling describes how the person moves the control stick so as to overcome the tendency for the unstable vehicle to run away, that is, to keep the dot of light near the center of the video display. The dynamic coupling between the moving dot of light and the person's movement of the control stick can be analyzed by measuring the pattern of correlation between these two variables. Experimental results indicate that the dynamic coupling representing the person can be approximated with two parameters, a gain and a time delay (Jex et al., 1966). The gain is a proportionality constant relating the displacement of the moving dot from the center marker to the motion of the control stick. The larger the gain is, the larger will be the movement of the control stick for a given displacement of the moving dot. The time delay represents the combined effects of perceptual, cognitive, and motor delays and can be considered a dynamic analog of a reaction time delay.

Given that the couplings in the system have been approximated, their joint effects on the overall stability of the behavior can be analyzed from the perspective of classical control theory (Jex et al., 1966). This technique considers the pattern of amplification and delays of the entire set of couplings to characterize overall system behavior. Performing such an analysis, one obtains two constraints on the gain that describes the person. First, it cannot be too large relative to the person's time delay. The combination of a high gain and a long time delay results in unstable oscillations in the overall system. Using too high a gain is analogous to turning the hot water spigot in a shower too quickly relative the time delay in the plumbing. Such behavior leads to overshooting and undershooting the desired temperature (e.g., Jagacinski, 1977). On the other hand, the gain cannot be too low, or else the unstable vehicle dynamics will dominate and cause the moving dot to go off the display. An intermediate level of gain is necessary in order to maintain overall stable performance.

If the time constant of the instability is gradually decreased so that the vehicle runs away more quickly, then the constraints on the person's gain become more restrictive. The range between the upper and lower bounds becomes narrower and narrower, until there is no gain that the person can adopt without the overall person–vehicle system becoming unstable. The time constant of the instability that just causes the person to lose control is a measure of the person's stabilization capability. The situation is somewhat analogous to balancing a stick on end (Pew, 1973). If the stick is long, the task is easy. However, if the stick were to become gradually shorter, the task would become more difficult. At some critical length, the person would no longer be able to balance the stick, and this stick length would be a measure of the person's stabilization capability.

The critical tracking task has been used to compare the stability of tracking performance by older and younger adults. Braune and Wickens (1985) found that 20- and 30-year-old subjects could stabilize a time constant of about 360 ms, whereas 40- and 50-year-old subjects could only stabilize a time constant of about 420 ms. These results can be considered global measures of the stability of subjects' tracking performance. Braune and Wickens (1985) additionally performed factor analyses on batteries of tasks and interpreted the critical tracking score as being related to perceptual–motor speed and perceptual–motor coordination, both of which correlated with age.

Can any more detailed insight into age-related decline in performance be gained from the preceding experimental results? The logic behind the critical task measurement technique is that performers adaptively adjust their gain to avoid a loss of stability as long as possible. As the task progresses that degree of freedom is eventually lost, and the performer's time delay then becomes the major limiting factor. For younger adults, the time constant at which performers lose control has been found to correlate with estimates of their effective time delay derived from Fourier analysis of tracking with a fixed unstable time constant (Jex & Allen, 1970); thus, there is convergence across different methods for measuring this aspect of tracking behavior.

Whether there is similar convergence for older adults has not been tested. There are several possible reasons for the older adults' poorer performance: (a) they may have a longer dynamic time delay; (b) they may not be as able as younger adults to adaptively alter their gain; or (c) they may be more variable in their motor control and thereby introduce larger perturbations for the unstable vehicle to amplify. These finer distinctions can be addressed because measurement techniques such as Fourier analysis exist for analyzing the dynamic transformation provided by the person. They are potentially important distinctions because they suggest different ways of trying to compensate for the poorer performance of the older adults.

Do the experimental results from the critical tracking task have any implications for the stability of driving behavior? Whether there is a strong correlation between performance in the critical tracking task and measures of the driving ability of older adults remains to be tested. A more general question is whether stability in one task correlates with stability in another task. Namely, if lengthening of a person's dynamic reaction time follows the same age-related pattern across tasks, then the stability of many perceptual–motor tasks may follow a similar longitudinal pattern within individuals. On the other hand, if there are many qualitatively distinct varieties of stability, or if there are many idiosyncratic limiting factors across stabilization tasks, or if the limiting factors depend strongly on the degree of experience with that task (e.g., Ackerman, 1989), then patterns of task performance within individuals may be much more complicated. The suggestion here is that research attempting to identify general underlying performance factors may benefit from exploring a variety of tasks for which stability is an important property (e.g., Braune & Wickens, 1985).

ADAPTIVITY

Consider for a moment the issue of adaptively adjusting a gain, that is, a proportionality constant in the coupling of the stimulus stream to the response stream. One constraint on its adjustment is that the overall system behavior must be stable. However, unlike the constraints of the task discussed previously, this constraint is often a fairly broad one that leaves room for many different styles of system behavior depending on the particular value of stable gain that is chosen. If one's goal is to minimize some measure of error (e.g., deviations from the center of a driving lane), that goal will suggest one value of gain. On the other hand, the goal of achieving some trade-off between minimizing error and avoiding abrupt changes in position might call for a lower gain. For example, an airline pilot might try to minimize error from an intended glideslope in performing a landing on a moving carrier at sea. On the other hand, the same pilot might be more willing to trade off glideslope error and smoothness of the plane's trajectory when performing as a commercial pilot with civilian passengers and approaching a longer, stationary runaway.

Miller (1965) found that given appropriate feedback, a young adult was able to vary gain adaptively in order to trade off tracking error and control stick movement with various relative weightings. There have been few other studies that have explicitly varied this trade-off, yet it is an important aspect of perceptual–motor coordination. At a very abstract level of comparison, this trade-off in perceptual–motor coordination is analogous to the trade-off between hits and false alarms in a signal detection task (Swets, 1992), speed and accuracy in a choice-reaction time task (Pachella, 1974), or speed and endpoint accuracy in a target acquisition task (Meyer, Smith, Kornblum, Abrams, & Wright, 1990). It represents a degree of freedom available to the performer that can introduce large individual differences in the actual performance of people with the same behavioral capabilities.

More particularly, this trade-off is a potential confounding factor when comparing the perceptual–motor coordination of older and younger adults. If older adults exhibit lower gains than younger adults, then are they simply placing a higher weighting on movement smoothness, or is their trade-off function for error and movement smoothness different from that of younger adults? There are several possible experimental approaches in dealing with this issue. One is to assess the entire trade-off function in a manner analogous to the way researchers measure the speed–accuracy trade-off function for discrete target acquisition. A second approach is to try to infer the criterion that subjects are optimizing from their performance. This latter approach is used by optimal control theory (Levison, 1981), which explicitly models dependence of the control gains on perceptual–motor lags, time delays, perceptual and motor noises, and the subjective weightings of error and effort or smoothness that the performer is attempting to optimize.

There is some evidence indicating that older adults have greater difficulty adjusting their gains than younger adults. Jagacinski, Liao, and Fayyad (1995) examined sinewave tracking in older and younger adults. This task is quite different from the critical tracking task mentioned previously. In that task, the motion of the moving dot was unpredictable, and performers used an error nulling strategy based on feedback control. For sinewave tracking, the desired pattern is well known to the performer. Rather than relying primarily on feedback control, the performer can achieve better performance by generating a sinusoidal pattern with some internal pattern generator and then adaptively adjusting the amplitude, frequency, and phase of the pattern to match the target pattern (e.g., Magdaleno, Jex, & Johnson, 1969; Noble, Fitts, & Warren, 1955). From this perspective, sinewave tracking is primarily an adaptive control task.

Experimental results indicate that older adults are almost as good as younger adults in synchronizing with a sinusoidal target pattern

(Jagacinski et al., 1995). However, they exhibit much smaller amplitudes than younger adults as the sinusoidal frequency approaches 1 Hz. The limitation does not appear to be a peripheral limitation on movement velocity. Rather, it appears to be a limitation on the older adults' adaptive matching capability, or a result of increased motor noise, or both. Older adults have also been shown to be slower in adaptively readjusting movement parameters for planned discrete movements (Stelmach, Goggin, & Amrhein, 1988).

Another way of thinking about this poorer performance is that older adults fail to converge toward a complete matching of the target pattern. Just as one could classify the performance of a fixed control law subjected to perturbations as stable or unstable, one can similarly apply the concept of stability to adaptive control systems (e.g., Narendra & Annaswamy, 1989). The stability of the overall adaptive system is demonstrated if it can be shown that it minimizes some cost function (e.g., a Lyapunov function) that involves both the error generated by the control law and deviations of the adjustable parameters (e.g., gains) from their target values. The notion of stability is thus extended to a higher level to include the dynamics of the adaptive adjustment as well as the dynamics of the underlying control law. From this perspective, adaptivity can be considered a more general form of stability than is captured in the stability a single fixed control law. Loss of adaptivity can then be considered as another form of loss of stability. Whether this conceptualization proves to be a fruitful way of describing age-related changes in adaptivity remains to be tested.

Even if one is able to adjust the parameters of a given control law, the variety of behaviors required to perform a complex task may not be achievable by that single control law. In that case, another form of adaptivity is to develop a set of control laws. Each control law in the set is used in a delimited class of situations, and together they permit better overall performance than any single control law. For example, a pilot might use very different control laws for takeoff, cruising, approach to landing, and final descent (e.g., Baron, Zacharias, Muralidharan, & Lancraft, 1980; Baron & Corker, 1989). Similarly, a car driver might use very different control laws for normal highway driving, obstacle avoidance, negotiating an intersection, and backing up.

This form of adaptivity requires at least two levels of organization. At the lower level of organization is each particular control law, which has a goal that it is trying to achieve, a set of stimulus streams that serve as inputs, and a dynamic transformation of these inputs that generates an output or movement. At the higher level of organization is a set of conditions for starting, stopping, and interrupting the activity of each control law. The higher level might function as a production system that activates only one of the control laws at a time (e.g., Jagacinski, Plamondon, & Miller, 1987 for a review), or it might function as a gating network that permits multiple control laws to be active simultaneously and to different degrees (e.g., Jacobs & Jordan, 1993).

Adaptation in this complex structure includes tuning the parameters of individual control laws. However, it also includes tuning the conditions under which each of the control laws are activated (e.g., Jacobs & Jordan, 1993). An extension of the stability concept is needed here to determine when a coordinated set of control laws will be globally stable. Within this conceptualization, one can explore a variety of adaptivities. For example, under what conditions does a performer decide that a particular set of control laws cannot be adequately tuned for a given task and then proceed to learn and incorporate a new control law into the existing set? Age differences in these aspects of adaptivity might be significant.

Another form of hierarchical structure involves using multiple perceptual cues in parallel to exert control on successively embedded time scales. For example, in automobile driving the control of heading angle can be considered to be embedded within the loop structure for the control of lateral position (e.g., Hess, 1987; McRuer, Weir, Jex, Magdaleno, & Allen, 1973). The driver's response to heading angle deviations will be faster than and form part of the response to lateral deviations according to this conceptualization. Whether older adults have greater difficulty using multiple cues in this manner remains to be tested.

WHAT'S WRONG WITH BEING A LITTLE SLOWER?

Much recent research on aging has provided evidence that older adults are slower information processors (e.g., Birren, 1974; Myerson et al., 1990; Salthouse, 1985). If one is working on a self-paced task, and all of the subprocesses are time-scaled, so that they are completed proportionately more slowly, then the task will take longer, but it will still be completed in the same manner as before. Suppose, however, the slowing among subprocesses is not uniform. If the flow of information is in the form of a serial chain or even a network of parallel and serial elements (e.g., Schweickert & Fisher, 1987), overall performance will be slower as determined by subprocesses along the (most) critical path. However, the convergence of the various subprocesses toward the final behavioral goal will be maintained. On the other hand, if the flow of information forms a loop structure, then that convergence could be disrupted; that is, stability could be lost. The performer may have to adjust some parametric aspects of a control law or actually construct new control laws for performing the task.

For example, suppose the performer must interact with a dynamic process that remains invariant as the person ages and becomes a slower information processor. Namely, a loop structure exists in which only part of the system is slowing down, so one would expect some disruption of performance. If the acceleration due to gravity remains constant, but one's ability to react to perturbations in a gravitational field is slowed by an increased reaction time or by impaired perception, one may fall more easily (e.g., Lord, Clark, & Webster, 1991; Woollacott, Shumway-Cook, & Nashner, 1982). One does not need control theory to reach this conclusion. However, control theory may be useful in understanding the relative importance of various sources of information and of the types of disturbances that lead to a loss of stability. The dynamics of the body can be described in terms of a series of linked segments and applied torques (e.g., Koozekanani, Stockwell, McGhee, & Firoozmand, 1980). Control strategies can be explored analytically (e.g., Iqbal, Hemami, & Simon, 1993) or more qualitatively in terms of patterns of temporal covariation among the movement of various joints (e.g., Riccio, 1993). Insight into the processes underlying postural control may be achieved by describing stability as an emergent property of perceptual and biomechanical couplings.

As a second example, tracking studies (e.g., Jagacinski et al., 1995; Welford (1958/1973) indicate that the rapidity of the input signal can seriously degrade the performance of older adults relative to younger adults, even when the form of the input is known in advance. In the context of a driving task, older adults could drive more slowly to reduce the rate of variation of the input signal, that is, the roadway. This solution would be acceptable on an untraveled country road. However, if there is ambient traffic, then slowing down can increase the relative velocity between one's own vehicle and other vehicles, which permits less time for traffic avoidance maneuvers. Thus, slowing down to lower the effective rate of change of bends in the roadway has a dangerous side effect. Part of the system has been slowed, but part of it (other traffic) has not, and the resulting behavior may no longer be stable. It seems remarkable that so much of the research on behavioral slowing investigates tasks for the which the consequences of being slower are relatively benign. We hope that this work will expand to place greater emphasis on tasks involving dynamic interactions with the environment.

A somewhat tangential point is that the issue of whether behavioral slowing in older adults is general across subprocesses within some delimited domain has some theoretical parallels with the issue of how people of any particular age produce variations in their rates of perceptual–motor performance. One can consider three types of slowing: (a) the stochastic variations in rate that occur when a performer is trying to maintain a constant rate of performance across trials (e.g., Gentner, 1987); (b) deliberate changes in rate of performance, such as expressively playing a piano piece slower or faster (e.g., Repp, 1994), or varying the speed of one's golf shot to produce a desired distance; and (c) age-related slowing. In the first two instances of slowing (and speeding), all of the components of an action do not typically slow down proportionately, although sometimes they do (Gentner, 1987; Repp, 1994). Similarly, some researchers argue that age-related slowing is uniform across subprocesses within a delimited task domain (e.g., Myerson et al., 1990), whereas others argue for differential rates of slowing (e.g., Cerella, 1985). The observability of various stages of perceptual–motor acts permits additional tests of generalized slowing. Whether the underlying mechanisms involved in stochastic and deliberate variation in speed of performance are systematically related to factors underlying age-related slowing needs additional investigation.

COMPENSATION TECHNIQUES

As noted earlier, one contribution of control theory is that it explicitly considers the conditions of information flow that lead to stable behavior of some overall interactive system. A second contribution is that it considers different techniques for modifying the information flow in a system that is either unstable or too sluggish or too oscillatory. In doing so, control theory considers the implications of the modification in the context of the overall system dynamics. Sometimes modifications in one segment of information flow can have unintuitive effects on the overall system performance.

A simple compensation technique for overcoming information processing delays is to increase anticipation of some signal. Typists do not only look at the word they are presently typing but look ahead at what is coming up. Older typists tend to look ahead farther and are able to perform at levels comparable to younger typists (Bosman, 1993; Salthouse, 1984). Drivers do not look just in front of their vehicle but instead look down the road to see what is coming up (McLean & Hoffmann, 1973). The need for preview of this kind can be related via optimal control theory to the vehicle dynamics and the relative weighting of tracking error and control effort (e.g., Miller, 1976). An interesting issue is whether older and younger adults differ in their use of preview in vehicular control. Welford (1958/1973) varied the amount of preview available in a one-dimensional tracking task and found that preview reduced, but did not eliminate differences between older and younger adults. There was also some evidence that larger amounts of preview were more beneficial for older adults.

Preview is one of several anticipatory mechanisms used in controlling dynamic systems. If preview is unavailable (e.g., driving in fog), one might be restricted to anticipation based on local trends in the signal to be followed. *Lead generation* refers to the use of an additive combination of instantaneous position and velocity to predict how a signal will vary in the immediate future. Namely, an approximate prediction of the value of a signal T seconds from now is equal to the signal's present position plus T times the signal's velocity. Lead generation can thus function as a partial substitute for preview (e.g., Elkind, 1956). Lead can also be used to compensate for lag or sluggishness in an electromechanical part of a dynamic system. For example, drivers are believed to use lead generation to compensate for lag in the steering response (e.g., McRuer et al., 1973; Allen et al., 1989).

In tracking predictable signals without preview (e.g., a familiar road in fog), one could rely on lead generation, but one could also anticipate the entire pattern, and then act to null out small unpredictable errors between the anticipated pattern and the actual pattern. For example, in rapid sinewave tracking, performers are believed to rely primarily on whole pattern generation rather than on lead generation (e.g., Magdaleno et al., 1969; Noble et al., 1955).

Compensation techniques to assist anticipation by older adults might try to augment any of these strategies depending on the task. As noted previously, Welford (1958/1973) found that providing explicit signal preview helped the tracking performance of both older and younger adults. Jagacinski, Greenberg, Liao, and Wang (1993) found that providing a supplementary auditory display of target position or velocity helped both older and younger performers to anticipate a predictable modulated sinewave signal. However, there were important gender differences. Males were helped by supplementary velocity information, but females were helped by supplementary position information. Overall, these results are encouraging because they indicate that older adults can benefit from multimodal information in the context of a control task. Whether auditory cues will ever be useful in providing anticipatory roadway cues for night or reduced visibility driving remains to be explored.

Besides providing anticipation regarding input signals, supplementary displays can also provide information about what control actions to exert. Janiga and Mayne (1977) demonstrated the use of auditory cues to issue advisory steering commands for stabilizing a skidding vehicle. The use of supplementary proprioceptive inputs to a driver's steering wheel when there is a large deviation from control theoretic estimates of desired performance may also be useful (Schumann, Lowenau, & Naab, in press). These examples involve nonvisual cues on the assumption that the visual modality is already highly occupied during driving. When additional visually demanding devices are recommended for vehicles, their potential impact on the stability of performance needs to be carefully evaluated, especially for older adults, who may operate such devices more slowly (e.g., Hancock, Dewing, & Parasuraman, 1993). Control theory models of vehicular control embedded in a hierarchical model of multitask performance may be very useful (e.g., Levison, 1993). Although the present discussion has emphasized driving, these aiding techniques may be useful in many other perceptual–motor tasks in which the stability of performance is important.

Although the preceding research has explored fixed schemes for improving performance, the same schemes could be implemented in an adaptive fashion. For example, model reference adaptive control is a technique by which the nominal input to a given system is transformed to make the system's performance mimic that of another target system (e.g., Astrom & Wittenmark, 1989; Narendra & Annaswamy, 1989). Rather than specifying the transformation a priori, this approach adaptively adjusts the transformation to achieve the desired behavior. The stability of this type of adaptive control is well understood for linear stationary systems (Narendra & Annaswamy, 1989). The challenge in applying these ideas to human performance is that the human possesses an as yet poorly understood degree of nonlinearity and adaptivity. This approach can be considered an adaptive successor to earlier work by Birmingham and Taylor (1954) in which subjects were given a "quickened" error signal rather than the true error signal in order to make their tracking performance with complex dynamics more anticipatory. The application of such techniques to the perceptual–motor performance of older adults has received little attention.

Finally, it should be noted that new developments in nonlinear systems analysis (e.g., Kelso, Ding, & Schoner, 1993, for a review) have led to new categories of stability, for example, chaotic behavior. These new distinctions may expand the set of control techniques available for stabilizing physiological subsystems (e.g., Garfinkel, Spano, Ditto, & Weiss, 1992) and perhaps in the future for assisting human performance. Furthermore, this area has prompted researchers to explore the implications of stability in domains as diverse as perception and memory (e.g., Skarda & Freeman, 1987) and postural control (Dijkstra,

Schoner, Giese, & Gielen, 1994). Issues of stability could thus become a unifying theme across many presently disparate areas of behavioral research. This approach is still in its early stages of development, but may prove important for understanding age-related changes in performance (e.g., Mandell & Shlesinger, 1990).

In summary, the present chapter has suggested that the stability of behavior is an important topic in the study of aging. Although much of the laboratory work on age-related slowing has used information processing tasks requiring discrete responses to a sequence of independent stimuli, some of the most important implications of age-related slowing may be in the control of dynamic processes over extended periods of time. New ways of measuring varieties of stability may provide insights into compensatory strategies for maintaining behavioral stability in older adults.

Areas of application of this approach may include a wide variety of behaviors such as postural control, sports activity, vehicular control, navigation, and decision making. Although control theoretic techniques from the engineering literature will provide a starting point, the effective adaptation of these techniques to the behavior of highly nonlinear, very stochastic, and highly individualized older adults is a significant challenge.

REFERENCES

Ackerman, P. L. (1989). Individual differences and skill acquisition. In P. L. Ackerman, R. J. Sternberg, & R. Glaser, (Eds.), *Learning and individual differences: Advances in theory and research* (pp. 165–217). New York: W. H. Freeman.

Allen, R. W., McRuer, D. T., & Thompson, P. M. (1989). Dynamic systems analysis programs with classical and optimal control applications of human performance models. In G. R. McMillan, D. Beevis, E. Salas, M. H. Strub, R. Sutton, & L. van Breda (Eds.), *Applications of human performance models to system design* (pp. 169–184). New York: Plenum Press.

Astrom, K. J., & Wittenmark, B. (1989). *Adaptive control.* Reading, MA: Addison-Wesley.

Baron, S., & Corker, K. (1989). Engineering-based approaches to human perforemance modeling. In G. R. McMillan, D. Beevis, E. Salas, M. H. Strub, R. Sutton, & L. van Breda (Eds.), *Applications of human performance models to system design* (pp. 203–217). New York: Plenum Press.

Baron, S., Zacharias, G., Muralidharan, R., & Lancraft, R. (1980). *PROCRU: A model for analyzing flight crew procedures in approach to landing* (NAS2-10035). Moffett Field, CA: Ames Research Center (NASA).

Birmingham, H. P., & Taylor, F. V. (1954). A design philosophy for man-machine control systems. *Proceedings of the IEEE, 54,* 1748–1758.

Birren, J. E. (1974). Translations in gerontology—from lab to life: Psychophysiology and speed of response. *American Psychologist, 29,* 808–815.

Bosman, E. A. (1993). Age-related differences in the motoric aspects of transcription typing skill. *Psychology and Aging, 8*, 87–102.

Braune, R., & Wickens, C. D. (1985). The functional age profile: An objective decision criterion for the assessment of pilot performance capacities and capabilities. *Human Factors, 27*, 681–693.

Cerella, J. (1985). Information processing rates in the elderly. *Psychological Bulletin, 98*, 67–83.

Dijkstra, T. M. H., Schoner, G., Giese, M. A., & Gielen, C. C. A. M. (1994). Frequency dependence of the action–perception cycle for postural control in a moving visual environment: Relative phase dynamics. *Biological Cybernetics, 71*, 489–501.

Elkind, J. I. (1956). *Characteristics of simple manual control systems* (Tech. Rep. No. 111, MIT Lincoln Laboratory, Lexington, MA).

Flach, J. (1990). Control with an eye for perception: Precursors to an active psychophysics. *Ecological Psychology, 2*, 83–111.

Garfinkel, A., Spano, M. L., Ditto, W. L., & Weiss, J. N. (1992). Controlling cardiac chaos. *Science, 257*, 1230–1235.

Gentner, D. (1987). Timing of skilled motor performance: Tests of the proportional duration model. *Psychological Review, 94*, 255–276.

Hancock, P. A., Dewing, W. L., & Parasuraman, R. (1993, April). The human factors of intelligent travel systems. *Ergonomics in Design*, 12–15, 35–39.

Hess, R. A. (1987). Feedback control models. In G. Salvendy (Ed.), *Handbook of human factors* (pp. 1212–1242). New York: Wiley.

Iqbal, K., Hemami, H., & Simon, S. (1993). Stability and control of a frontal four-link biped system. *IEEE Transactions on Biomedical Eel. Psychological Review, 94*, 255–276.

Jacobs, R. A. , & Jordan, M. I. (1993). Learning piecewise control strategies in a modular neural network architecture. *IEEE Transactions on Systems, Man, and Cybernetics, 23*, 337–345.

Jagacinski, R. J. (1977). A qualitative look at feedback control theory as a style of describing behavior. *Human Factors, 19*, 331–347.

Jagacinski, R. J., Greenberg, N., Liao, M., & Wang, J. (1993). Manual performance of a repeated pattern by older and younger adults with supplementary auditory cues. *Psychology and Aging, 3*, 429–439.

Jagacinski, R. J., Liao, M., & Fayyad, E. A. (1995). Generalized slowing in sinewave tracking by older adults. *Psychology and Aging, 10*, 8–19.

Jagacinski, R. J., Plamondon, B. D., & Miller, R. A. (1987). Describing movement control at two levels of abstraction. In P. A. Hancock (Ed.), *Human factors psychology* (pp. 199–247). Amsterdam: North Holland.

Janiga, D. V., & Mayne, R. W. (1977). Use of a nonvisual display for improving the manual control of an unstable system. *IEEE Transactions on Systems, Man, and Cybernetics, SMC-7*, 530–537.

Jex, H. R., & Allen, R. W. (1970). Research on a new human dynamic response test battery. *Proceedings of the sixth annual conference on Manual Control*. Wright-Patterson AFB, OH.

Jex, H. R., McDonnell, J. D., & Phatak, A. V. (1966). A "critical" tracking task for manual control research. *IEEE Transactions on Human Factors in Electronics, HFE-7*, 138–144.

Kelso, J. A. S., Ding, M., & Schoner, G. (1993). Dynamic pattern formation: A primer. In L. B. Smith & E. Thelen, (Eds.), *A dynamic systems approach to development: Applications* (pp. 13–50). Cambridge, MA: MIT Press.

Koozekanani, S. H., Stockwell, C. W., McGhee, R. B., & Firoozmand, F. (1980). On the role of dynamic models in quantitative posturography. *IEEE Transactions on Biomedical Engineering, 27*, 605–609.

Levison, W. H. (1981). A methodology for quantifying the effects of aging on perceptual–motor capability. *Human Factors, 23,* 87–96.

Levison, W. H. (1993). A simulation model for the driver's use of in-vehicle information systems. *Transportation Research Record, 1403,* 7–13.

Lord, S. R., Clark, R. D., & Webster, I. W. (1991). Postural stability and associated physiological factors in a population of aged persons. *Journal of Gerontology: Medical Sciences, 46,* M69–76.

Magdaleno, R. E., Jex, H. R., & Johnson, W. A. (1969). Tracking quasi-predictable displays. *Proceedings of the fifth annual NASA-University Conference on Manual Control* (pp. D1.1–D1.25), MIT, Cambridge, MA.

Mandell, A. J., & Shlesinger, M. F. (1990). Lost choices: Parallelism and topological entropy decrements in neurobiological aging. In S. Krasner (Ed.), *The ubiquity of chaos* (pp. 35–46). Washington, DC: American Association for the Advancement of Science.

McLean, J. R., & Hoffmann, E. R. (1973). The effects of restricted preview on driver steering control and performance. *Human Factors, 15,* 421–430.

McRuer, D. T., Weir, D. H., Jex, H. R., Magdaleno, R. E., & Allen, R. W. (1973). Measurement of driver/vehicle multiloop response properties with a single disturbance input. *Proceedings of the ninth annual Conference on Manual Control,* MIT Cambridge, MA.

Meyer, D. E., Smith, J. E. K., Kornblum, S., Abrams, R. A., & Wright, C. E. (1990). Speed–accuracy trade-offs in aimed movements: Toward a theory of rapid voluntary action. In M. Jeannerod (Ed.), *Attention and performance XIII* (pp. 173–226). Hillsdale, New Jersey: Lawrence Erlbaum Associates.

Miller, D. C. (1965). The effects of performance-scoring criteria on compensatory tracking behavior. *IEEE Transactions on Human Factors in Electronics, HFE-6,* 62–65.

Miller, R. A. (1976). On the finite preview problem in manual control. *International Journal of Systems Science, 7,* 667–672.

Milsum, J. H. (1966). *Biological control systems analysis.* New York: McGraw-Hill.

Myerson, J., Hale, S., Wagstaff, D., Poon, L. W., & Smith G. A. (1990). The information-loss model: A mathematical theory of age-related cognitive slowing. *Psychological Review, 97,* 475–487.

Narendra, K. S., & Annaswamy, A. M. (1989). *Stable adaptive systems.* Englewood Cliffs, NJ: Prentice-Hall.

Noble, M., Fitts, P. M., & Warren, C. E. (1955). The frequency response of skilled subjects in a pursuit tracking task. *Journal of Experimental Psychology, 49,* 249–256.

Pachella, R. G. (1974). The interpretation of reaction time in information processing research. In B. H. Kantowitz, (Ed.), *Human information processing* (pp. 41–82). New York: Lawrence Erlbaum Associates.

Pew, R. W. (1973). Performance assessment via the critical task and dowel balancing. *Proceedings of the ninth annual Conference on Manual Control,* MIT, Cambridge, MA.

Pew, R. W. (1974). Human perceptual–motor performance. In B. H. Kantowitz (Ed.), *Human information processing: Tutorials in performance and cognition* (pp. 1–39). Hillsdale, NJ: Lawrence Erlbaum Associates.

Repp, B. P. (1994). Relational invariance of expressive microstructure across global tempo changes in music performance: An exploratory study. *Psychological Research, 56,* 269–284.

Riccio, G. E. (1993). Information in movement variability about the qualitative dynamics of posture and orientation. In K. M. Newell & D. M. Corcos, (Eds.), *Variability and motor control* (pp. 317–357). Champaign, IL: Human Kinetics.

Salthouse, T. A. (1984). Effects of age and skill in typing. *Journal of Experimental*

Psychology: General, 113, 345–371.
Salthouse, T. A. (1985). Speed of behavior and its implications for cognition. In J. E. Birren & K. W. Schaie (Eds.), *Handbook of the psychology of aging* (pp. 400–426). New York: Van Nostrand Reinhold.
Schumann, J., Lowenau, J., & Naab, K. (in press). The active steering wheel as a continuous support for the driver's lateral control task. In A. G. Gale (Ed.), *Vision in vehicles V*. Amsterdam: North Holland.
Schweickert, R., & Fisher, D. L. (1987). Stochastic network models. In G. Salvendy (Ed.), *Handbook of human factors* (pp. 1177–1199). New York: Wiley.
Skarda, C. A., & Freeman, W. J. (1987). How brains make chaos in order to make sense of the world. *Behavioral and Brain Sciences, 10*, 161–195.
Stelmach, G. E., Goggin, N. L., & Amrhein, P. C. (1988). Aging and the restructuring of precued movements. *Psychology and Aging, 3*, 151–157.
Swets, J. A. (1992). The science of choosing the right decision threshold in high-stakes diagnostics. *American Psychologist, 47*, 522–532.
Verrillo, R. T., & Verrillo, V. (1985). Sensory and perceptual performance. In N. Charness (Ed.), *Aging and human performance* (pp. 1–46). Chicester, England: Wiley.
Welford, A. T. (1973). *Ageing and human skill*. Westport, CT: Greenwood Press. (Original work published in 1958)
Welford, A. T. (1982). Motor skills and aging. In J. A. Mortimer, F. J. Pirozzolo, & G. J. Maletta (Eds.), *The aging motor system* (pp. 152–187). New York: Praeger.
Woollacott, M. H., Shumway-Cook, A. & Nashner, L. (1982). Postural reflexes and aging. In J. A. Mortimer, F. J. Pirozzolo, & G. J. Maletta (Eds.), *The aging motor system* (pp. 98–119). New York: Praeger.

CHAPTER 5

Aging and Dual-Task Performance

Arthur F. Kramer
John L. Larish
University of Illinois
at Urbana-Champaign

One of the best exemplars of a mental activity in which large and robust age-related differences have been consistently obtained is dual-task processing. In dual-task or divided attention paradigms subjects are instructed to concurrently perform two tasks. In some varieties of this paradigm subjects are instructed to treat one task as primary and the other task as secondary. In other situations subjects are instructed to treat the tasks as equally important. Dual-task "costs" are assessed by comparing performance of each of the tasks when performed together to their respective single task control conditions. The dual-task decrements have been calculated as both absolute costs (e.g., dual-task performance minus single-task performance) and relative costs ([dual minus single] divided by single). In both cases, the decrement measures represent an attempt to employ the single task conditions as baselines against which to compare dual-task performance. In situations in which reaction time (RT) serves as the dependent measure, relative cost measures are more conservative estimates of age differences in dual-task performance given that older subjects tend to respond more slowly than younger subjects on single tasks (Guttentag, 1989; Somberg & Salthouse, 1982; but see Ackerman, Schneider, & Wickens, 1984; Baron & Mattila, 1989). In general, the study of dual-task processing in the laboratory represents an attempt to understand the manner in which humans cope with processing demands inherent in many real-world situations such as driving an automobile, cooking dinner while carrying on a telephone conversation, typing a manuscript while composing a letter, walking down a flight of stairs while planning a meeting, and so on. In fact, there have been a number of studies that have found that performance in divided attention and attention switching tasks is predictive of the quality of real-world performance in tasks such as flying an aircraft (Crosby & Parkinson, 1979; Damos, 1978; Gopher, 1982; North & Gopher, 1976), driving buses (Kahneman, Ben-Ishai, & Lotan, 1973) and automobiles (Avolio, Kroeck, & Panek, 1985; Ball & Owsley, 1991).

Given the theoretical and practical importance of dual-task performance coupled with the numerous reports of age-related decrements in the concurrent performance of multiple tasks one would expect that a considerable effort would have been made to examine training strategies that could be used to reduce age-related decrements in dual-task performance. Unfortunately, very few such studies have been conducted. In this chapter we address this issue by examining four main issues of relevance to aging and dual-task performance. We begin by briefly reviewing the literature on age-related differences in dual-task performance, and in particular the models that have been proposed to account for these differences. We then review the literature on training approaches to dual-task performance in light of their potential to reduce age-related decrements. Next, we describe the relatively limited literature that has examined age-related differences in the acquisition and transfer of dual-task processing skills. Finally, we discuss the gaps in the aging and training literature and suggest how these important issues might be resolved.

DUAL-TASK PROCESSING AND AGING

In his summary of the dual-task and aging literature, Craik (1977) suggested that, "One of the clearest results in the experimental psychology of aging is the finding that older subjects are more penalized when they must divide their attention, either between two input sources, input and holding, or holding and responding" (p. 391). In recent years there have been a number of critical reviews of the methodological details of the earlier dual-task studies that suggest caution in interpreting the age-related differences in performance found in the 1960s and 1970s (Guttentag, 1989; Somberg & Salthouse, 1982). However, more recent and methodologically sophisticated examinations of the relationship between aging and dual-task decrements, with few exceptions, obtained results which confirm the earlier findings (Crossley & Hiscock, 1992; Korteling, 1991, 1993; Lorsbach & Simpson, 1988; McDowd, 1986; McDowd & Craik, 1988; Park, Smith, Dudley, & Lafronza, 1989; Ponds, Brouwer, & van Wolffelaar, 1988;

Salthouse, Rogan, & Prill, 1984; but see Somberg & Salthouse, 1982; Wickens, Braune, & Stokes, 1987). In fact, in a recent comprehensive review of age-related differences in attentional processes Hartley (1992) concluded, in agreement with Craik's earlier assessment, that there was strong evidence across a wide variety of tasks and dependent measures for substantial decrements in dual-task processing during aging.

It is important to mention, however, that although there is a general consensus about the robustness of the dual-task or divided attention effects there is considerable disagreement as to the theoretical mechanisms that underlie these age-related differences in performance. One proposal concerns the relative complexity of single and dual tasks (McDowd, 1986; Salthouse, 1982). McDowd and Craik (1988) stated that, "It does not seem that the division of attention presents some especial difficulty to older people. Rather, division of attention is one of several equivalent ways to increase overall task complexity. In turn, age differences are exaggerated as tasks are made more complex" (p. 267). McDowd and Craik examined the complexity hypothesis by manipulating the difficulty (i.e., through manipulations that would presumably influence depth of processing) and complexity (i.e., number of choices) of a variety of single- and dual-task combinations. According to the Complexity hypothesis, older adults should be proportionally slower than younger adults as the complexity of the tasks being performed increases, regardless of whether the tasks are performed in a single- or dual-task paradigm. McDowd and Craik's findings provided partial support for their hypothesis because, for most of their tasks, increases in complexity or difficulty served to increase age-related differences in performance. Furthermore, when young mean RTs for different tasks were regressed on old mean RTs, both the single and dual tasks were well fit by a linear function with a slope of 1.6. This result was taken as evidence that division of attention in dual-task paradigms functions in a way that is very similar to an increase in single-task complexity.

The complexity hypothesis as applied to single- and dual-task aging differences shares much in common with a earlier argument that age-related differences in processing speed can be accounted for by a general slowing factor (Birren, 1974; Birren, Woods, & Williams, 1980; Cerella, 1985; Salthouse, 1985). The General Slowing proposal, like the Complexity hypothesis, suggests that older adults' response speed can be well predicted by a linear function in the following form: Old = s * young + b, with s (slope) approximately equal to 1.5 and b (intercept) equal to 0. More recently, other nonlinear functions have been found to provide slightly better accounts of the relationship between the processing speed of young and old adults (Cerella, 1990; Myerson, Hale, Wagstaff, Poon, & Smith, 1990).

Although the complexity hypothesis, and its "general slowing" parent, provides a relatively good account of the single-task/dual-task data there are several pieces of evidence which suggest that age-related differences in dual-task processing may involve more than a generalized complexity effect. First, although the Complexity hypothesis predicts that older adults' responses will be proportionally slower than younger subjects' responses, a number of recent dual-task studies found disproportionate age-related dual-task costs (e.g., relative costs greater than 1.0; Crossley & Hiscock, 1992; Madden, 1986; Park et al., 1989; Ponds et al., 1988; Salthouse et al., 1984). Second, some studies found larger age-related differences in performance in less rather than more complex tasks (Crossley & Hiscock, 1992; Korteling, 1991; McDowd & Craik, 1988; Rogers, Bertus, & Gilbert, 1994). Finally, a number of studies found selective rather than general age-related differences in dual-task performance (Jennings, Brock, & Nebes, 1990; Salthouse et al., 1984; Wickens et al., 1987). For example, Park et al. (1989) found age-related differences in encoding but not in retrieval when a categorization and a number monitoring task were concurrently performed.

In addition to the exceptions to the complexity hypothesis described previously, it is important to note that this hypothesis is descriptive rather than explanatory. Thus, an important question is why older adults are at a disadvantage with increasing single- or dual-task complexity. One proposal is that there is a decrease in capacity or resources during aging, and, therefore, more difficult single- and dual-tasks will show proportionally larger age-related decrements, because they require more resources than easier tasks. Resources have been conceptualized in terms of working memory capacity (Baddeley & Hitch, 1974; Craik, 1977; Welford, 1977), attentional or mental energy (Freidman & Polson, 1981; Kahneman, 1973; Wickens, 1980), and the rate of performing different mental operations (Cerella, 1985; Salthouse et al., 1984).

Studies consistent with the diminished resource hypothesis found that older subjects showed larger dual-task processing decrements than younger subjects showed in tasks that rely heavily on working memory (Park et al., 1989; Parkinson, Lindholm, & Urell, 1980; Salthouse et al., 1984). Dual-task age-related decrements also were reported in perceptual and motor tasks (Hawkins, Kramer, & Capaldi, 1992; Korteling, 1991; Ponds et al., 1988). Thus, it appears conceivable that some variant of the resource hypothesis might account, in part, for age-related decrements in dual-task performance.

It is important to note, however, that there have been a number of critical reviews of the resource metaphor in recent years. These criticisms focused both on methodological and theoretical issues. For example, Navon (1984) argued that the graded tradeoffs in the performance of two concurrently performed tasks, the centerpiece of many resource models, may be due to demand characteristics rather than a real limit to available resources (see also Kantowitz, 1985). Other authors argued that resource models have been oversold, because, at best, they account for only a small subset of dual-task performance effects (Allport, 1987; Hirst & Kalmar, 1987; Neumann, 1987; Pashler, 1994).

Several alternative accounts of dual-task decrements were proposed. One proposal is that dual-task interference can be explained in terms of different forms of crosstalk or outcome conflicts that occur between parallel processes (Hirst & Kalmar, 1987; Navon, 1984). It was suggested that crosstalk occurs as a result of the confusability of similar types of stimulus materials, similar transformations, or similar response patterns. For example, crosstalk will occur when nontargets in one task belong to the same semantic category as targets in another task (Navon & Miller, 1987) or when the same operations, such as checking for spelling errors or performing arithmetical calculations, are carried out on stimulus materials from two distinct tasks (Hirst & Kalmar, 1987). Thus, in this class of models the emphasis is on explicating the nature and breadth of processing that takes place in different processing mechanisms.

Other authors (Kieras & Meyer, 1994; Pashler, 1994) suggested that dual-task interference can be explained in terms of bottlenecks, in which some operations may require a single mechanism that can only be dedicated to one task at a time. If two tasks require such a mechanism, a bottleneck results, such that the processing in one task must await the completion of processing for the other task. Thus, in essence, bottleneck models suggest that tasks alternate in their use of a single mechanism rather than share resources, in a graded fashion, as argued in the resource or capacity models.

At present, there is no clear winner with respect to these competing models of dual-task processing and performance. Each of the models appears to be capable of accounting for a subset of dual-task decrements reported in the literature. However, there has been a conspicuous absence of the examination of nonresource models, such as the crosstalk and bottleneck models, in the context of aging and dual-task processing (for a notable exception see Korteling, 1991, 1993, 1994). The potential application of these models to the study of age differences in dual-task processing will be discussed later in this chapter.

Another proposal that was offered to account for age-related differences in dual-task processing is that older subjects have more difficulty in the management or coordination of multiple tasks (Korteling, 1991; Madden, 1986; Salthouse et al., 1984). There are several pieces of evidence that support this hypothesis. One important finding is that older adults are less proficient than younger adults in the rapid and strategic redeployment of attention among two or more tasks or processes (Korteling, 1991; McDowd, Vercruyssen, & Birren, 1991). One example of this lack of control or attentional flexibility was illustrated in a study by Hawkins et al. (1992) in which older adults had more difficulty than younger adults when they were required to switch rapidly between an auditory and a visual task. Another example is provided by Jennings et al. (1990), who found that older subjects were less well prepared for rapidly presented stimuli when required to perform an arithmetic task concurrently with a monitoring task. The proposal of age-related differences in task coordination or attentional flexibility is also consistent with findings that older adults exhibit less flexibility than young adults in varying their speed–accuracy criteria (Hertzog, Vernon, & Rypma, 1993; Sharps & Gollin, 1987; Strayer, Wickens, & Braune, 1987; Welford, 1958), adjusting response speed following errors (Rabbitt, 1979), selecting among different mnemonic strategies (Brigham & Pressley, 1988), and coordinating patterns of movements between their hands (Stelmach, Amrhein, & Goggin, 1988).

Other evidence, however, appears to be at odds with the coordination hypothesis. This evidence was provided in studies that required subjects to emphasize differentially the performance on two concurrent tasks in different blocks of trials. Performance under these different processing priorities is then plotted in an Attention Operating Characteristic (AOC; Kinchla, 1980; Sperling & Melcher, 1978), such that performance in one task is plotted against performance in the other concurrently performed task. Thus, for example, points might be plotted for instructional conditions in which subjects are told to perform Task A alone, optimize their performance on Task A and treat Task B of secondary importance, emphasize both tasks equivalently, optimize their performance on Task B and treat Task A as secondary, and perform Task B alone. The shape of the resultant AOC function provides an indication of a subjects ability to distribute their attention between the two tasks. A number of studies that used this procedure found that young and old adults appear equally facile at varying their processing priorities between two tasks (Jennings et al., 1990; Ponds et al., 1988; Salthouse et al., 1984; Somberg & Salthouse, 1982). At first glance this finding appears inconsistent with the coordination hypothesis. However, it is important to note that the processing priority manipulations employed in these studies were between blocks of trials, whereas the studies that obtained results consistent with the coordination hypothesis most often assessed processing flexibility on a trial-by-trial basis. Thus, it is conceivable that older and younger adults are equally facile at varying their processing priorities and strategies in static situations, but that older subjects have more difficulty varying processing priorities in dynamically changing tasks and environments.

In summary, based on the literature reviewed in the foregoing discussion, it is clear that large and robust age-related differences in dual-task performance are obtained in many situations. It also seems prudent, at the present time, to assume that these performance differences are the result of age-related changes in several underlying mechanisms. In the subsequent section we examine the influence of practice and training strategies on the learning, performance and transfer of dual-task skills.

TRAINING FOR DUAL-TASK PERFORMANCE

Two general classes of training strategies have been employed in dual-task settings, part-task and whole-task training techniques (Damos, 1991; Lintern & Wickens, 1991). Part-task training has been defined as practice on a subset of components of a task or skill prior to practice on the whole task. For example, in learning to pilot an aircraft, students typically practice a number of component skills, such as preflight procedures, map reading, instrument interpretation, and communication procedures, prior to their actually flying the aircraft.

A number of part-task training strategies have been described, with their common feature being the division of the whole task into components followed by the training of individual components either separately or in various combinations (Wightman & Lintern, 1985). The major advantage of this class of techniques is that it serves to reduce the magnitude of the processing demands imposed upon subjects by the whole task. In turn, the reduction of processing demands has been linked to a more rapid development of skill in the part-task components than might otherwise be achieved if training were accomplished in the context of the whole task (Brown & Carr, 1989; Schneider, 1985). For example, Nissen and Bullemer (1987) trained subjects on a repeating sequence of 10 stimuli in either a single-task (e.g., repeating sequence only) or dual-task (e.g., with an auditory running memory task) context. In a transfer task in which subjects performed only the repeating sequence task, the single-task training subjects achieved higher levels of performance than the dual-task training subjects did. Furthermore, those trained in the dual-task context performed no better than a third group of subjects who were trained on a random sequence of stimuli (see also Noble, Trumbo, & Fowler, 1967). Thus, it would appear that, in some situations, reducing processing demands by employing part-task training strategies can enhance the rate of learning of the tasks.

There are also a number of potential disadvantages associated with part-task training, particularly with regard to the performance of the trained tasks or task components in dual-task settings. First, several investigators demonstrated that dual tasks are more than the sum of their parts or component tasks (Bahrick, Noble, & Fitts, 1954; Bahrick & Shelly, 1959; Damos & Wickens, 1980). For example, Schneider and Fisk (1982) found continued improvements in dual-task processing long after the performance of the constituent single tasks had stabilized. Thus, it would appear that there is more to dual-task performance than a reduction in the resource demands and subsequent automatization of the single tasks. Second, there appear to be critical attentional control and task coordination strategies that are not easily acquired during part-task training. Damos and Wickens (1980) found that subjects developed specific strategies for coordinating two tasks (e.g., time-sharing versus time-switching) during whole-task training and that these strategies transferred to a different set of tasks. No such transfer was found for part-task training (see also Fabiani et al., 1989; Hunt & Lansman, 1982). Finally, the manner in which part-tasks are defined appears to be critical to training success (Wightman & Lintern, 1985). Unfortunately, there is yet no agreed on method for parsing a task into its part-task constituents. One promising proposal, however, is that part-tasks should be defined as components with consistent stimulus-response mappings (Fisk & Gallini, 1989; Fisk, Lee, & Rogers, 1991; Fisk & Rogers, 1991b). However, even in this circumstance it is clear that some amount of dual-task training is required to achieve efficient dual-task processing (Kramer & Strayer, 1988; Schneider & Fisk, 1982).

Whole-task training involves the training of all components of a task, or in the case of dual-tasks, both tasks, at the same time. This is often accomplished by instructing subjects to treat the two tasks, or multiple components of a single task, as of equal importance. The main advantage of this training strategy is that it enables subjects to develop task coordination and attentional control strategies. As indicated previously, whole-task training is necessary to reduce the dual-task decrements that are found when two tasks are performed together (Damos & Wickens, 1980; Lintern & Wickens, 1991; Schneider & Fisk,

1982). However, the main disadvantage of whole-task training is the possibility that the processing demands will be so excessive that subjects are prevented from learning either of the tasks (Nissen & Bullemer, 1987; Noble et al., 1967).

In summary, it appears that the strength of part-task training is a weakness of whole-task training and vice-versa. Thus, the reduction in processing demands associated with training separate or part tasks leads to automaticity, given the availability of consistent stimulus–response mappings (Kramer, Strayer, & Buckley, 1990; Rogers & Fisk, 1991; Schneider & Shiffrin, 1977), while the increased demands associated with whole-task training can slow or prevent learning of the individual tasks. Conversely, task coordination and attentional control strategies are acquired with the whole but not the part-task training strategies. Given the relative strengths and weaknesses of these two strategies an important question is whether a hybrid part–whole task training procedure would promote efficient acquisition and transfer of skill in dual-task paradigms.

In fact, there have been a small number of studies which suggest that hybrid training strategies might be quite effective in dual-task settings. Schneider and Fisk (1982) trained subjects on two versions of a visual search task, one version was consistently mapped (CM) and the other variably mapped (VP). In the CM task the relationship between stimuli and responses was fixed across trials. In the VM task the relationship between stimuli and responses varied across trials.

Previous studies suggested that given sufficient practice, performance would eventually become automatized on the CM task (Schneider & Shiffrin, 1977; Shiffrin & Schneider, 1977). This, in fact, occurred in the Schneider and Fisk study. After extensive single task practice on the CM and VM search tasks subjects were required to perform both of the tasks together. Initially, performance declined in the dual relative to the single task conditions. However, after subjects were taught to emphasize the VM task rather than the CM task performance in the dual CM–VM conditions improved to that of the single task baseline conditions. This study suggests that both single or part-task training and whole-task training are necessary for the acquisition of efficient dual-task performance.

Another hybrid training strategy was employed by Gopher and colleagues (Gopher, 1993; Gopher, Weil, & Siegel, 1989). Brickner and Gopher (1981) argued that the advantages of both part-task and whole-task training strategies could be achieved with a training procedure in which subjects performed both tasks together (e.g., whole-task training) but varied their emphasis between the two tasks (e.g. part-task training) in different blocks of trials. Thus, in this embedded part–whole task training strategy subjects could learn to coordinate and control their attention between the two tasks while still capitalizing on the reduced processing requirements as the priorities were shifted between the two tasks.

In an effort to test this hypothesis Brickner and Gopher had subjects perform a self-paced letter typing task with a digit classification task. Six subjects were assigned to each of two conditions; a fixed priority (FP) group in which the subjects were to emphasize both of the tasks equally and a variable priority (VP) training group in which, across different blocks, subjects were to vary their priorities between the two tasks (e.g., for the two tasks; 25%–75%, 35%–65%, 50%–50%, 65%–35%, 75%–25% priorities). Priorities were indicated by a continuously moving bar graph that was individually scaled on the basis of each subject's performance on a previous block of trials.

Several interesting results were obtained. First, the VP subjects outperformed the FP subjects during training. That is, the VP subjects showed faster acquisition of skilled performance on the tasks and a higher level of mastery at the conclusion of training than did subjects trained with the FP strategy. Second, the VP subjects were more successful at reducing performance decrements than the FP subjects when difficulty of the tasks was varied. Finally, the VP subjects performance was superior to the FP subjects when subjects were transferred to externally paced versions of the two tasks. These results suggest that acquisition and transfer of dual-task skills can be aided by embedding part-task training strategies within the context of the whole task (e.g., VP group), when compared to whole-task training (e.g., FP group). Unfortunately, however, the Brickner and Gopher (1981) study did not include a part-task training group for comparison like that used by Schneider and Fisk (1982).

Gopher and colleagues have gone on to conduct a number of additional studies which have, in general, found results consistent with the Brickner and Gopher (1981) study. In one such study Gopher et al. (1989) trained subjects, using the VP training procedure, in a complex video game-like task called Space Fortress. The Space Fortress task involved a number of component skills including manual control, aiming, and visual discrimination. Subjects who had been trained with the VP strategy outperformed other subjects who had been trained with a whole-task training strategy. VP subjects were also found to be less sensitive to interference from an extraneous task than were subjects trained with a whole-task training procedure (Fabiani et al., 1989). In a more recent study (Gopher, Weil, & Bareket, 1994) flight students who had received 10 hours of practice on the Space Fortress task with the VP training strategy were found to be more successful in completing flight training than subjects who had not received the VP training. In summary, the VP training, a hybrid part–whole task training strategy appears to capitalize on the advantages of the part and whole-task training procedures without incurring the costs.

AGE-RELATED DIFFERENCES IN TRAINING FOR DUAL-TASK PERFORMANCE

There is now a small but growing body of literature that examines the question of whether practice, and in some cases specific training strategies, produces similar improvements in the dual-task performance of young and elderly adults. McDowd (1986) reasoned that practice on dual tasks might serve to reduce age-related differences in performance given previous reports of reductions in age-related differences in single task performance with extensive practice (e.g., Murrell, 1970; Mowbray & Rhoades, 1959; Nebes, 1978; but see Salthouse, 1990, for a different conclusion). Six young and six old adults performed a visual tracking and auditory choice RT task for 6 hours. Although both old and young subjects showed improvements in dual-task performance across practice sessions the age-related difference was insensitive to practice. Greenwood and Parasuraman (1991) came to a similar conclusion when they examined changes in the performance of young and old adults across 2 days of practice on a letter matching and probe RT task. Interestingly, however, probe RT continued to improve across the 2 days of practice for the old adults, whereas RT appears to have asymptoted after the first day of practice for the younger adults. Therefore, it appears conceivable that the performance gap between old and young adults might have narrowed with additional practice.

In a study reported by Baron and Mattila (1989), 12 young and 12 old adult men received 44 hours of practice with a memory scanning procedure in which lists of visual and auditory stimuli were presented both separately and together. Subjects were instructed to make one response on a probe trial if a target was present and another response if a target was not present. The stimuli which served as targets and distractors in these lists varied over trials (e.g., a varied mapping procedure was used). Targets occurred on 50% of the probe trials. Although it might be argued that the dual-list conditions do not really constitute a dual-task because the two lists required only a single response on any particular trial, the results of the study are intriguing nonetheless.

In general the older subjects performed the task more slowly than the younger subjects did in both the single- and dual-list conditions. Practice on the task produced only small improvements in performance for both young and older subjects. The small practice effect is not particularly surprising because the mapping between stimuli and responses was varied over trials (Fisk & Rogers, 1991b; Schneider & Shiffrin, 1977). However, when a time limit on responding was imposed such that subjects were rewarded if they responded faster than the 75th percentile of their previous block of trials, the age-related difference in single versus dual-list conditions was reduced. Furthermore, this reduced age-related decrement remained even when the time contingency was removed.

These results suggest that it may be possible, with particular training strategies, to reduce the age-related decrements in dual-task processing. However, while this study provides some intriguing data there are number of unanswered questions. First, as mentioned earlier, it is unclear whether this procedure constitutes a dual task, given the simultaneous presentation of two different lists of items that required only a single response. In fact, Logan and Stadler (1991) argued, on the basis of empirical data, that in similar situations subjects will often use a superspan strategy in which they combine two lists of items into a single list and perform a single search through the items of this combined list. Second, given the varied mapping of stimuli to responses in this paradigm, it was impossible to assess whether training would lead to automatized processing for both the old and young subjects. Fisk and Rogers (1991a) reported that with consistent mapping of stimuli to responses both old and young subjects develop automatic processing in memory but not visual search tasks (but see Strayer & Kramer, 1994). Third, the lack of a separate set of transfer tasks makes it impossible to determine whether training leads to a generalizable or specific information processing skill. That is, would the old and young subjects be capable of employing the time-limit strategy in the learning of new tasks and skills? Fourth, there was no detailed analysis of changes in the strategies that subjects employed in the dual-list conditions. A substantial number of techniques have now been developed that enable one to assess the degree to which subjects are timesharing or quickly switching between two tasks (Falmagne, 1968; Sperling & Melcher, 1978; Sperling & Dosher, 1986; Strayer & Kramer, 1990). These analysis techniques, which include the examination of cumulative distribution functions, fixed-point properties of mixture distributions, and contingency analyses, would be quite useful in explicating the influence of training on the fine structure of dual tasks.

Rogers et al. (1994) reported a study in which 20 young and 20 old adults were extensively trained (> 7000 trials) on varied (VM) and consistently mapped (CM) versions of a visual search task. At the conclusion of training the visual search task was then performed concurrently with a variably mapped (VM) memory search task for an additional three experimental sessions. Thus, in essence, Rogers et al. employed a part-task training procedure by practicing one of the tasks prior to dual-task performance.

Several interesting results were obtained. First, both young and old adults displayed large dual-task costs in the performance of the CM and VM visual search tasks when these tasks were first performed with the memory search task. Such a result is not surprising given that attentional control and task coordination skills are not easily acquired during part-task training (Damos & Wickens, 1989; Hunt & Lansman, 1982). Second, there was no significant improvement in the performance of the VM versions of the visual and memory search tasks, for either the young or old adults, across the three dual-task sessions. Finally, the young but not the older adults showed substantial reductions in dual-task performance costs when they performed the CM version of the visual search task with the memory search task. The authors interpreted these results as suggesting that the older adults did not automatize processing in the visual search task.

It is interesting to note, however, that the reduction in dual-task performance costs was not observed for the younger adults until the third session of dual-task practice. Thus, if the older adults acquired dual-task processing skills at a slower rate than the younger adults, three practice sessions might not have been sufficient to observe improvements for the older adults. The authors also reported that the older subjects performed the visual search task more accurately than the younger adults. Given Baron and Mattila's (1989) report of reduced dual-task decrements, as well as a narrowing of the age difference in dual-task performance, with speed rather than accuracy emphasis, it seems possible that older adults' emphasis on accuracy may have further slowed their improvement in dual-task conditions. In summary, Rogers et al.'s (1994) finding of differential age-related practice effects in dual-task conditions is important in that it begins to define the conditions under which older adults show less benefit from practice than younger adults. However, the extent to which these age-related learning differences are amenable to training strategy (e.g., speed versus accuracy emphasis) and more extensive practice is an open question.

Salthouse and Somberg (1982) performed what is now a classic study to examine the influence of practice on the acquisition of new skills by young and old adults. In particular, they were interested in the types of processing changes that take place over the course of extensive practice and whether or not such changes differ between groups of young and old adults. They described and investigated three types of processing changes that might occur during the course of practice. One was a reduction in the need for processing resources or attention and a concomitant automatization of a task or task component. Another was a change in the specific types of information that were being processed by the subjects such as the types of information which might be used to discriminate one visually presented stimulus from another. The final hypothesis was that practice might lead to a change in the specific processes or operations to which the stimuli are subjected. Thus, some processing steps might be omitted or processing steps might take place in a parallel rather than in a serial fashion.

Salthouse and Somberg (1982) explored these hypotheses by practicing eight young and eight older subjects for 51 hours on a number of elementary tasks that were presented within the context of an impoverished video game they called Space Trex. The tasks included signal detection, memory scanning, visual discrimination and temporal prediction. Although the paradigm cannot be classified as a dual-task, because the elementary tasks were not performed concurrently, the results are quite instructive with regard to practice effects. The three hypotheses described above were examined by occasionally imposing transfer tasks throughout the 51 hours of practice. For example, the resource or attention reduction hypothesis was examined by occasionally requiring subjects to perform a secondary task concurrently with the training tasks. Variants of the elementary tasks were also used as transfer tasks to assess the degree to which learning was specific to the particular stimuli that were employed in the training tasks. Possible changes in the processing operations were examined by inspecting the specific dependent variables employed in each of the elementary tasks (e.g., change in slope in the memory scanning task).

Several important results were obtained in the study. First, both young and older adults improved their performance throughout the practice sessions, although the initial age-related difference in performance was maintained, for most of the tasks and dependent variables, across the course of practice. Second, evidence was obtained for changes in each of the hypothesized processes. Probe RTs decreased with practice, suggesting a reduction in the need for resources or attention by the elementary tasks with practice. The amount of transfer to different stimuli varied across the elementary tasks with near perfect transfer in the signal detection task and poor transfer in the visual discrimination task. Evidence was also provided for changes in the processing operations in a subset of tasks. Memory search slopes decreased with practice for both young and old subjects. Given that the stimuli and responses in this task were consistently mapped, it is quite likely that the search process was becoming automatized during practice (Fisk & Rogers, 1991b; Shiffrin & Schneider, 1977). Third, it appeared that changes in these processes were quite similar for both young and old subjects. Finally, performance improvements achieved at the conclusion of practice were maintained across a 1-month retention interval.

In summary, the literature on age-related differences in dual-task practice/training effects is quite limited despite the importance of this issue for everyday leisure and workplace activities. However, a common finding in the studies that have been performed, with the notable exception of the recent report by Rogers et al. (1994), is that older adults are capable of improving their performance in dual-task situations. At present it is uncertain whether age-related decrements in dual-task processing can be reduced or eliminated through practice or the application of specific training strategies. We discovered only one study (Baron & Mattila, 1989) that investigated the influence of more than a single training strategy on dual-task learning and performance. It is also unclear as to the influence of practice and training on the nature of dual-task processing. The research of Salthouse and Somberg (1982) certainly provided important insights into the qualitative and quantitative changes that take place during skill acquisition with older adults, but much remains to be investigated, especially within the realm of dual-task processing (see also Fisk & Rogers, 1991a).

In an effort to further examine the question of whether the learning and performance of dual-tasks by young and old adults could be enhanced through training, we recently conducted a study in which we examined the influence of practice on the dual-task performance of 30 old and 30 young adults (for a full report of this study see Kramer, Larish, & Strayer, 1995). More specifically, we compared the efficacy of two different dual-task training strategies, fixed priority (FP) training and variable priority training (VP) in the learning of single and dual-tasks as well as transfer of training to novel single and dual-tasks. As described previously, Gopher and colleagues (Brickner & Gopher, 1981; Gopher et al., 1989, 1994) argued, on the basis of empirical data, that subjects trained to vary their processing priorities among two or more tasks will show faster rates of learning, superior asymptotic performance and higher rates of transfer to other dual-task situations than subjects trained in the more traditional way, that is, with fixed processing priorities. Thus, Gopher's results suggest that subjects in the VP training group are learning a fairly generalizable dual-task processing skill, at least within the constraints of the tasks that have been employed in his studies.

Despite the impressive success that Gopher and colleagues demonstrated with VP training, there are, at present, still a number of unanswered questions with regard to this training strategy. First, the tasks that were examined in the training paradigms were largely psychomotor. Thus, one important question is whether the VP training strategy is applicable to tasks that are more cognitive in nature. This issue was examined in our study by employing tasks which included substantial memory and decision making components. Second, the VP training strategy was employed only with young adults. Thus, a second important question is whether this training strategy is appropriate for older adults. Finally, Gopher and colleagues employed a restricted set of transfer tasks in their studies. For example, Brickner and Gopher (1981) transferred subjects to a dual-task pair with one old (pretrained) and one new task. Our study employed two novel tasks in the transfer conditions.

Subjects in our study we trained on the two tasks illustrated in Fig. 5.1. The monitoring task required subjects to keep track of the position of the cursor on each of the six gauges and to reset each cursor as soon as it exceeded a critical value (i.e., 9). A critical aspect of this task was that the cursors were invisible until sampled, with only a single cursor being viewable at a time. This aspect of the task rendered it necessary

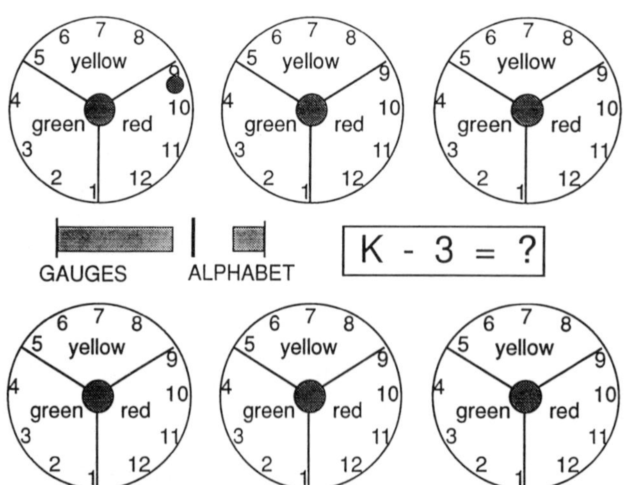

FIG. 5.1 A graphic illustration of the monitoring and alphabet arithmetic tasks. The bars in the center left of the figure were used to provide continuous performance feedback to the subjects during training.

for subjects to construct a mental representation of the movement of the cursors, a relatively difficult and dynamic memory task. Subjects were also trained on an alphabet arithmetic task which required that they add and subtract numbers from letters (e.g., M − 3 = J). The alphabet arithmetic task was chosen because previous studies have found that the computation of the answer becomes automatized with practice (Logan, 1988). Thus, the inclusion of this task enabled us to assess the automatization of a component of the dual-task.

Finally, as indicated in Fig. 5.1 a set of bargraphs was included in the training display in an effort to provide continuous feedback to subjects as to whether they were performing as instructed. In the FP group the bar graphs were calibrated so that they abutted the centrally located vertical line when subjects were responding faster than the 50th percentile of their previous single task RT distribution (with equivalent accuracy) for the same task. In the VP training condition task priority was varied across trials such that subjects would either maximize performance on one task or the other or treat both tasks as equally important.

Following three 2-hour sessions of training with either the FP or VP strategy, subjects were transferred to the two tasks illustrated in Fig. 5.2. In the scheduling task subjects assigned incoming boxes, illustrated in the top left corner of the figure, to one of four moving lines. The goal of the task was to assign each new box to the shortest line, that is, the line with the smallest total area of boxes. Subjects were required to assign boxes as quickly and as accurately as possible. The difficultly was varied by using a single box height in one condition, boxes with

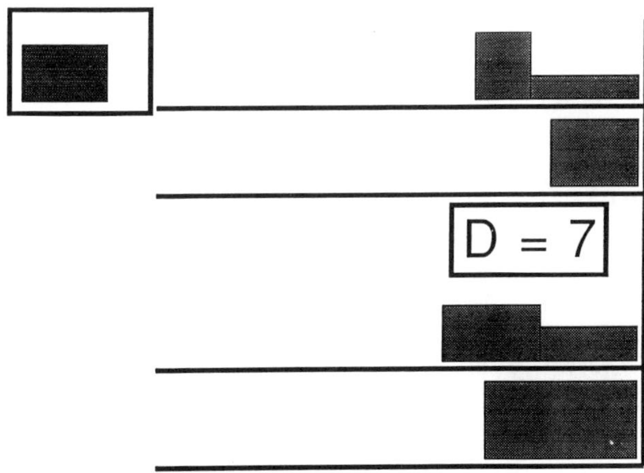

FIG. 5.2 A graphic illustration of the scheduling and running memory tasks performed by the subjects in the transfer phase of the study.

three different heights and widths in another condition, and boxes with five different heights and widths in a third condition. The paired associate running memory task is illustrated in the centrally located box in Fig. 5.2 (e.g., D = 7). The subject viewed a series of letter–number pairs and was occasionally probed to indicate whether a letter–number pair matched the last presentation of the pair (e.g., D = 7?). Task difficulty was varied by using the letters A–C, A–D, and A–E for the easy, medium, and difficult conditions, respectively. Continuous feedback was not presented in the transfer sessions, but subjects were asked to perform both of the new tasks as well as possible.

Several interesting results were obtained in the training and transfer phases of the study. First, as illustrated for the alphabet arithmetic task in Fig. 5.3, VP training resulted in improved dual-task performance for both the old and young adults. On the other hand, FP training was relatively ineffective in reducing dual-task performance deficits. Second, although the younger adults' dual-task performance improvement was relatively continuous with VP training, the older adults' initial dual-task performance was better with the FP than the VP strategy. It is likely that these early costs for the old adults were due to the requirement to keep track of the priority instructions and feedback in the VP condition, in essence an additional task not associated with the FP training strategy. Third, perhaps the most important result was that both the young and old VP trained subjects learned the transfer tasks more quickly and showed substantially smaller dual-task deficits on these tasks than did the FP trained subjects. These results are illustrated for the scheduling task in Fig. 5.4.

In summary, the results of our study suggest, along with the findings of Baron and Mattila (1989), that training techniques that emphasize flexible task coordination strategies can enhance the rate of learning and level of mastery of dual-tasks. Furthermore, such strategies appear to be generalizable to other tasks and settings, although the limits of generalizability require further study. Of course, additional research is necessary to examine the efficacy of different training strategies for the dual-task performance of young and old adults.

AGE-RELATED DIFFERENCES IN DUAL-TASK TRAINING AND PERFORMANCE: UNRESOLVED ISSUES

Although it is clear from the literature surveyed in the preceding sections that we are beginning to explicate some of the important factors that contribute to the successful acquisition, transfer, and retention of skills in dual-task settings, there are a number of gaps in

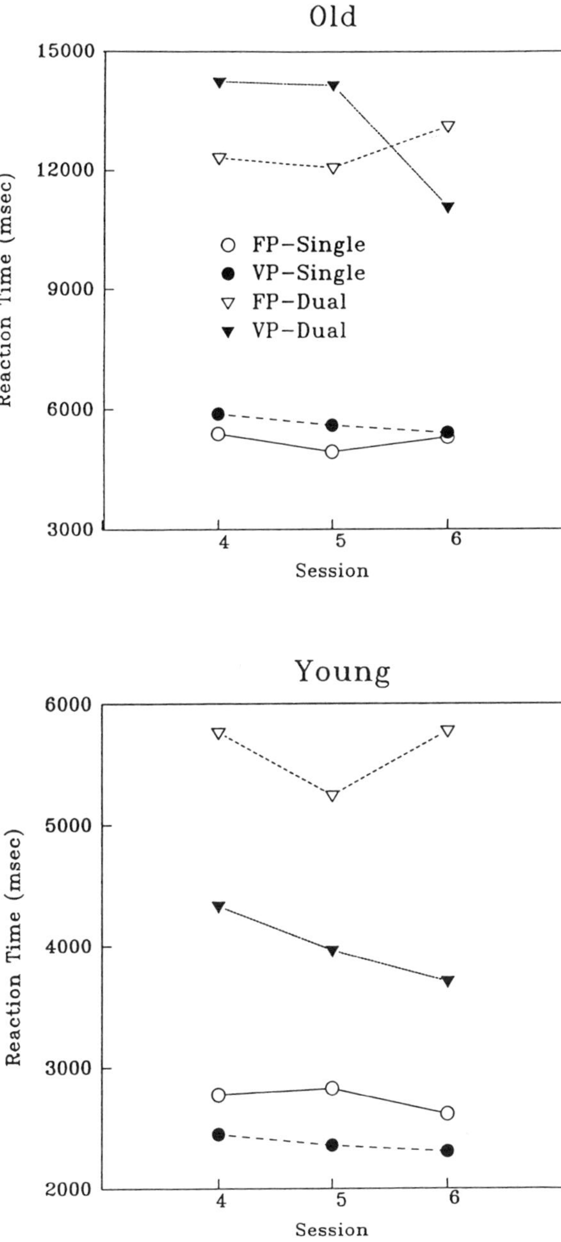

FIG. 5.3 Single- and dual-task reaction time data from the three training sessions for the FP and VP subjects in the alphabet arithmetic task. Note that the range of the reaction time values on the ordinate differs for the young and old adults.

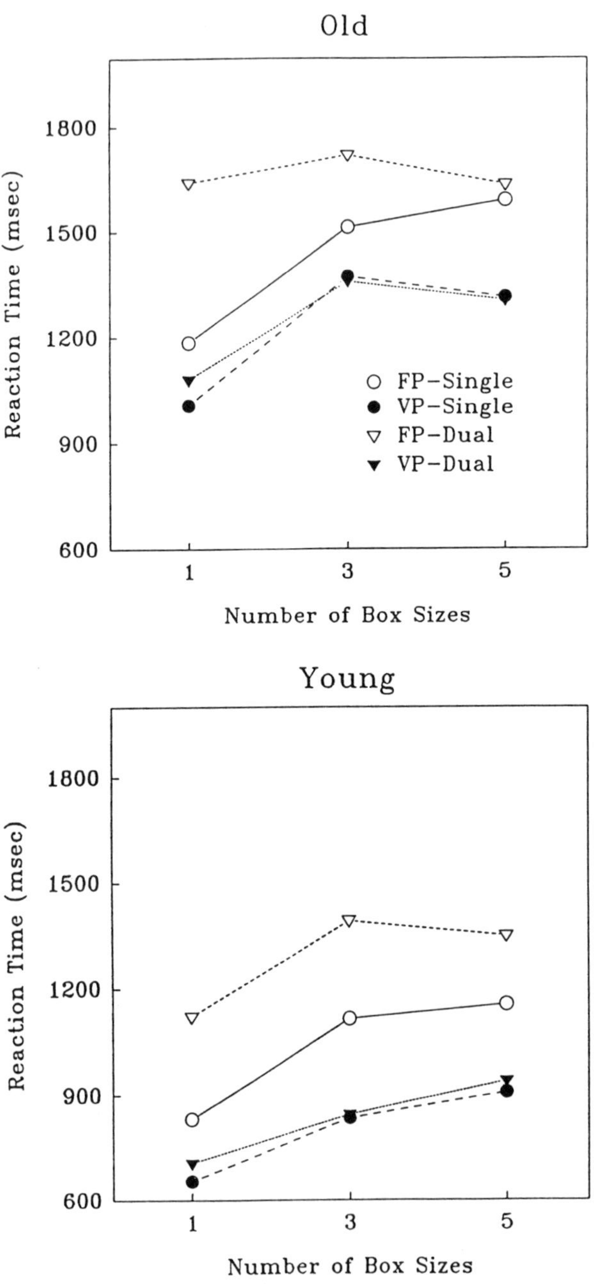

FIG. 5.4 Single- and dual-task reaction time data from the transfer sessions for the FP and VP subjects in the scheduling task.

our knowledge base that require additional research. For instance, there has been relatively little systematic examination of age-related differences in dual-task performance or training effects within the context of modern day models of dual-task processing, such as multiple resource, crosstalk, or bottleneck models. Each of these models makes testable predictions about the situations in which dual-task performance decrements will be found. For example, Pashler (1984) argued that a bottleneck in the selection of actions is responsible for the great majority of performance decrements observed in simple dual-tasks. An important question is whether aging results in a quantitative difference in this form of interference, perhaps due to the lengthening of response selection processing with age, or instead whether bottlenecks in additional processing operations are observed with older adults. In a similar vein, multiple resource models (Freidman & Polson, 1981; Wickens, 1992) are explicit in their predictions about the nature of task and process interactions. For example, Wickens (1992) suggested that processing resources can be conceptualized along three different dimensions, stages of processing, codes (hemispheres) of processing, and modalities of input and output. In this theoretical framework, task interference will be observed to the extent that concurrently performed tasks require the same types of resources. Unfortunately, there has been little systematic research that examined the extent to which the pattern of resource interactions varies with age.

The notion that dual-task interference or facilitation can be explained in terms of the similarity of stimulus materials, transformations, or response patterns was examined in the context of aging. Korteling (1991, 1993) reported a series of studies in which young and old adults concurrently performed two compensatory tracking tasks. Older adults were less able to utilize redundancies in the two tasks to benefit performance and were more negatively influenced by incompatible display/control relationships than were younger adults. Although these data are interesting and potentially important with respect to the delineation of age-related differences in interference and facilitation attributable to similarity or crosstalk, additional research is needed to examine the influence of practice and training strategies on these performance effects. Furthermore, the relationship between general or specific inhibitory failures during aging (Hasher & Zacks, 1988; Kramer, Humphrey, Larish, Logan, & Strayer, 1994) and crosstalk effects in dual-task performance appears to be a promising avenue for future research.

A second gap in the research on age-related differences in dual-task processing concerns the methodologies that have been brought to bear on the examination of dual-task performance strategies. For example, although declines in the availability of some general form of processing capacity has often been assumed to be the basis of age-related differences in dual-task performance, there has been little quantitative analysis of processing strategies.

Resource or capacity models assume that resources are divided in a graded fashion among concurrently performed tasks. On the other hand, bottleneck models argue that some processing operations take place in an all-or-none fashion. In this case, dual-task performance decrements occur because of time delays in accessing processing mechanisms. These two strategies have been referred to as time-sharing and time-switching, respectively. An important unresolved issue is whether aging is associated with a shift from one strategy to the other or instead whether the efficiency with which one or both of these strategies are utilized declines during aging.

Several quantitative techniques are available to discriminate between time-sharing and time-switching strategies. For example, contingency analysis (Sperling & Dosher, 1986; Sperling & Melcher, 1978) involves the construction of a two-way table that displays the probability that performance of Task A will be accurate as a function of the accuracy of performance on Task B. If subjects are employing a time-sharing strategy, the 2 × 2 contingency table will show statistical independence, the probability of a correct response on one task will not be dependent on whether the response to the other task was right or wrong. On the other hand, time-switching will be indicated by a statistical dependence between the correctness of responses on the two tasks. An alternative technique for discriminating between time-sharing and time-switching strategies is to examine the reaction time cumulative density functions to determine whether or not they pass through a common (fixed) point. Falmagne (1968) first noted the fixed point property of mixture distributions. According to this property, all linear combinations of two partially overlapping density functions must pass through the same fixed point. Thus, density functions that pass through the same fixed point would indicate that two different strategies were being used in dual-task conditions; that is, subjects would be switching attention between the two tasks. Both the contingency analysis and fixed point properties were used successfully in previous studies (Bonnel, Possami, & Schmitt, 1987; Sperling & Melcher, 1978; Strayer & Kramer, 1990) to discriminate between time-sharing and time-switching strategies. Such techniques would be quite useful in characterizing age-related differences in dual-task performance (see also Yantis, Meyer, & Smith, 1991, for other tests of mixture distributions).

Third, there have been few attempts, particularly with older adults, to assess the generalizability and long-term stability of skills learned during dual-task training. Given that the goal of training is usually to support post-training performance, at least in real-world settings, it is surprising that this important issue has not been investigated more thoroughly. In any event, there are several aspects of post-training performance that would appear to be important to assess. One is the extent to which the skills learned during training can be retained. Salthouse and Somberg (1982) have found good retention one month after training, for both young and older adults, on the elementary tasks that were trained in their paradigm. However, we were able to find only a single study in which the retention of dual-task skills were assessed post-training. Ball, Beard, Roenker, Miller, and Griggs (1988) trained young and old adults to perform concurrently an identification task at fixation and a detection task in the periphery of the visual field. Training improved subjects' ability to perform the peripheral task and this improvement lasted, for both young and old adults, across a 6-month retention interval.

It would also seem important to assess the extent to which skills trained in dual-task paradigms are resistant to distraction from extraneous stimuli or changes in the difficulty of the trained task. Gopher and colleagues found that subjects trained with the VP strategy were better able to cope with changes in task difficulty and the imposition of another task than subjects trained with the more traditional whole-task (e.g., FP group) training strategy. We have found similar VP training benefits for both young and old adults in our recent study.

Finally, it would appear important to determine whether the skills learned during training can be transferred to other tasks and settings. Although the issue of the generality of dual-task processing, or, as it has often been called, time-sharing skills, is still quite controversial (see Ackerman et al., 1984; Brookings & Damos, 1991; Lintern & Wickens, 1991, for an in-depth review of this issue) the Gopher et al. studies, along with our recent study, suggest that different training strategies might promote differential amounts of transfer. Studies that found an association between dual-task processing efficiency and performance in real-world skills also suggest that the dual-task processing skills might be more general than previously believed (Avolio et al., 1985; Ball & Owsley, 1991; Crosby & Parkinson, 1979; Damos, 1978; Gopher, 1982; North & Gopher, 1976). In any event, the issues of retention, resistance to distraction, and transfer of dual-task processing strategies are important and should be further explored, particularly with respect to aging.

Fourth, although the type and magnitude of feedback has been shown to have an important influence on the acquisition, retention and generalization of motor and verbal skills (Schmidt & Bjork, 1992), there has been a lack of systematic study of feedback in dual-task settings with either young or older adults. In the motor learning arena, Schmidt, Young, Swinnen, and Shapiro (1989) found faster acquisition of complex arm movements when feedback was provided on every trial compared to conditions in which summary feedback was provided after every 5 or 15 trials. However, when performance was assessed on a delayed retention test subjects who received less frequent feedback during training outperformed those subjects who received feedback on every trial. Similar effects have been reported for learning concepts in computer languages (Schooler & Anderson, 1990). A plausible interpretation of these results is that while frequent feedback may provide useful guidance early in practice it also becomes part of the task resulting in decrements in performance when it is removed. It is conceivable that subjects come to rely on the feedback rather than attempt to use cues which are inherent in the tasks to monitor their quality of performance. In fact, this interpretation is consistent with the findings obtained with the procedure of fading or augmented feedback in which feedback is initially presented frequently and later faded as subjects performance improves (Winstein & Schmidt, 1990). Within the multitask context, Lintern and colleagues (Lintern & Roscoe, 1980; Lintern, Thomley, Nelson, & Roscoe, 1984) found high rates of transfer of training when augmented feedback was used during the acquisition of a number of flight skills.

Additional research is needed to investigate the efficacy of different feedback schedules for acquisition, transfer, and retention of dual-task skills for both young and elderly adults. Given that aging is associated with deficits in metacognitive skills such as self-monitoring and information management (Dempster, 1992; Hasher & Zacks, 1988; Murphy, Schmitt, Caruso, & Sanders, 1987; Tipper, 1991), it is reasonable to assume that older subjects will have more difficulty than younger adults with the transition from training tasks that provide continuous performance feedback to transfer tasks that do not provide explicit feedback. Thus, the fading of feedback during training may prove to be particularly beneficial to older adults to the extent that it encourages them to internalize performance monitoring processes.

In conclusion, we have attempted in this brief exposition to provide a sketch of the current state of research on aging and multi-task performance. Although there is now a relatively strong consensus concerning the robustness of age-related decrements in dual-task performance, much remains to be discovered about the mechanisms and strategies that underlie these processing changes and the extent to which performance decrements can be mediated through practice and training. In our concluding section, we have endeavored to describe a set of research issues which we believe have important theoretical and practical implications for our understanding of age-related differences in multitask performance.

REFERENCES

Ackerman, P., Schneider, W., & Wickens, C. (1984). Deciding the existence of a time sharing ability: A combined methodological and theoretical approach. *Human Factors, 26,* 71–82.

Allport, A. (1987). Selection for action: some behavioral and neurophysiological considerations of attention and action. In H. Heuer & A. Sanders (Eds.), *Perspectives on perception and action* (pp. 395–420). Hillsdale, NJ: Lawrence Erlbaum Associates.

Avolio, B., Kroeck, K., & Panek, P. (1985). Individual differences in information processing ability as a predictor of motor vehicle accidents. *Human Factors, 27,* 577–587.

Baddeley, A., & Hitch, G. (1974). Working memory. In G. Bower (Ed.), *The Psychology of Learning and Motivation* (pp. 47–90). New York: Academic Press.

Ball, K., Beard, B., Roenker, D., Miller, R., & Griggs, D. (1988). Age and visual search: Expanding the useful field of view. *Journal of the Optical Society of America, 5,* 2210–2219.

Ball, K., & Owsley, C. (1991). Identifying correlates of accident involvement for the older driver. *Human Factors, 33,* 583–595.

Bahrick, H., Noble, M., & Fitts, P. (1954). Extra-task performance as a measure of learning a primary task. *Journal of Experimental Psychology, 48,* 298–302.

Bahrick, H., & Shelly, C. (1959). Time sharing as an index of automatization. *Journal of Experimental Psychology, 56,* 288–293.

Baron, A., & Mattila, W. (1989). Response slowing of older adults: Effects of time-limit contingencies on single and dual-task performance. *Psychology and Aging, 4,* 66–72.

Birren, J. (1974) Translations in gerontology—From lab to life: Psychophysiology and speed of response. *American Psychologist, 29,* 808–815.

Birren, J., Woods, A., & Williams, A. (1980). Behavioral slowing with age: Causes, organization and consequences. In L. Poon (Ed.), *Aging in the 1980's: Psychological issues* (pp. 293–308). Washington, D.C.: American Psychological Association.

Bonnel, A., Possami, C., & Schmitt, M. (1987). Early modulation of visual input: A study of attentional strategies. *Quartely Journal of Experimental Psychology, 39,* 757–776.

Brickner, M., & Gopher, D. (1981). *Improving time-sharing performance by enhancing voluntary control of processing resources* (Rep. No. HEIS-81-3). Haifa, Israel: Technion-III, Faculty of Industrial Engineering and Management, Research Center for Work Safety and Human Engineering.

Brigham, M., & Pressley, M. (1988). Cognitive monitoring and strategy choice in younger and older adults. *Psychology and Aging, 3,* 249–257.

Brookings, J., & Damos, D. (1991). Individual differences in multiple task performance. In D. Damos (Ed.), *Multiple task performance* (pp. 363–385). London: Wiley.

Brown, T., & Carr, T. (1989). Automaticity in skill acquisition: Mechanisms for reducing interference in concurrent performance. *Journal of Experimental Psychology: Human Perception and Performance, 15,* 686–700.

Cerella, J. (1985). Information processing rates in the elderly. *Psychological Bulletin, 98*, 67–83.
Cerella, J. (1990). Aging and information processing rate. In J. Birren & K. W. Schaie (Eds.), *Handbook of psychology of aging* (pp. 201–221). New York: Academic Press.
Craik, F.I.M. (1977). Age differences in human memory. In J. Birren & K. Schaie (Eds.), *Handbook of the psychology of aging* (pp. 384–420). New York: Van Nostrand Reinhold.
Crosby, J., & Parkinson, S. (1979) A dual-task investigation of pilots' skill level. *Ergonomics, 22*, 1301–1313.
Crossley, M., & Hiscock, M. (1992). Age-related differences in concurrent task performance of normal adults: Evidence for a decline in processing resources. *Psychology and Aging, 7*, 499–506.
Damos, D. (1978). Residual attention as a predictor of pilot performance. *Human Factors, 20*, 435–440.
Damos, D. (1991). Dual-task methodology: Some common problems. In D. Damos (Ed.), *Multiple task performance* (pp. 101–119). London: Wiley.
Damos, D., & Wickens, C. (1980). The identification and transfer of timesharing skills. *Acta Psychologica, 46*, 15–39.
Dempster, F. N. (1992). The rise and fall of the inhibitory mechanism: Toward a unified theory of cognitive development and aging. *Developmental Review, 12*, 45–75.
Fabiani, M., Buckley, J., Gratton, G., Coles, M., Donchin, E., & Logie, R. (1989). The training of complex task performance. *Acta Psychologica, 71*, 259–299.
Falmagne, J. (1968). Note on a simple fixed-point property of binary mixtures. *British Journal of Mathematical and Statistical Psychology, 21*, 131–132.
Fisk, A. D., & Gallini, J. (1989). Training consistent components of tasks: Developing an instructional system based on automatic/controlled processing principles. *Human Factors, 31*, 453–463.
Fisk, A. D., Lee, M., & Rogers, W. (1991). Recombination of automatic processing components: The effects of transfer, reversal and conflict situations. *Human Factors, 33*, 267–280.
Fisk, A. D., & Rogers, W. (1991a). Development of skilled performance: An age related perspective. In D. Damos (Ed.), *Multiple task performance* (pp. 415–443). London: Wiley.
Fisk, A. D., & Rogers, W. (1991b). Toward an understanding of age-related memory and visual search effects. *Journal of Experimental Psychology: General, 120*, 131–149.
Freidman, A., & Polson, M. (1981). The hemispheres as independent resource systems: Limited capacity processing and cerebral specialization. *Journal of Experimental Psychology: Human Perception and Performance, 7*, 1030–1058.
Gopher, D. (1982). A selective attention test as a predictor of success in flight training. *Human Factors, 24*, 173–184.
Gopher, D. (1993). The skill of attention control: Acquisition and execution of attention strategies. In S. Kornblum & D. Meyer (Eds.), *Attention and performance XIV* (pp. 299–322). Hillsdale, NJ: Lawrence Erlbaum Associates.
Gopher, D., Weil, M., & Bareket, T. (1994). Transfer of skill from a computer game trainer to flight. *Human Factors, 36*, 387–405.
Gopher, D., Weil, M., & Siegel, D. (1989). Practice under changing priorities: An approach to training of complex skills. *Acta Psychologica, 71*, 147–179.
Greenwood, P., & Parasuraman, R. (1991). Effects of aging on the speed and attentional cost of cognitive operations. *Developmental Neuropsychology, 7*, 421–434.
Guttentag, R. (1989). Age differences in dual-task performance: Procedures, assumptions and results. *Developmental Review, 9*, 146–170.
Hartley, A. (1992). Attention. In F. Craik & T. Salthouse (Eds.), *Handbook of aging and*

cognition (pp. 3–49). Hillsdale, NJ: Lawrence Erlbaum Associates.
Hasher, L., & Zacks, R. (1988). Working memory, comprehension, and aging: A review and a new view. In G. K. Bower (Ed.), *The psychology of learning and motivation* (pp. 193–225). New York: Academic Press.
Hawkins, H. L., Kramer, A. F., & Capaldi, D. (1992). Aging, exercise, and attention. *Psychology and Aging, 7,* 643–653.
Hertzog, C., Vernon, M. C., & Rypma, B. (1993). Age differences in mental rotation task performance: The influence of speed/accuracy tradeoffs. *Journal of Gerontology: Psychological Sciences, 48,* 150–156.
Hirst, W., & Kalmar, D. (1987). Characterizing attentional resources. *Journal of Experimental Psychology: Human Perception and Performance, 116,* 68–81.
Hunt, E., & Lansman, M. (1982). Individual differences in attention. In R. Sternberg (Ed.), *Advances in the psychology of human intelligence* (pp.207–254). Hillsdale, NJ: Lawrence Erlbaum Associates.
Jennings, R., Brock, K., & Nebes, R. (1990). Age and specific processing capacities: A cardiovascular analysis. *Journal of Psychophysiology, 4,* 51–64.
Kahneman, D. (1973). Attention and effort. Englewood Cliffs, NJ: Prentice-Hall.
Kahneman, D., Ben-Ishai, R., & Lotan, M. (1973) Relation of a test of attention to road accidents. *Journal of Applied Psychology, 58,* 113–115.
Kantowitz, B. (1985). Channels and stages in human information processing: A limited analysis of theory and methodology. *Journal of Mathematical Psychology, 29,* 135–174.
Kieras, D., & Meyer, D. (1994). *The EPIC architecture for modeling human information processing and performance: A brief introduction* (EPIC Rep. No. 1 [TR-94/ONR-EPIC-1]), University of Michigan, Department of Psychology).
Kinchla, R. (1980). The measurement of attention. In R. Nickerson & R. Pew (Eds.), *Attention and performance VIII* (pp. 189–215). Hillsdale, NJ: Lawrence Erlbaum Associates.
Korteling, J. (1991). Effects of skill integration and perceptual competition on age-related differences in dual-task performance. *Human Factors, 33,* 35–44.
Korteling, J. (1993). Effects of age and task similarity on dual-task performance. *Human Factors, 35,* 99–114.
Korteling, J. (1994). Effects of aging, skill modification, and demand alternation on multiple-task performance. *Human Factors, 36,* 27–43.
Kramer, A., Humphrey, D., Larish, J., Logan, G., & Strayer, D. (1994). Aging and inhibition: Beyond a unitary view of inhibitory processing in attention. *Psychology and Aging, 9,* 491–512.
Kramer, A. F., Larish, J., & Strayer, D. L. (1995). Training for attentional control in dual-task settings: A comparison of young and old adults. *Journal of Experimental Psychology: Applied, 1,* 50–76.
Kramer, A. F., & Strayer, D. L. (1988). Assessing the development of automatic processing: Dual-task and event-related brain potential methodologies. *Biological Psychology, 26,* 231–267.
Kramer, A. F., Strayer, D. L., & Buckley, J. (1990). Development and transfer of automatic processing. *Journal of Experimental Psychology: Human Perception and Performance, 16,* 505–522.
Lintern, G., & Roscoe, S. (1980). Visual cue augmentation in contact flight simulation. In S. Roscoe (Ed.), *Aviation Psychology* (pp. 227–238). Ames, IA: Iowa University Press.
Lintern, G., Thomley, K. Nelson, B., & Roscoe, S. (1984). *Content, variety, and augmentation of simulated visual scenes for teaching air-to-ground attack. (Navtraequipcen 81-C-0105-3). Orlando, FL: Naval Training Equipment Center.*
Lintern, G., & Wickens, C. (1991). Issues for acquisition and transfer of timesharing and

dual-task skills. In D. Damos (Ed.), *Multiple task performance* (pp. 123–138). London: Wiley.

Logan, G., & Stadler, M. (1991) Mechanisms of performance improvement in consistent-mapping memory search: Automaticity or strategy shift? *Journal of Experimental Psychology: Learning, Memory and Cognition, 17,* 478–496.

Lorsbach, T., & Simpson, G. (1988). Dual–task performance as a function of adult age and task complextiy. *Psychology and Aging, 3,* 210–212.

Madden, D. (1986). Adult age differences in the attentional capacity demands of visual search. *Cognitive Development, 1,* 335–363.

McDowd, J. (1986). The effects of age and extended practice on divided attention performance. *Journal of Gerontology, 41,* 764–769.

McDowd, J., & Craik, F. (1988). Effects of aging and task difficulty on divided attention performance. *Journal of Experimental Psychology: Human Perception and Performance, 14,* 267–280.

McDowd, J., Vercruyssen, M., & Birren, J. (1991). Aging, divided attention, and dual-task performance. In D. Damos (Ed.), *Multiple task performance* (pp. 387–414). Bristol, PA: Taylor & Francis.

Mowbray, G., & Rhoades, M. (1959). On the reduction of choice reaction time with practice. *Quarterly Journal of Experimental Psychology, 2,* 16–23.

Murphy, M., Schmitt, F., Caruso, M., & Sanders, R. (1987). Metamemory in older adults: The role of monitoring in serial recall. *Psychology and Aging, 2,* 331–339.

Murrell, K. (1970) The effect of extensive practice on age differences in reaction time. *Journal of Gerontology, 25,* 268–274.

Myerson, J., Hale, S., Wagstaff, D., Poon, L., & Smith, G. (1990). The information loss model: A mathematical theory of age-related cognitive slowing. *Psychological Review, 97,* 475–487.

Navon, D. (1984). Resources—a theoretical soup stone? *Psychological Review, 91,* 216–234.

Navon, D., & Miller, J. (1987). The role of outcome conflict in dual-task performance. *Journal of Experimental Psychology: Human Perception and Performance, 13,* 435–448.

Nebes, R. (1978). Vocal versus manual response as a determinant of age differences in simple reaction time. *Journal of Gerontology, 33,* 884–889.

Neumann, O. (1987). Beyond capacity: A functional view of attention. In H. Heuer & A. Sanders (Eds.), *Perspectives on perception and action* (pp. 229–276). Hillsdale, NJ: Lawrence Erlbaum Associates.

Nissen, M., & Bullemer, P. (1987). Attentional requirements of learning: Evidence from performance measures. *Cognitive Psychology, 19,* 1–32.

Noble, M., Trumbo, D., & Fowler, F. (1967) Further evidence on secondary task interference in tracking. *Journal of Experimental Psychology, 73,* 146–149.

North, R., & Gopher, D. (1976). Measures of attention as predictors of flight performance. *Human Factors, 18,* 1–14.

Parkinson, S., Lindholm, J., & Urell, T. (1980). Aging, dichotic memory, and digit span. *Journal of Gerontology, 35,* 87–95.

Park, D., Smith, A., Dudley, W., & Lafronza, V. (1989). Effects of age and a divided attention task presented during encoding and retrieval on memory. *Journal of Experimental Psychology: Learning, Memory and Cognition, 15,* 1185–1191.

Pashler, H. (1984). Processing stages in overlapping tasks: Evidence for a central bottleneck. *Journal of Experimental Psychology: Human Perception and Performance, 10,* 358–377.

Pashler, H. (1994). Dual-task interference in simple tasks: Data and theory. *Psychological Bulletin, 116,* 220-244.

Ponds, W., Brouwer, W., & van Wolffelaar, P. (1988). Age differences in divided attention in a simulated driving task. *Journal of Gerontology, 6,* 151–156.

Rabbitt, P. (1979). How old and young subjects monitor and control responses for accuracy and speed. *British Journal of Psychology, 70,* 305–311.

Rogers, W., Bertus, E., & Gilbert, K. (1994). Dual-task assessment of age differences in automatic process development. *Psychology and Aging, 9,* 398–413.

Rogers, W., & Fisk, A. D. (1990). A reconsideration of age-related reaction time slowing from a learning perspective: Age-related slowing is not just complexity based. *Learning and Individual Differences, 2,* 161–179.

Rogers, W., & Fisk, A.D. (1991). Age-related difference in the maintenance and modification of automatic processes: Arithmetic Stroop interference. *Human Factors, 33,* 45–56.

Salthouse, T. (1982). *Adult cognition: An experimental psychology of aging.* New York: Springer-Verlag.

Salthouse, T. (1985) Speed of behavior and its implications for cognition. In J. Birren & K. Schaie (Eds.), *Handbook of psychology of aging* (pp. 400–426). New York: Van Nostrand.

Salthouse, T. (1990). Influence of experience on age-differences in cognitive functioning. *Human Factors, 34,* 551–569.

Salthouse, T., & Babcock, R. (1991). Decomposing adult age differences in working memory. *Developmental Review, 27,* 763–776.

Salthouse, T., Rogan, J., & Prill, K. (1984). Division of attention: Age differences on a visually presented memory task. *Memory & Cognition, 12,* 613–620.

Schmidt, R., & Bjork, R. (1992). New conceptualizations of practice: Common principles in three paradigms suggest new concepts for training. *Psychological Science, 3,* 207–217.

Schmidt, R., Young, D., Swinnen, S., & Shapiro, D. (1989). Summary knowledge of results for skill acquisition: Support for the guidance hypothesis. *Journal of Experimental Psychology: Learning, Memory and Cognition, 15,* 352–359.

Schneider, W. (1985). Training high performance skills: Fallacies and guidelines. *Human Factors, 27,* 285–300.

Schneider, W., & Fisk, D. (1982). Concurrent automatic and controlled visual search: Can processing occur without resource cost? *Journal of Experimental Psychology: Learning, Memory and Cognition, 8,* 261–278.

Schneider, W., & Shiffrin, R. (1977). Controlled and automatic human information processing: I. Detection, search and attention. *Psychological Review, 84,* 1–66.

Schooler, L., & Anderson, J. (1990). The disruptive potential of immediate feedback. In (Eds.), *Proceedings of the Cognitive Science Society* (pp. 00–00). Hillsdale, NJ: Lawrence Erlbaum Associates.

Sharps, M., & Gollin, E. (1987). Speed and accuracy of mental rotation in young and elderly adults. *Journal of Gerontology, 42,* 342–344.

Shiffrin, R., & Schneider, W. (1977). Controlled and automatic human information processing: II. Perceptual learning, automatic attending and a general theory. *Psychological Review, 84,* 127–190.

Somberg, B., & Salthouse, T. (1982). Divided attention abilities in young and old adults. *Journal of Experimental Psychology: Human Perception and Performance, 8,* 651–653.

Sperling, G., & Dosher, B. (1986). Strategy and optimization in human information processing. In K. Boff, L. Kaufman & J. Thomas (Eds.), *Handbook of human perception and performance* (Vol. 1, pp. 2-1–2-65). New York: Wiley.

Sperling, G., & Melcher, M. (1978). The attention operating characteristic: Examples from visual search. *Science, 202,* 315–318.

Stelmach, G., Amrhein, P., & Goggin, N. (1988). Age differences in bimanual corrdination. *Journal of Gerontology, 43,* 18–23.

Strayer, D. L., & Kramer, A. F. (1990). Attentional requirements of automatic and controlled processes. *Journal of Experimental Psychology: Learning, Memory and Cognition, 16,* 67–82.

Strayer, D. L., & Kramer, A. F. (1994). Aging and skill acquisition: Learning-performance distinctions. *Psychology and Aging, 9,* 589–605.

Strayer, D., Wickens, C., & Braune, R. (1987). Adult age differences in speed and capacity of information processing: 2. An electrophysiological approach. *Psychology and Aging, 2,* 99–110.

Tipper, S. (1991). Less attentional selectivity as a result of declining inhibition in older adults. *Bulletin of the Psychonomic Society, 29,* 45–47.

Welford, A. T. (1958). *Aging and human skill.* London: Oxford University Press.

Welford, A. (1977). Motor performance. In J. Birren & K. Schaie (Eds.), *Handbook of psychology of aging* (pp. 450–496). New York: Van Nostrand.

Wickens, C. (1980). The structure of attentional resources. In R. Nickerson & R. Pew (Eds.), *Attention and performance VIII* (pp. 239–257). Hillsdale, NJ: Lawrence Erlbaum Associates.

Wickens, C. (1992). *Engineering Psychology and Human Performance.* New York: HarperCollins.

Wickens, C., Braune, R., & Stokes, A. (1987). Age differences in the speed and capacity of information processing: 1. A dual-task approach. *Psychology and Aging, 2,* 70–78.

Wightman, D., & Lintern. G. (1985) Part-task training for tracking and manual control. *Human Factors, 27,* 201–312.

Winstein, C., & Schmidt, R. (1988) Variability in practice: Facilitation in retention and transfer through schema formation or context effects? *Journal of Motor Behavior, 20,* 133–149.

Yantis, S., Meyer, D., & Smith, J. (1991). Analyses of Multinomial mixture distributions: New tests for stochastic models of cognition and action. *Psychological Bulletin, 110,* 350–374.

CHAPTER 6

Aging and Memory: Implications for Skilled Performance

Fergus I. M. Craik
University of Toronto

Larry L. Jacoby
McMaster University

This chapter concerns age-related changes in human memory and the implications that these changes have for the acquisition and maintenance of various types of skilled performance. After surveying what is currently known and understood about the differences in memory abilities at various ages, we focus primarily on the contrast between consciously controlled and automatic processes. The basic idea is that behavior reflects a combination of automatic influences and consciously controlled processes. In general, it seems that age differences are smallest when processes are driven automatically by the stimulus or supported by the environment, that is, in cases in which the stimulus is strongly linked to the appropriate response, either by "wired in" functions or because the response is habitual. Age differences are greatest, on the other hand, when processes must be self-initiated in a consciously controlled manner and when a different attentional set from that induced by habit, or by a specific environment, must be established. This account is somewhat similar to the proposal made by Hasher and Zacks (1979), that age differences are greatest with effortful processing and least with automatic processing. Also, it has similarities to Rabbitt's (1979, 1982) suggestion that data driven processes hold up well with age, whereas memory (or conceptually) driven processes are impaired.

We argue that to understand memory and learning fully, it is necessary to separate the contributions of automatic and controlled processes. This may be especially true for age-related differences, in which case there is reason to believe that consciously controlled processing becomes less effective with increasing age, necessitating a greater dependence on habitual modes of responding. We outline a method—the *process dissociation procedure* (Jacoby, 1991)—that was developed for the purposes of decomposing task performance into automatic and controlled components and showing how the method can be applied to problems of aging. In this chapter we use the terms *automatic influence* and *habit* somewhat interchangeably. In our view, a single experienced event can influence later behavior in an automatic and unconscious way. If a set of similar events or similar situations gives rise to the same response over time, then the response may become habitual, that is, typically given and somewhat stereotyped, yet specific to that set of stimuli, tasks, or contexts.

AGING AND MEMORY

There is general agreement that memory abilities do decline with the advancing years but also that the age-related differences are much greater in some tasks than in others. One major factor appears to be whether the task can be classified as implicit or explicit—that is, whether subjects simply demonstrate the effects of past experience in their present behavior or whether they are explicitly asked to recollect details of the original episode. In general, age differences are rather small in implicit tasks such as fragment completion, stem completion, and perceptual identification, but are typically much larger in explicit tasks such as recall and recognition (Light & LaVoie, 1993).

The implicit–explicit difference is not the only factor, however. Within implicit tasks, Light and LaVoie (1993) pointed out that associative priming tasks tend to show larger age differences than do item priming tasks. Item priming tasks appear to utilize mainly perceptual information, whereas associative priming tasks have a greater conceptual component (Craik, Moscovitch, & McDowd, 1994). In line with these findings, a study by Jelicic, Craik, and Moscovitch (in press) found no age differences in a perceptual implicit task (word fragment completion) and small but significant age differences in a conceptual implicit task (category generation). They also found large age differences in two explicit memory tasks, regardless of whether the task had substantial perceptual and conceptual components (stem-cued recall) or relied primarily on conceptual information (free recall). The data are shown in Table 6.1, and they suggest that older people may have some problems in encoding or utilizing conceptual information (Craik, 1983; Eysenck, 1974). That is, an age-related decrement

TABLE 6.1
Mean Proportions Correct (*M*) and Standard Deviations (*SD*) for Younger and Older Adults on Four Tests

	Younger Adults		*Older Adults*	
Task and Measure	*M*	*SD*	*M*	*SD*
Fragment completion				
Target	.47	.11	.39	.14
Baseline	.32	.12	.25	.11
Priming	.15	.09	.14	.08
Category generation				
Target	.39	.11	.32	.08
Baseline	.16	.06	.15	.13
Priming	.23	.11	.17	.11
Stem-cued recall				
Target	.47	.13	.29	.11
Baseline	.00		.00	
Free recall				
Target	.41	.11	.25	.13

Note: From "Effects of Aging on Different Explicit and Implicit Memory Tasks," by M. Jelicic, F. I. M. Craik, and M. Moscovitch, in press. Adapted by permission of the authors.

was found when conceptual processing was required, even when the task was an implicit one.

Within explicit memory tasks, the size of the age difference also varies, presumably again as a function of the underlying processes involved. One factor appears to be the extent to which the task requires effortful, self-initiated processing on the part of the participant, especially, perhaps, at retrieval (Craik, 1983, 1986). Thus, free recall requires more self-initiated processing than does recognition, and age-related differences are typically larger in the former task (Craik & McDowd, 1987).

In the original formulation of these ideas, it was suggested that less self-initiated processing is needed when more environmental support is present, that is, when the external context induces or supports the mental operations appropriate for successful completion of the task. In this sense, recognition tasks (in which the original stimuli are reprovided) involve more environmental support than recall tasks (in which the participant must generate the retrieval information in a self-initiated manner). If older people have more difficulty with self-initiated processing activities, because of their resource demanding and effortful nature, it follows that they should benefit especially from the provision of environmental support (Craik, 1983). Put another way, it may be that older people are more reliant on environmental support; they will perform relatively well when support is present and poorly when it is absent. Further, to the extent that older people require environmental support for processing operations that are carried out by younger people in the absence of such support, provision of support will improve performance in the old but not in the young (who can accomplish the processing in a self-initiated manner).

When the idea of environmental support is applied generally, it suggests that whenever encoding or retrieval conditions improve so that performance levels increase in younger participants, performance levels in older people should improve even more. That is, a pattern of compensation should be seen, with older people deriving more benefit from improved conditions. This pattern was observed in some early experiments reported by Craik and Byrd (1982); but in a later review article, Light (1991) pointed out that the great majority of studies showed that as encoding or retrieval conditions improved, older participants benefitted to the same extent as did their younger counterparts. Craik and Jennings (1992) agreed that many experiments showed equal benefit to young and old but cited cases in which compensation did occur and even cases in which young participants showed greater benefits. Craik and Jennings suggested that equal benefits may reflect situations in which the beneficial processing is achieved rather automatically (e.g., pictures rather than words, the generation effect); on the other hand, compensation occurs when the beneficial condition induces processing that is already carried out spontaneously by younger participants under the less effective encoding condition. Finally, greater benefits to younger participants may occur when processing possibilities are relatively open-ended—younger people carry out more self-initiated elaborate processing operations at encoding and/or retrieval.

This analysis is plausible but unsatisfactory as it stands. Any set of findings can be fitted post hoc to one or other of the theoretical patterns. If it is indeed the case that performance can be enhanced by self-initiated, consciously controlled processes, by automatic processes, or by some unknown mixture of the two, then it is clearly necessary to be able to measure the influence of the two types of processing separately. As described in a following section, this is precisely the purpose of the Process Dissociation Procedure, or PDP (Jacoby, 1991). Application of the PDP should yield a principled account of the circumstances under which various patterns of age-related encoding and retrieval benefits are observed.

NEGATIVE EFFECTS OF AUTOMATIC RESPONDING

After extended practice on real-life skills, many of the routine operations become automated and are thus no longer under conscious control. In general, this loss of control is beneficial, because it frees up working memory for other tasks. Occasionally, however, situations call for an override of habitual responding, with negative consequences if the automated responses are not inhibited. Everyday examples typically involve some unaccustomed deviation from a familiar routine, for example, the necessity to pick up a package from a store that is off our usual daily driving route to work; we are especially likely to forget to make the appropriate turn if our attention is on other matters. The tendency to be "absent-minded," and therefore vulnerable to such slips of action, appears to be greater when we are preoccupied with some problem; the tendency also appears to be greater in older people, at least anecdotally.

In the context of previous work distinguishing automatic and controlled processes in cognition (e.g., Posner & Snyder, 1975; Shiffrin & Schneider, 1977) Jacoby and his colleagues (Jacoby, 1991; Jacoby, Toth, & Yonelinas, 1993; Jennings & Jacoby, 1993) have proposed that there are two independent sources of influence on behavior—habit (automatic influence) and conscious control—of which the latter declines in effectiveness with increasing adult age whereas the former remains essentially constant. These ideas are similar to the framework proposed by Hasher and Zacks (1979) and later augmented by the same authors (Hasher & Zacks, 1988). They suggested that processing operations are either automatic or effortful and that only the latter decline in efficiency with increasing age. In the later paper, Hasher and Zacks proposed that inhibitory processes also decline with age, leading to heightened distractibility and to the continuation of off-track and irrelevant types of processing during memory encoding and retrieval. Jacoby's emphasis was on an age-related decline in conscious control rather than on a decline in inhibition. In turn, the decline in control leaves a relatively more dominant role for automatic and habitual responding. Importantly, the remedy is therefore not so much to inhibit habit as to enhance conscious control if we wish to restore cognitive functioning in older people.

In most cases, of course, we do follow familiar routines in our everyday activities, so automatic influences are perfectly adequate to provide general guidance for our actions, with conscious control serving to provide the fine tuning to deal with minor local perturbations. Similarly, conscious recollection of an intention or a command may often work in concert with preformed automatic influences, or automatic influences may be recruited to boost recollection, as when we put our keys and glasses in set locations or place a letter to be mailed by the door. In other cases automatic influences and conscious recollection work in opposition, with conscious control providing the appropriate guidance to behavior providing it is brought into play.

The notion of environmental support is relevant here in that we typically learn both automated routines and specific events in particular contexts; reinstatement of those environmental contexts is therefore likely to enhance automatic, habitual responding as well as recollection of some earlier event (Jacoby, 1994). In all of these cases, however, the environment supports recollection and induces automatic responding in unknown proportions. Craik's (1983, 1986) suggestions concerning environmental support were restricted to the beneficial effects of context on conscious recollection; he did not take into account the complicating factor of induced automatic influences, which may or may not support an appropriate response. Both conscious and unconscious influences must be considered for understanding age-related deficits, and also for relating these impairments to other patterns of performance such as those shown by patients with frontal lobe dysfunction. It has been suggested that these patients suffer from a reduction in consciously controlled processing and as a result are both dependent on environmental support to function effectively and, at the same time, are more at the mercy of inappropriate or maladaptive contextual stimulation (Lhermitte, 1983). These findings are relevant because of the evidence that supports the association between aging and the deterioration of frontal lobe functioning (Craik, Morris, Morris, & Loewen, 1990; Parkin & Walter, 1992) and that older people therefore function, in some respects at least, like patients with mild frontal lobe impairment (Stuss, Craik, Sayer, Franchi, & Alexander, in press).

Our main point is that many, if not all, cognitive operations in the realms of perception, attention, memory, and thinking can be characterized in terms of the balance between consciously controlled processes and unconscious, automatic influences. In many cases, these independent sources work together to influence the same outcome but their relative proportions are unknown. In other cases automatic processes and conscious control can be set in opposition to each other, leading to different responses. The PDP provides a technique by which the two sets of processing operations may be teased apart and quantified, thereby allowing their relative influence, and their changes with age, to be assessed.

THE ADVANTAGES OF OPPOSITION

Before turning to the PDP work we will describe some experiments in which automatic responses were set in opposition to processes of conscious recollection. As one example, Jacoby, Woloshyn, and Kelley (1989) explored the effect of recent presentation of a name on how famous the named person is judged to be in a later test. The idea is that recent presentation will increase the familiarity of the name in the subsequent fame judgment and that familiarity acts as an automatic cue to fame, even in the absence of any conscious recollection of who the person is or what he or she is famous for. In the fame paradigm, recollection and automatic influences are set in opposition by use of an exclusion test. People read a list of nonfamous names. Next, these old names are mixed with famous and new nonfamous names, and presented for fame judgments. Participants are correctly informed that all of the names they read in the first list are nonfamous, so if they recognize a name on the fame test as one from the first list they can be certain that the name is nonfamous. Thus conscious recollection of a name from the first list opposes any increase in familiarity the name might gain from being read in that list. A "false fame" effect for old nonfamous names will result if recollection fails and leaves automatic influences in the form of familiarity unopposed.

Using this paradigm, Dywan and Jacoby (1990) tested groups of young and elderly participants and obtained the results shown in Table 6.2. The fame judgment test contained names of genuinely famous people (e.g., Christopher Wren), mixed with made-up (nonfamous) names that had either been presented in the study list (old nonfamous) or were presented for the first time (new nonfamous). Table 6.2 shows that the elderly participants correctly identified more famous names than did the young—the elderly people were better informed. The

TABLE 6.2
Proportions of Names Classified as Famous by Young and Elderly Subjects in a Fame Judgment Test

	Young Adults		*Elderly Adults*	
Type of Name	*M*	*SD*	*M*	*SD*
Famous	.54	.16	.70	.14
New nonfamous	.25	.22	.14	.15
Old nonfamous	.14	.14	.20	.17

Note: From "Effects of Aging on Source Monitoring: Differences in Susceptibility to False Fame," by J. Dywan and L. L. Jacoby, 1990, *Psychology and Aging, 5*, p. 383. Adapted by permission.

results of interest emerge from the contrast between old and new nonfamous names. The young participants incorrectly classified 0.25 of new nonfamous names as "famous," but classified fewer old nonfamous names as "famous" (0.14); the implication is that these people remembered some of the old nonfamous names from the study list, and were therefore able to conclude that they were not famous names. The corresponding proportions of new and old nonfamous names incorrectly classified as "famous" by the elderly participants were .14 and .20, respectively, showing that for elderly people, prior presentation boosted the familiarity of old nonfamous names and that this enhanced familiarity was attributed to "fame" because it was largely unopposed by recollection that the names had been presented previously. We may therefore conclude that older people are less able to remember, or "monitor," the source of previously presented information (Hashtroudi, Johnson, & Chrosniak, 1989; McIntyre & Craik, 1987) and that they are thus more likely to make action slips in cases in which information comes to mind "automatically" and is poorly opposed by consciously controlled processes that would otherwise flag the action as inappropriate. It may be noted in passing that the fame judgment case (like the cases reported by Hashtroudi et al., 1989, and by McIntyre & Craik, 1987) is one in which older participants are less able than their younger counterparts to recollect details of the original episodic context; this age-related failure is contrasted in a later section with cases in which older people show a greater vulnerability to the misleading effects of prior context.

As a further illustration of the opposition logic, Jacoby and his colleagues conducted a study in which young people first studied a visually presented list in which words were presented either once, twice, or three times. They were then given a list of auditorily presented words, again with instructions to remember the words for a later test. Finally, they were given a recognition test list which contained words from both List 1 (visual) and List 2 (auditory) with instructions to respond "yes" only to List 2 words. The question of interest was whether participants would erroneously repond "old" to List 1 words and whether that tendency is affected by whether the List 1 word was presented once, twice, or three times. One final factor in the experiment was the imposition of a response deadline; participants had to decide whether a word was from the new or old list within either 700 msec or 1200 msec. The results showed that, with the shorter deadline, the probability of responding "old" to a List 1 word increased from 1 to 3 visual presentations, whereas with the longer deadline that probability decreased from 1 to 3 visual presentations. Jacoby accounts for this striking result by suggesting that within 700 msec, subjects can utilize only automatic information, that more visual presentations increase the accessibility of automatic information, thereby making the word appear very familiar and so leading to an "old" response. In contrast, at 1200 msec conscious recollection is available, and now further visual presentations increase the probability that the person will recognize that the word was on the visual list, thereby decreasing the likelihood that he or she will classify it as an auditory word.

So far this experiment has been carried out with young participants only, but some predictions may be made if it is repeated either with age or with divided attention as the crucial variable instead of response deadline. That is, whereas younger participants would continue to show a decrease in the number of false alarms as a function of visual repetitions, older participants should show an increase, indicating again that their less effective control processes fail to hold the automatic influences in check. Similarly, if the recognition test was conducted under divided attention conditions, false alarms should again increase with repetitions, showing that, with limited processing resources, the automatically available information was dominant.

PROCESS DISSOCIATION

The PDP measures cognitive control by contrasting results from a condition in which automatic and consciously controlled processes act in opposition with results from a condition in which the two types of process act in concert. In a situation in which the participant can exert no conscious control, these conditions will obviously yield the same levels of performance; by the same token, performance levels will differ between the conditions by an amount that reflects the degree of cognitive control. Jacoby et al. (1993) provided one illustration of how the method may be used in a memory context. In their experiment, words were presented for study and then tested by presentation of their first letters as a cue for recall (e.g., motel; mot _ _). The nature of the test was also varied; for an "inclusion" test, the word stem was accompanied by the message "old," and participants were instructed to use the stem as a cue for recall of a previously presented word or, if they could not do so, to complete the stem with the first word that came to mind. An inclusion test thus corresponds to a standard test of cued recall with instructions to guess when recollection fails. For an "exclusion" test, a word stem was accompanied by the message "new" and participants were instructed to complete the stem if possible but that they should not use a previously presented word as a completion for the stem. That is, participants were told to exclude old words and complete stems only with new words. Completing a stem with an old word for an exclusion test would correspond to an action slip. The two types of test were randomly intermixed.

For an inclusion test, participants could complete a stem with an old (previously presented) word either because they consciously recollected the old word, with a probability R, or because, even though recollection failed (1 − R), the old word came automatically to mind (A) as a completion; that is:

$$\text{Inclusion} = R + A(1 - R)$$

For an exclusion test, in contrast, a stem would be completed with an old word (contrary to instructions) only if recollection failed and the word came automatically to mind; that is:

$$\text{Exclusion} = A(1 - R)$$

Thus, the difference between the inclusion test (trying to use old words) and exclusion test (trying not to use old words) provides a measure of the probability of recollection. Given that estimate, the probability of an old word automatically coming to mind as a completion can be computed. One way of doing this is to divide the probability of responding with an old word in an exclusion test by (1 − R); that is:

$$R = \text{Inclusion} - \text{Exclusion}$$

$$A = \text{Exclusion} \div (1 - R)$$

An experiment conducted in Jacoby's lab extended these procedures to examine age-related differences in memory performance. When an inclusion or exclusion test immediately followed presentation of its completion word (0 spacing), performance of the elderly and of the young was close to ceiling. This finding is important in that it shows that the elderly were able to understand and follow instructions. In contrast, when a large number of items intervened between the presentation of a word and its inclusion or exclusion test (48 spacing), the elderly performed much more poorly than did the young. The data are shown in Table 6.3.

For the exclusion test, older participants were more likely to mistakenly complete a stem with an old word than were younger participants. Doing so amounts to an action slip, because for the exclusion test,

TABLE 6.3
Inclusion Scores, Exclusion Scores, and Estimates of Conscious Recollection (R) and Automatic Influences (A) for Younger and Older Adults

Measure	*Young Adults*	*Older Adults*
Inclusion	.70	.55
Exclusion	.26	.39
Recollection (R)	.44	.16
Automatic (A)	.46	.46

Note: From "Measuring Recollection: Strategic vs. Automatic Influences of Associative Context," by L. L. Jacoby, in C. Umilta and M. Moscovitch (Eds.), *Attention and Performance XV*, p. 670. Adapted by permission.

effects of automatic influences of memory for earlier reading a word should be opposed by recollection—a consciously controlled use of memory. The poorer performance of the older adults on the exclusion test can be explained as resulting from a deficit in recollection, as can their poorer performance on the inclusion test. Placing recollection and automatic influences in opposition, as was done by the exclusion test, can provide evidence of the existence of the two types of processes (Jacoby et al., 1993). However, it is necessary to combine results from the exclusion and inclusion tests to estimate the separate contributions of consciously controlled and automatic processes.

The estimates shown in Table 6.3 provide evidence that the older adults experienced a deficit in recollection as compared to younger participants but that automatic influences of memory were unchanged. The estimates of automatic influences were well above the baseline probability (.33) of completing a stem with a target word when that word had not been presented earlier. The difference between estimated automatic influences and baseline performance serves as a measure of automatic influences of memory —the effect of studying a word on the probability of the word later automatically coming to mind as a completion for a stem.

Results from this experiment showed age-related differences in memory to be very similar to effects produced by divided versus full attention to the study presentation of a word in an experiment by Jacoby et al. (Experiment 1b, 1993). That earlier experiment used the same materials but tested only young participants. Results showed that divided, as compared to full, attention during study reduced the probability of recollection (.00 vs. .25) but left automatic influences unchanged (.46 vs. .47). For the divided attention versus full attention experiment, study and test were in separate phases rather than intermixed, and, on average, the spacing between study of a word and its test was approximately 48 intervening items. The correspondence between age-related differences in memory and effects of full versus divided attention supports Craik's (1982) claim that dividing attention during study can mimic the effects of aging on memory.

To sum up this section, Jacoby (1991) suggested earlier that responses in memory retrieval tasks are driven by two distinct sets of processes: automatic processes, which give rise to feelings of familiarity, and controlled processes, which support conscious recollection of the original event, including details of the target item and its context. Typically these processes work together, but situations can be devised in which they are in opposition; the process-dissociation procedure utilizes the two types of situation to yield independent measures of automatic and controlled processes. We have focused on the applications of these ideas to memory, but they also apply to many other cognitive situations in which highly practiced habitual responses may or may not be in conflict with the appropriate response on one particular occasion. One well-researched example is the Stroop effect, in which easily read color names conflict with the discrepant names of the colors themselves; this effect has also been decomposed by means of the PDP technique into its constituent automatic and controlled aspects (Lindsay & Jacoby, 1994).

The PDP approach is not without its critics. For example, Curran and Hintzman (1995) argued that some items are both more familiar (reflecting automatic influences) and better recollected, and so the assumption of independence is violated. Their argument may be valid, but it also was shown that even if there is a high correlation at the item level, the bias in estimates of automatic influences is trivial (Jacoby, Begg, & Toth, in press). Another reservation is that a given task is likely to draw differentially on automatic and controlled processes at different times—for example, driving on an empty highway as opposed to driving on a busy city street. This point is also valid and provides an interesting topic for further research, although it should be remembered that the current laboratory versions of the PDP technique do measure aspects of performance on a given task at a given time and place.

With regard to aging, the results of the fame experiment (Dywan & Jacoby, 1990) and the results shown in Table 6.3 suggest strongly that the strength and effectiveness of habitual or automatic influences are unchanged across the lifespan, but that the effectiveness of conscious control declines with age, leaving habitual responding more dominant. The unchanging effectiveness of the automatic component with age is also supported by the absence of age-related effects on implicit memory tasks—at least of a perceptual variety (Table 6.1; Light & La Voie, 1993).

Why does conscious control (and associated processes such as recollection) decline with age? Presumably the answer lies in some set of changing biological processes—it is difficult to argue that the loss of control is adaptive in any sense. Hasher and Zacks (1988) proposed the influential idea that the effects of inhibitory control decrease with age and that this decrease results in a number of cognitive deficits. They suggested specifically that the capacity of working memory is apparently reduced in the elderly as a result of a failure to inhibit intrusive thoughts and to screen out irrelevant contextual stimulation. This is an appealing account in many ways; it ties in, for example, with the observation that older people have trouble "concentrating" and are more distractable (Hoyer, Rebok, & Sved, 1979; Park, Smith, Dudley, & Lafronza, 1989). However, rather than argue that working memory capacity is reduced as a secondary consequence of decreased inhibition, we prefer to argue that decreased effectiveness of executive control is the primary age-related dysfunction and that this reduction in control permits prepotent habitual responses to run off. Decreased executive control, which may be thought of as a reduction in the efficiency of the central executive component of working memory (Baddeley, 1986; Baddeley & Hitch, 1974), is very much a hallmark of the behavior of patients with prefrontal lesions (Lhermitte, 1983; Fuster, 1989; Shallice, 1988; Stuss & Benson, 1984). One possibility, therefore, is that normal aging is associated with a specific loss of efficiency of processes mediated by prefrontal structures and that the behavior of normal older people thus bears some resemblance to the behavior of patients with frontal dysfunction.

Roberts, Hager, and Heron (1994) have proposed an interactive model along these lines. In their version, the ability to inhibit a prepotent response (reflexive eye saccades, in their experiments) depends on the strength of the prepotency, the efficiency of the working memory system, and the working memory demands of a concurrent task. That is, if working memory is engaged with a demanding secondary task, as in conditions of divided attention, inappropriate prepotent responses will not be inhibited, and normal participants will behave somewhat like patients with prefrontal dysfunction. Clearly, this analysis is very much like the one argued for here and in previous publications (Jacoby, 1991; Jacoby et al., 1993). It is also in good agreement with the ideas that (a) working memory functions are less effective in older people (Baddeley, 1986; Craik, Morris, & Gick, 1990; Hasher & Zacks, 1988; Salthouse, 1990b); (b) the behavior of older people resembles that of patients with frontal disorders in some respects (Craik, Morris, Morris, & Loewen, 1990); (c) the division of attention in normal young adults makes them behave like older individuals (Craik, 1982); and (d) older people are particularly vulnerable to the disruptive effects of divided attention (Craik, 1977).

In summary, conscious control may decline in the elderly as a result of the less effective functioning of prefrontal structures (Albert & Kaplan, 1980; Craik, Morris, Morris, & Loewen, 1990; Whelihan & Lesher, 1985). In turn, this age-related loss of executive control will have the previously discussed consequences on memory, attention, and other cognitive functions. We now turn to the implications of this perspective for skilled performance in older people.

IMPLICATIONS FOR SKILLED PERFORMANCE IN THE ELDERLY

In this final section of the chapter we review the implications of the present set of ideas for the understanding of the acquisition, maintenance, and loss of skilled procedures in older people. Since the ideas are relatively novel, we concentrate on possible applications of the theoretical notions rather than on work already accomplished. In this way we hope that the chapter will serve a heuristic function with respect to new research. We also restrict our examples largely to the domain of cognition, rather than to that of perceptual–motor skill.

Context Reinstatement

Two sets of results that seem paradoxical at first sight can be explained very sensibly in light of the foregoing discussion. The first result is that older people have greater difficulty in remembering the source of acquired information (Hashtroudi et al., 1989; McIntyre & Craik, 1987), suggesting strongly that they are less able to recollect details of the episodic context. The second result is that older and impaired people's behavior sometimes appears to be more influenced by contextual reinstatement. For example, Nebes, Boller, and Holland (1986) asked patients with Alzheimer's disease (AD) and individuals in a control group to generate an appropriate last word for incomplete sentences that either were highly constrained (e.g., "Father carved the turkey with a ____ ") or had few semantic constraints (e.g., "They went to see the famous ____ "). With minimal guidance from the context the AD patients showed typical word finding difficulties and performed less well than the controls. With the highly constrained sentences, however, the patients performed fairly normally, both in terms of appropriateness of the ending and speed of response. The apparent conflict between impaired memory for contextual detail on the one hand and greater reliance on contextual reinstatement on the other hand is resolved by the point that the first case represents an age-related decrease in controlled recollection, whereas the second case represents the continued effectiveness of the automatic influences of contextual reinstatement. These automatic influences may even appear to be greater for the older person if they are relatively unopposed by appropriate controlled processes. Thus, older skilled performers may be more reliant than their younger counterparts on the reinstatement of compatible contexts (between acquisition and utilization of the skill) but also more vulnerable to the disruptive effects of incompatible context reinstatement.

As discussed earlier, action slips can be described as the expression of automatic or habitual responses that emerge in the absence of conscious control. It seems likely that such slips are associated with particular contexts; they do not occur randomly but in response to certain environmental triggers. In the case of an elderly person's "telling the same story twice" (Koriat, Ben-Zur, & Sheffer, 1988), it is probable that specific individuals act as retrieval cues to increase the probability that a particular story will come to mind. Thus, an important question concerns the role of context in "activating" habits. Devising better methods for measuring the separate effects of recollection and habit is important for improving both the diagnosis and the management of such deficits. Knowledge of conditions that allow the establishment and maintenance of habits can be used to design special environments in which older people can better function.

A central question here concerns the qualitative type of contextual or environmental change that is most effective in activating specific automatic response tendencies. It is well established that implicit memory tasks such as perceptual identification, word fragment, and word stem completion are heavily dependent on the reinstatement of perceptual features for their successful performance. Is this reliance on perceptual reinstatement generally true of all habitual responses? That seems quite unlikely. Examples of conceptual factors interacting with habitual responses include being set to interpret written and spoken words in one of several languages that a person speaks, failing to see how objects can be used to solve a problem when they occur in a different functional context ("functional fixedness"), and the effectiveness of conceptually similar solutions in helping people solve analogical reasoning problems (Gick & Holyoak, 1980, 1983).

The problem for future work is therefore to determine which types of contextual reinstatement are maximally effective for various types of habitual response. The starting point for such research should presumably be the notions of encoding specificity (Tulving & Thomson, 1973) or transfer-appropriate processing (Morris, Bransford, & Franks, 1977; Roediger, Weldon, & Challis, 1989), which state in essence that the most effective retrieval cue for a learned item is some integral part of the item's functional encoding. In turn, this approach points to the need for a satisfactory analysis and classification of automatic responses, and their integration with environmental contexts.

Learning Automatic Responses

If we accept the idea that older people have less effective controlled processes, and that their performance is therefore dominated (relatively) by prepotent automatic responses, it becomes of immediate interest to ask about the acquisition, maintenance, and vulnerability to interference of these automatic responses. In particular, how easy is it for people of different ages to acquire new automatic responses, and how do such newly acquired habits differ from deeply ingrained habits of long standing?

New behavioral sets are quite easy to establish; the Wisconsin Card Sorting Test (WCST) is an obvious case in point. In this test, subjects discover a rule by which cards must be sorted, and then the rule is changed without the subject being informed. Normal controls discover the new rule and abandon the old one fairly quickly, but patients with frontal lesions perseverate with the now-inappropriate old rule for some time. Normal older people also show some tendency to persevere unadaptively with the original rule (Craik, Morris, Morris, & Loewen, 1990; Whelihan & Lesher, 1985). The question for research is therefore how rapidly older people can acquire new automatic responses, and how amenable these newly acquired habits are to change when change is indicated.

One paradigm that may prove useful here is one introduced by Jacoby and Hay (1993). In the first (training) phase of their experiments, word fragments were presented with a cue word (e.g., knee b _ n _), and participants were to predict which of two words would be used to complete the fragment. After they had made their prediction, participants were shown the "correct" completion. Probabilities were varied such that one completion (knee bone) was presented on 75% of the trials and another completion (knee bend) was presented on the remaining 25% of the trials. The training phase was designed to establish associations of varying strengths between the cue words and completions, much as would result from a behavior being performed a varying proportion of times in a particular context. Associations established in this first phase could either facilitate or interfere with performance on a task required in the second phase of the experiment. In Phase 2, short lists of pairs to be remembered were followed by the presentation of cues and fragments. Participants were to complete fragments with words presented in the immediately preceding list. For some pairs, the completion presented in that list was the more common completion from Phase 1; thus, the effects of automatic responding were congruent with recollection and would facilitate performance. For other pairs, the less common completion from Phase 1 was presented so as to make automatic responding incongruent with recollection, thus producing interference. The incongruent pairs correspond to the action slip case—automatic influences would induce errors.

For the equations used to estimate recollection and automatic influences, performance on congruent pairs was treated as performance in an inclusion condition, and performance on incongruent pairs was treated as performance in an exclusion condition. Computing estimates in that way, Jacoby and Hay found that their estimates of automatic influences showed probability matching (e.g., Estes, 1976). That is, the estimated probability of giving a completion in Phase 2 due to automatic influences was very close to the objective probability of that completion in Phase 1. Effects on recollection and automatic influences were dissociated. Manipulating the objective probability of a completion in Phase 1 had an effect on estimates of automatic influences that produced probability matching across a range of probabilities, but had no effect on estimates of recollection. In contrast, requiring fast responding in Phase 2 reduced the probability of recollection but left estimated automatic influences invariant. A further experiment comparing the performance of young and elderly people showed a deficit in recollection for the elderly but no age-related difference in estimated automatic influences of memory. These dissociations are the same as those found with the inclusion–exclusion procedure, and provide converging evidence to support assumptions underlying the two ways of implementing the PDP.

The result with older participants suggests that older people acquire new automatic responses as readily as do their younger counterparts. This is a surprising result, although it is in accord with work by Howard and Howard (1992) showing that the learning of serial patterns is age invariant. Not all researchers have found age invariance in the development of new automatic procedures, however (Dulaney & Rogers, 1994; Fisk & Rogers, 1991; Rogers & Fisk, 1991), so an important further question concerns the characteristics of new automatic procedures that are either age invariant in their learning phase, or show age-associated differences. A related question for research is whether particular learning methods are particularly effective for older learners of new implicit knowledge; two candidates here are active versus passive learning procedures (cf. Reber, 1989) and techniques involving errorless learning (Baddeley & Wilson, 1994).

AUTOMATICITY, CONTROL, AND COGNITIVE FLEXIBILITY

Given that measures of recollection (R) and automatic influences (A) can be calculated for particular participants performing specific tasks, to what extent would we expect these measures to correlate across tasks for the same people, and across individuals for the same tasks? Put another way, are R and A characteristics of individuals, of tasks, or of their interactions? When we think of skilled tasks in everyday life—driving a car, playing a sport, riding a bicycle, speaking a second language—it becomes clear that the automated portions of these skills are very unlikely to share common elements. Rather, the automatic aspects are likely to be task specific (Jacoby et al., 1993; Ste. Marie & Jacoby, 1993). On the other hand, the consciously controlled R component of performance is likely to show more generality across tasks for the same individual. This is one of the main points made in this chapter—that younger and older adults differ in the amount of conscious control that they can exert. Even here, however, there is likely to be some degree of specificity in the R measure; that is, through natural aptitude and practice, tasks will vary in the amount of control that a particular person can bring to bear.

Some evidence on these questions can be gleaned from correlation studies. For example, Jennings and Hay (in an unpublished study) obtained preliminary evidence that memory complaints as measured by a cognitive failures questionnaire are correlated with contributions of R but not A to performance on laboratory tests of memory. Another source of evidence is the degree of correlation among tasks measuring working memory. If working memory (WM) is one fixed set of mechanisms or processes, as implied by the Baddeley and Hitch model (Baddeley, 1986; Baddeley & Hitch, 1974) then WM tasks should intercorrelate quite highly. Typically, this was not found, however (Daneman & Tardif, 1987; Roberts et al., 1994), suggesting at least some degree of task specificity in R or central executive control. This lack of correlation suggests that the concept of working memory might be better reformulated as an umbrella term for the computational aspects of a whole variety of types of knowledge and skilled procedures. Whereas there may well be some individual difference that dictates in general terms how well or how poorly an individual can manipulate knowledge in a controlled manner (with some resemblance to Spearman's g perhaps), it is also likely that other aspects of R reflect specific person/task interactions. Further interesting research questions emerge from this analysis when it is applied to cognitive aging; are there age differences in the acquisition of control? Do such differences depend on the task, and on the individual's knowledge of similar tasks? How does maintenance of a previously learned skill (such as driving, word processing, or speaking a second language) interact with age, and with the R and A components of performance? Answers to at least some of these questions can probably be gleaned from the existing literature on skill and aging (see, e.g., Charness, 1985; Salthouse, 1990a).

A further question concerns the retraining of older workers and learners, and the extent to which cognitive flexibility can be built in to a training procedure. As discussed previously, new behavioral sets can be established fairly readily, even in an experimental setting. One example is the WCST in which patients with frontal lobe dysfunction discover the principle underlying the correct classification of multidimensional stimuli but then have great difficulty in abandoning that principle when it becomes irrelevant to a new rule that the tester has imposed. To the extent that normal older people behave like young patients with frontal disorders (Craik, Morris, Morris, & Loewen, 1990; Parkin & Walter, 1992), older learners should also have difficulty in switching to take changed conditions into account.

The WCST is one in which a newly aquired habit may continue to influence behavior if unopposed by conscious control processes. Patients with frontal lobe dysfunction, for example, apparently do not realize that their responses are now inappropriate, or, at least, they fail to initiate new responses. Two questions for research then, are first whether there are age differences in the development of awareness that current response patterns are inadequate, and second, whether age groups differ in the ability to inhibit inappropriate automatic responses and to establish a new set of appropriate responses. One of the most interesting findings from work on patients with frontal lobe disorders is that they show a deficit in controlled responding despite awareness of the information that would allow such control to operate. For example, on the WCST, these patients can often state the principles underlying the task, thus showing awareness, yet fail to utilize these principles in their actual performance—an example of the so-called *dysexecutive syndrome* (Stuss & Benson, 1984). Experiments should also check for the presence of this dissociation between awareness and performance in older people.

A final—and crucial—topic concerns age-related differences in cognitive control. To what extent do older people retain conscious control of highly practiced tasks? How flexible is cognitive control in the elderly, and how easy or difficult is it to train or retrain recollection and other forms of controlled processing?

We plan to examine these questions in a series of laboratory experiments. One specific question concerns age differences in the time taken to form a cognitive set. Previous work has suggested that older people are impaired in their ability to use prior information to set themselves for an upcoming stimulus (Byrd, 1981). A related question concerns the ease or difficulty with which people of different ages can override an existing set. The phenomenon of functional fixedness provides a paradigm case here. The uses of certain objects become fixed by experience, and participants in problem-solving situations have difficulty seeing alternative unusual uses for these objects. It seems likely that functional fixedness effects are greater in older people; can people be trained to think laterally in order to overcome such preexisting sets?

Once an appropriate set is established—a temporary goal or intention for example—how easily is it maintained by people of different ages? Older people complain that they are easily distracted and so, for example, tend to forget why they went into a particular room. The question of set maintenance, then, is similar to the maintenance of information in short term or working memory, which is a well researched topic in cognitive aging (Craik, 1977; Salthouse, 1990b). One difference is that we are now talking about maintaining an intention, as compared with a string of words or digits, and, to that extent, the topic also bears some resemblance to questions of prospective memory, for which age-related differences are also found (Cockburn & Smith, 1991; Dobbs & Rule, 1987).

On the question of training recollection in the elderly, Jennings and Jacoby (in an unpublished study) have obtained encouraging preliminary results using a technique in which participants learn a list of words (List 1) and are then given a second list made up of List 1 words plus new words, and a repetition of each new word at lags of 0, 3, or 12 intervening items. Participants are told that the second list is a recognition test, in which they say "yes" to List 1 words but "no" to new (List 2) words, both on a new word's first and second presentation. The second presentation of a new item is crucial, because its earlier presentation will increase its familiarity, thus increasing the likelihood that it will mistakenly be called a List 1 word. However, if participants recollect the first presentation of a List 2 word, they will correctly reject it; this recollection and rejection is very easy at a lag of 0, but gets increasingly difficult as the lag increases between the first and second presentation of the List 2 word. In an initial study, Jennings and Jacoby found that older adults performed significantly worse than the younger adults when as few as 3 items intervened between first and second presentations—reflecting a time interval of less than 10 seconds! However, after extensive training involving positive feedback for correct responding and a gradual increase in the lag intervals, older people were able to perform at the level of young people with a lag of 28 intervening items. This result suggests that recollection (and perhaps other aspects of controlled processing) can be trained using this method of gradual shaping.

CONCLUSIONS

In summary, the present analysis of age differences in memory and related cognitive processes has some similarities and some dissimilarities to previous approaches. We agree with Hasher and Zacks (1979) that age differences are least with automatic processing and greatest with controlled processing. The present analysis is also in agreement with Craik's (1983, 1986) point that self-initiated processing is more difficult for the elderly. However, the present approach differs somewhat from the view expressed by Hasher and Zacks (1988) that an age-related loss in the efficiency of inhibitory processes underlies many cognitive deficits; we argue rather that an age-related reduction in the effectiveness of controlled processing is primary, resulting in a relative dominance of prepotent automatic responses. Crucially, the present set of suggestions relies on Jacoby's (1991) procedure for separating automatic influences from conscious control, and this separation opens up new perspectives on such issues as the effects of contextual support, learning and maintenance of new habitual responses, and the learning and maintenance of controlled procedures such as recollection and executive intentions.

ACKNOWLEDGMENTS

The research reported in this chapter was supported by grants from the Natural Sciences and Engineering Research Council of Canada to both authors. We are grateful for very useful comments on the chapter from Richard L. Marsh and Wendy A. Rogers.

REFERENCES

Albert, M. S., & Kaplan, E. (1980). Organic implications of neuropsychological deficits in the elderly. In L. W. Poon, J. Fozard, L. Cermak, D. Arenberg, & L. Thompson

(Eds.), *New directions in memory and aging* (pp. 403–432). Hillsdale, NJ: Lawrence Erlbaum Associates.

Baddeley, A. D. (1986). *Working memory*. Oxford: Clarendon Press.

Baddeley, A. D., & Hitch, G. J. (1974). Working memory. In G. H. Bower (Ed.), *The psychology of learning and motivation* (Vol. 8, pp. 47–90). New York: Academic Press.

Baddeley, A. D., & Wilson, B. A. (1994). When implicit learning fails: Amnesia and the problem of error elimination. *Neuropsychologia, 32*, 53–68.

Byrd, M. (1981). *Age differences in memory for prose passages*. Unpublished doctoral dissertation, University of Toronto, Canada

Charness, N. (Ed.). (1995). *Aging and human performance*. Chichester, England: Wiley.

Cockburn, J., & Smith, P. T. (1991). The relative influence of intelligence and age on everyday memory. *Journals of Gerontology: Psychological Sciences, 46*, 32–36.

Craik, F. I. M. (1977). Age differences in human memory. In J. E. Birren & K. W. Schaie (Eds.), *Handbook of the psychology of aging* (pp. 384–420). New York: Reinhold.

Craik, F. I. M. (1982). Selective changes in encoding as a function of reduced processing capacity. In F. Klix, J. Hoffmann, & E. van der Meer (Eds.), *Cognitive research in psychology* (pp. 152–161). Berlin, FRG: Deutscher Verlag der Wissenschaften.

Craik, F. I. M. (1983). On the transfer of information from temporary to permanent memory. *Philosophical Transactions of the Royal Society, B302*, 341–359.

Craik, F. I. M. (1986). A functional account of age differences in memory. In F. Klix & H. Hagendorf (Eds.), *Human memory and cognitive capabilities, mechanisms and performances* (pp. 409–422). Amsterdam, North Holland: Elsevier Science.

Craik, F. I. M., & Byrd, M. (1982). Aging and cognitive deficits: The role of attentional resources. In F. I. M. Craik & S. Trehub (Eds.), *Aging and cognitive processes* (pp. 191–211). New York: Plenum.

Craik, F. I. M., & Jennings, J. M. (1992). Human memory. In F. I. M. Craik & T. A. Salthouse (Eds.), *The handbook of aging and cognition* (pp. 51–110). Hillsdale, NJ: Lawrence Erlbaum Associates.

Craik, F. I. M., & McDowd, J. M. (1987). Age differences in recall and recognition. *Journal of Experimental Psychology: Learning, Memory, and Cognition, 13*, 474–479.

Craik, F. I. M., Morris, R. G., & Gick, M. L. (1990). Adult age differences in working memory. In G. Vallar & T. Shallice (Eds.), *Neuropsychological impairments of short-term memory* (pp. 247–267). Cambridge, England: Cambridge University Press.

Craik, F. I. M., Morris, L. W., Morris, R. G., & Loewen, E. R. (1990). Aging, source amnesia and frontal lobe functioning. *Psychology and Aging, 5*, 148–151.

Craik, F. I. M., Moscovitch, M., & McDowd, J. M. (1994). Contributions of surface and conceptual information to performance on implicit and explicit memory tasks. *Journal of Experimental Psychology: Learning, Memory, and Cognition, 20*, 864–875.

Curran, T., & Hintzman, D. (1995) Violations of the independence assumption in process dissociation. *Journal of Experimental Psychology: Learning, Memory, and Cognition, 21*, 531–547.

Daneman, M., & Tardif, T. (1987). Working memory and reading skill re-examined. In M. Coltheart (Ed.), *Attention and performance XII* (pp. 491–508). Hillsdale, NJ: Lawrence Erlbaum Associates.

Dobbs, A. R., & Rule, B. G. (1987). Prospective memory and self-reports of memory abilities in older adults. *Canadian Journal of Psychology, 41*, 209–222.

Dulaney, C. L., & Rogers, W. A. (1994). Mechanisms underlying reduction in Stroop interference with practice for young and old adults. *Journal of Experimental Psychology: Learning, Memory and Cognition, 20*, 470–484.

Dywan, J., & Jacoby, L. L. (1990). Effects of aging on source monitoring: Differences in susceptibility to false fame. *Psychology and Aging, 5*, 379–387.

Estes, W. K. (1976). The cognitive side of probability learning. *Psychological Review, 83*, 37–64.

Eysenck, M. W. (1974). Age differences in incidental learning. *Developmental Psychology, 10*, 936–941.

Fisk, A. D., & Rogers, W. A. (1991). Toward an understanding of age-related memory and visual search effects. *Journal of Experimental Psychology: General, 120*, 131–149.

Fuster, J. M. (1989). The prefrontal cortex in delay tasks: Evidence from reversible lesion and unit recording in the monkey. In H. S. Levin, H. M. Eisenberg, & A. L. Benton (Eds.), *Frontal lobe function and dysfunction*. (pp. 59–71). New York: Oxford University Press.

Gick, M. L., & Holyoak, K. J. (1980). Analogical problem solving. *Cognitive Psychology, 12*, 306–355.

Gick, M. L., & Holyoak, K. J. (1983). Schema induction and analogical transfer. *Cognitive Psychology, 15*, 1–38.

Hasher, L., & Zacks, R. T. (1979). Automatic and effortful processes in memory. *Journal of Experimental Psychology: General, 108*, 356–388.

Hasher, L., & Zacks, R. T. (1988). Working memory, comprehension, and aging: A review and a new view. In G. H. Bower (Ed.), *The psychology of learning and motivation* (Vol. 22, pp. 193–225). New York: Academic Press.

Hashtroudi, S., Johnson, M. K., & Chrosniak, L. D. (1989). Aging and source monitoring. *Psychology and Aging, 4*, 106–112.

Howard, D. V., & Howard, J. H. (1992). Adult age differences in the rate of learning serial patterns: Evidence from direct and indirect tests. *Psychology and Aging, 7*, 232–241.

Hoyer, W. J., Rebok, G. W., & Sved, S. M. (1979). Effects of varying irrelevant information on adult age differences in problem solving. *Journal of Gerontology, 14*, 553–560.

Jacoby, L. L. (1991). A process dissociation framework: Separating automatic from intentional uses of memory. *Journal of Memory and Language, 30*, 513–541.

Jacoby, L. L. (1994). Measuring recollection: Strategic vs. automatic influences of associative context. In C. Umilta & M. Moscovitch (Eds.), *Attention and performance XV* (pp. 661–679). Cambridge, MA: Bradford.

Jacoby, L. L., Begg, I., & Toth, J. P. (in press). In defense of independence: Violations of assumptions underlying the process-dissociation procedure? *Journal of Experimental Psychology: Learning, Memory and Cognition.*

Jacoby, L. L., & Hay, J. (1993, November). *Action slips, proactive interference, and probability matching*. Paper presented at the 34th annual meeting of the Psychonomic Society, Washington, DC.

Jacoby, L. L., Toth, J. P., & Yonelinas, A. P. (1993). Separating conscious and unconscious influences of memory: Measuring recollection. *Journal of Experimental Psychology: General, 122*, 139–154.

Jacoby, L. L., Woloshyn, V., & Kelley, C. M. (1989). Becoming famous without being recognized: Unconscious influences of memory produced by dividing attention. *Journal of Experimental Psychology: General, 118*, 115–125.

Jelicic, M., Craik, F. I. M., & Moscovitch, M. (in press). Effects of aging on different explicit and implicit memory tasks. *The European Journal of Cognitive Psychology.*

Jennings, J., & Jacoby, L. L. (1993). Automatic versus intentional uses of memory: Aging, attention and control. *Psychology and Aging, 8*, 283–293.

Koriat, A., Ben-Zur, H., & Sheffer, D. (1988). Telling the same story twice: Output monitoring and age. *Journal of Memory and Language, 27*, 23–39.

Lhermitte, F. (1983). Utilization behavior and its relation to lesions of the frontal lobes. *Brain, 106*, 237–255.

Light, L. L. (1991). Memory and aging: Four hypotheses in search of data. *Annual*

Review of Psychology, 43, 333–376.

Light, L. L., & LaVoie, D. (1993). Direct and indirect measures of memory in old age. In P. Graf & M. E. J. Masson (Eds.), *Implicit memory* (pp. 207–230). Hillsdale, NJ: Lawrence Erlbaum Associates.

Lindsay, D. S., & Jacoby, L. L. (1994). Stroop process dissociations: The relationship between facilitation and interference. *Journal of Experimental Psychology: Human Perception and Performance, 20*, 219–234.

McIntyre, J. S., & Craik, F. I. M. (1987). Age differences in memory for item and source information. *Canadian Journal of Psychology, 41*, 175–192.

Morris, C. D., Bransford, J. D., & Franks, J. J. (1977). Levels of processing versus transfer appropriate processing. *Journal of Verbal Learning and Verbal Behavior, 16*, 519–533.

Nebes, R. D., Boller, F., & Holland, A. (1986). Use of semantic context by patients with Alzheimer's disease. *Psychology and Aging, 1*, 261–269.

Park, D. C., Smith, A. D., Dudley, W. N., & Lafronza, V. N. (1989). The effects of age and a divided attention task presented at encoding and retrieval on memory. *Journal of Experimental Psychology: Learning, Memory and Cognition, 15*, 1185–1191.

Parkin, A. J., & Walter, B. M. (1992). Recollective experience, normal aging, and frontal dysfunction. *Psychology and Aging, 7*, 290–298.

Posner, M. I., & Snyder, C. R. R. (1975). Attention and cognitive control. In R. L. Solso (Ed.), *Information processing in cognition: The Loyola Symposium* (pp. 55–83). Hillsdale, NJ: Lawrence Erlbaum Associates.

Rabbitt, P. M. A. (1979). Some experiments and a model for changes in attentional selectivity with old age. *Bayer-Symposium VII—Brain function in old age* (pp. 82–94). New York: Springer-Verlag.

Rabbitt, P. M. A. (1982). How do old people know what to do next? In F. I. M. Craik, & S. E. Trehub (Eds.), *Aging and cognitive processes* (pp. 79–98). New York: Plenum.

Reber, A. S. (1989). Implicit learning and tacit knowledge. *Journal of Experimental Psychology: General, 118*, 219–235.

Roberts, R. R., Jr., Hager, L. D., & Heron, C. (1994). Prefrontal cognitive processes: Working memory and inhibition in the antisaccade task. *Journal of Experimental Psychology: General, 123*, 374–393.

Roediger, H. L., III, Weldon, M. S., & Challis, B. H. (1989). Explaining dissociations between implicit and explicit measures of retention: A processing account. In H. L. Roediger, III & F. I. M. Craik (Eds.), *Varieties of memory and consciousness* (pp. 3–41). Hillsdale, NJ: Lawrence Erlbaum Associates.

Rogers, W. A., & Fisk, A. D. (1991). Age-related differences in the maintenance and modification of automatic processes: Arithmetic Stroop interference. *Human Factors, 33*, 45–56.

Salthouse, T. A. (1990a). Cognitive competence and expertise in aging. In J. E. Birren & K. W. Schaie (Eds.), *Handbook of the psychology of aging* (3rd ed., pp. 311–319). New York: Academic.

Salthouse, T. A. (1990b). Working memory as a processing resource in cognitive aging. *Developmental Review, 10*, 101–124.

Shallice, T. (1988). *From neuropsychology to mental structure*. Cambridge: Cambridge University Press.

Shiffrin, R. M., & Schneider, W. (1977). Controlled and automatic human information processing. II. Perceptual learning, automatic attending, and a general theory. *Psychological Review, 84*, 127–190.

Ste. Marie, D. M., & Jacoby, L. L. (1993). Spontaneous vs. directed recognition: The relativity of automaticity. *Journal of Experimental Psychology: Learning, Memory and Cognition, 19*, 777–788.

Stuss, D. T., & Benson, D. F. (1984). Neuropsychological studies of the frontal lobes.

Psychological Bulletin, 95, 3–28.

Stuss, D. T., Craik, F. I. M., Sayer, L., Franchi, D., & Alexander, M. P. (in press). Comparison of elderly subjects to patients with frontal lesions: Evidence from word list learning. *Psychology and Aging*.

Tulving, E., & Thomson, D. M. (1973). Encoding specificity and retrieval processes in episodic memory. *Psychological Review*, *80*, 352–373.

Whelihan, W. M., & Lesher, E. L. (1985). Neuropsychology changes in frontal functions with aging. *Developmental Neuropsychology*, 1, 371–380.

CHAPTER 7

Intelligence as Process and Knowledge: An Integration for Adult Development and Application

Phillip L. Ackerman
University of Minnesota

Nearly a century ago, Binet and Simon ushered in the "modern" approach to the conceptualization and measurement of intelligence. The techniques created by Binet and Simon and their followers for assessment of children are ubiquitous today in the assessment of children and adults alike. However, Binet and Simon made a little remembered distinction between the psychological method and the pedagogical method of intellectual assessment. The modern general intelligence tests (Stanford–Binet and Wechsler scales) and primary mental abilities tests (Thurstone, 1938) approach adult assessment from the perspective of the psychological method, which is generally seen as predominantly a measure of intelligence-as-process (such as reasoning, memory, and so on). The pedagogical method, that is, the assessment of what the individual knows, may not be particularly useful in predicting school performance for children for whom a common curriculum is in use. However, in broad agreement with and extending Cattell's investment theory, I propose that, for adults, what an individual knows (e.g., knowledge structures), becomes an ever-increasingly important determinant of intellectual life through occupational and postoccupational developmental periods.

This chapter provides an overview of a theoretical approach to the integration of intellect-as-process and intellect-as-knowledge that includes broad adult developmental considerations of personality and interests (Ackerman, 1994, 1996a, 1996b). Recent research on typical intellectual engagement (Ackerman & Goff, 1994; Goff & Ackerman, 1992) is reviewed, along with studies that relate adult cognition, personality, motivation, and interests with knowledge (Rolfhus & Ackerman, 1996). Implications for understanding the nature of intellectual development across the lifespan are discussed, as are potential applications for the prediction of basic knowledge/skill acquisition and maintenance, and occupational success over the adult life course.

BACKGROUND

The standard view of intelligence as a construct, from the perspectives of Binet and Simon, Terman, Wechsler, and many others who have contributed to the prototype of one-on-one intelligence testing, provides a starting point for this discussion. Adopting this perspective, as Boring (1923/1961) suggested, we have an operational definition of measured intelligence: "Intelligence is what the tests test." Boring, of course, said more about the construct:

> If we agree, then, to define intelligence as what the tests of intelligence test, there is a good deal that we can say about it. We can say everything that has been experimentally observed. We can say that it is a "common factor" in many abilities, that it is something like power, that it can be measured roughly although not very finely, that it is only one factor among many in the mental life, that it develops mostly in childhood, that it develops little or not at all in adult life, and that it is largely predetermined at five years of age." (p. 214)

Although Boring stated this principle in the early 1920s, the description he provided reflects much of the current construct of general intelligence. However, when it comes to prediction of adult intellectual performance, such a definition leaves much to be desired. Modern tests of intellectual ability with the exceptions of general declarative knowledge elicited in information tests, mostly assess *intelligence-as-process*. The reason for this, as Binet and Simon (1961a, 1961b, 1961c) described, was their attempt to separate different methods of intellectual assessment, as follows:

> 1. *The medical method*, which aims to appreciate the anatomical, physiological, and pathological signs of inferior intelligence.
> 2. *The pedagogical method*, which aims to judge of [sic] the intelligence according to the sum of acquired knowledge.
> 3. *The psychological method*, which makes direct observations and measurements of the degree of intelligence. (Binet & Simon, 1905/1961b, p. 93)

Binet and Simon argued as follows:

> It is understood that we here separate natural intelligence from instruction. It is the intelligence alone that we seek to measure, by disregarding in so far as possible, the degree of instruction which the subject possesses. He should, indeed, be considered by the examiner as a complete ignoramus knowing neither how to read nor write. The necessity forces us to forego a great many exercises having a verbal, literary or scholastic character. These belong to a pedagogical examination. (Binet & Simon, 1905/1961b, p. 93)

That is, Binet and Simon attempted to provide an estimate of individual differences in intellectual ability that was, to a great degree, separated from influences of prior experience, social privilege, and other confounds of socioeconomic status (SES). Binet and Simon provided cogent arguments for using the psychological method over the pedagogical method for the purpose of assessing schoolchildren. To anticipate arguments treated later in this chapter, though, for assessment of adult intellect and for the prediction of individual differences in skilled performance by adults, it seems clear that assessment via the pedagogical method for intelligence-as-knowledge is in order (especially as procedural skills are included in a wide-ranging definition of intellectual performance). First, however, a review of intelligence assessment is provided.

Intelligence of Children and Adolescents

In the Stanford–Binet and other tests for children and adolescents, intelligence tests measure reasoning, memory, perceptual speed, numerical facility, spatial visualization, and other abilities. Knowledge (information) makes up one small part of the test battery. With the exception of information, (and numerical facility, to some degree) most tests have been structured to remove specific cultural or prior knowledge requirements. This strategy was originally based on Binet's view that the intelligence test should not penalize children from impoverished backgrounds, and has since been carried forward by the testing industry so as to minimize differences in scores among different SES's and racial or ethnic groups. This is not to say that such intelligence tests are culture-free—rather the developers typically attempt to reduce SES and other group differences within a dominant culture (for a review, see Anastasi, 1982).

The original criterion of interest for the intelligence test was school success or failure—previous and current intelligence tests predict this criterion well. Tests of reasoning, information, memory, and so on, are positively correlated with school performance. In the aggregate, substantial correlations between the intelligence tests and scholastic performance are found widely (e.g., see Anastasi, 1982). There is, indeed, no essential difficulty with this approach to the testing of children and adolescents in this fashion for the school performance criterion. Abstract reasoning, memory, and so on, have been demonstrated repeatedly as necessary ingredients for scholastic success. Moreover, the range and depth of knowledge for academic pursuits is substantially limited for this population—at least until late adolescence. For those critics who claim that intelligence tests are all about academic learning and too little about the real world, there is no argument. Intelligence tests are about academic learning because that is the primary criterion that establishes the validity of the tests.

Adult Intelligence

It is argued here that adult intelligence tests are potentially limited in validity (construct, criterion-related, and content). From a construct perspective, and with substantial hindsight, the problems for intelligence testing started during World War I, when intelligence or IQ[1] tests that were originally designed for predicting school success were adapted for the ostensible task of predicting job performance (and classification) in military occupations. Of course, the trouble was noticed very early after the end of the war, in a series of popular press accounts about the so-called mental age (MA) of the average army conscript (reported to be MA = 13 yrs). Over the years, the response to such criticisms has been that the MA concept is not appropriately applied to adults (e.g., it makes little sense to talk of an individual with a chronological age of 50, and a MA of 25). The "solution" to this problem was the development of normative standardization of test scores, so that intelligence is considered solely as a position in a normal distribution of performance, with respect to a particular age-norm group. The adult version of the Stanford–Binet and the Wechsler Adult Intelligence Scale (WAIS) do not change the fundamental nature of the intelligence assessment content. Indeed, the Wechsler Intelli-

[1]Computation of an IQ or Intelligence Quotient score was proposed by Stern (1914) as a means toward providing a stable measure of standing across age groups and tests. The IQ is based on the Mental Age (MA) score derived from an intelligence test. MA refers to the average score obtained on the test by groups of examinees at specific ages. For example, if a student obtained a score equal to that of the average 8-year-old, that student's MA = 8. The IQ is computed by dividing the student's MA from the intelligence test by the student's actual, or chronological age (CA), and then multiplying the result by 100 (i.e., IQ = MA/CA × 100). Thus, a student with a MA of 8 and a CA of 8 would have an IQ of 100. A student with a MA of 10 and CA of 8 would have an IQ of 125.

gence Scale for Children (WISC) and the Wechsler Preschool and Primary Scale of Intelligence (WPPSI) downward revisions of the WAIS contain the same content scales as the WAIS.

The problems, though, are deeper than the MA concept. From a *criterion-related* validity perspective, with the exception of some applications (such as military training success and college grades), the school performance criterion is not an appropriate universal criterion for an adult assessment of intelligence. Moreover, the intellectual repertoire of adults is vastly more complex than that of children and adolescents. The global intelligence IQ score actually does a relatively modest job of predicting relevant criteria for adults, such as occupational performance and advancement (certainly substantially lower correlations exist between IQ and occupational measures than those that exist for IQ and school grades). Such a case is supported by Hunter's (1983) model of job performance (task proficiency), in which "ability" has only an indirect role in determining performance—the direct effect of ability is on job knowledge, which in turn determines job performance.

Indeed, the primary source of validity for intellectual ability tests in college and graduate school comes in the first year of college grades or the first year of graduate and professional school grades. As students gain the declarative knowledge and procedural skills involved in respective school curricula, broad ability tests such as the Graduate Record Exam (GRE) Quantitative test show decreased validity (Lin & Humphreys, 1977). Figure 7.1 shows the general effect.

The decline in the validity of the broad ability tests, as shown in Fig. 7.1, for predicting school success for college and graduate school is general and pervasive (even taking restriction-of-range in talent into account). As academic specializations become distant from those that have predominant demands on verbal abilities (e.g., English and history have high verbal demands, but engineering and physics do not), the correlations between IQ and college grades tend to decline. Would we claim that engineering and physics disciplines require less intellect than English and history? Of course not. We might even be tempted to argue the opposite point. Why, then, do these declines in the validity of IQ show up across the academic spectrum for college and graduate school? The apparent reason, I believe, is that performance in such situations becomes less dependent on abilities such as abstract reasoning and memory and more determined by individual differences in prior knowledge. Without substantial knowledge of classical mechanics in physics, for example, understanding the theory of relativity or quantum mechanics is difficult, if not impossible. This is not to say that IQ does not play a role in determining individual

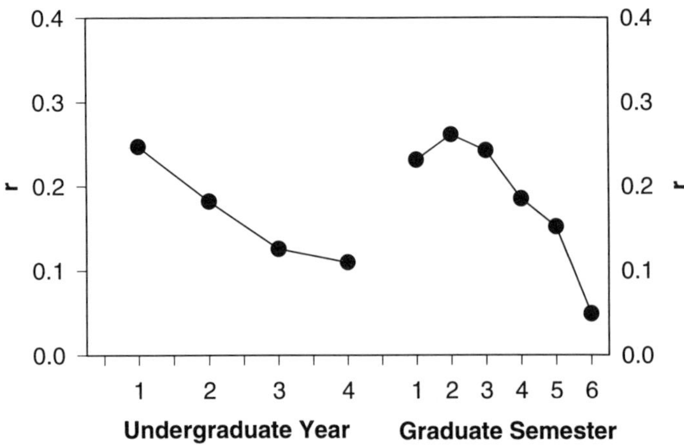

FIG. 7.1 Validity coefficients for GRE Quantitative tests for graduate students in math, chemistry and physics, over 4 undergraduate years and 6 graduate semesters. Postdiction of undergraduate grade point average; prediction of graduate grade point averages. From data reported by Lin and Humphreys (1977).

differences in learning outcomes for adults; it surely is an important determinant of such criteria. However, as adults complete their final years of education, and transfer into the workplace and further develop avocational knowledge, the depth and breadth of knowledge plays an increasingly important role in determining vocational and avocational competence.

The validity data from the GRE provide further support for this claim. For some areas of study, the respective GRE Advanced subject tests are singly more predictive of graduate school grades and completion of the PhD, more predictive, that is, than the Verbal and Quantitative tests (Anastasi, 1982; Conrad, Trismen, & Miller, 1977; Willingham, 1974). The GRE Advanced test is also reported to be of higher validity (than either the Verbal or Quantitative tests) for overall faculty rating and prediction of years to PhD completion. Further, the GRE Advanced tests are more highly predictive of post-PhD success (on-the-job ratings of scientific knowledge and citations of the individual's publications) than undergraduate GPA or letters of recommendation (Creager & Harmon, 1966). The importance of knowledge is not limited to individuals pursuing higher educational achievement; it is surely relevant to carpenters and computer-maintenance technicians as well. However, no substantive investigations of the knowledge bases for these professions have been carried out.

From a content validity perspective, the original designers of the modern IQ test (e.g., Terman & Merrill, 1937) suggested that: "At these levels [adult] the major intellectual differences between subjects reduce largely to differences in the ability to do conceptual thinking, and facility in dealing with concepts is most readily sampled by the use of verbal tests'' (p. 5.).

Aside from using items that were more acceptable to adults than were contained in the Stanford–Binet, and aside from abandoning the MA concept, Wechsler's test did very little to remedy the noted shortcomings of extant IQ tests in assessing adult intelligence (Wechsler, 1939). Indeed, with the Wechsler–Bellevue's de-emphasis on verbal content, it is possible that the Wechsler test actually taps less knowledge than the Stanford–Binet does. Neither of these instruments tap occupationally relevant knowledge; they mainly assess what Lenat and Guha (1990) call *consensus knowledge*—knowledge that is common to a dominant culture.

KNOWLEDGE STRUCTURES

In the past two decades, studies of expert performers, whether in physics (Chi, Glaser, & Rees, 1982), chess (Chase & Simon, 1973), or music (Ericsson, Krampe, & Tesch-Römer, 1993), have all come to the conclusion that the amount and structure of knowledge distinguishes levels of performance to a substantial degree (for a discussion, see Glaser, 1991). Indeed, investigators such as Ericsson et al. (1993) have suggested (a bit too hastily, in my opinion), that practice (and knowledge) is primary, and that individual differences in intelligence are unimportant for the acquisition of various types of expertise, from sports to music to scientific prominence. Nonetheless, such investigations, along with the broad emphasis on domain-related knowledge that has been emphasized in the artificial intelligence and expert system fields, recognize that the ''general-purpose problem solver'' approach is inadequate to account for performance in all but the most content-sterile domains (such as math and logic, e.g., see Lenat & Guha, 1990, for a discussion of knowledge-based problem solving from an artificial intelligence perspective).

From an individual differences perspective, the work by Sternberg and Wagner (1989, 1993) on tacit knowledge, and the work by Schmidt and Hunter (1993) on job knowledge, pointed to individual differences in level of knowledge as having substantial incremental validity for prediction of job performance and even success in postsecondary education. Such results are consistent with the current view that knowledge is fundamentally important to expressions of adult intellect (Ackerman, 1996a). Similarly, the work by Baltes and Staudinger

(1993), demonstrates advantages of older adults over younger adults on tests of wisdom, which are substantially knowledge-based.

Knowledge Structures: Ability Issues

Intelligence theorists have not ignored the role of knowledge in conceptualizations of intelligence (see, e.g., discussion in Ackerman, 1996a, 1996b). Indeed, one of the major types of intelligence proposed by Cattell and Horn (Horn & Cattell, 1966) is *crystallized intelligence*, which is defined as educational and experiential intelligence (Horn, 1965, 1968). Less well known is the full specification of the developmental trajectory of crystallized intelligence as described by Cattell (1971/1987), in his investment theory. He stated that problems occur

> When we begin to ask what happens to crystallized general intelligence, and the traditional intelligence tests that measure it, *after* school. The crystallized intelligence factor then goes awry both conceptually and in regard to the practical predictions to be made from traditional intelligence tests. In the twenty years following school, the judgmental skills that one should properly be measuring as the expression of learning by fluid ability must become different for different people. If these are sufficiently varied and lack any common core, the very concept of general intelligence begins to disappear.
>
> [The psychologist's] alternatives are then: (a) to sample behavior still more widely than in the traditional test, using a formula expressing the role of fluid intelligence in learning in each of many different fields (an approach which, in practice, might amount to producing as many different tests as there are occupations, etc.); (b) to change completely to fluid intelligence measures . . . or (c) to continue to measure by the "school version" of crystallized ability essentially learning on what the individual's intelligence was at the time of leaving school. (Cattell, 1971/1987, pp. 143–144)

A quick perusal of the literature on aging suggests that psychologists have almost exclusively selected options (b) and (c), to the detriment of discovering the knowledge structures of adult intellect. Many studies of adult intelligence have focused on delineating the relative effects of adult aging on crystallized intelligence, in comparison to abilities such as abstract reasoning and memory. Nearly all such investigations (e.g., Hertzog & Schaie, 1988; Schaie & Strother, 1968) demonstrated that verbal abilities (which usually are prototypical markers for crystallized intelligence (Gc) are well preserved until late adulthood, whereas measures of abstract reasoning, memory, spatial ability and so on show substantial age-related deficits.

Do these investigators claim that even though verbal abilities are preserved, older adults have lower intelligence than younger adults? No. Instead, such investigators discuss the relevance (or lack thereof) of various abilities for adult intellectual functioning, or argue about nature of the testing situation (e.g., see the exchange between Horn & Donaldson, 1976, 1977, and Baltes & Schaie, 1976). The issue whether the intelligence of older adults increases or decreases is generally side-stepped in such discussions (Baltes & Schaie, 1976). However, if we adopt the Boring (1923/1961) operational definition of intelligence, we should conclude that adult intelligence declines substantially with age. The way out of this dilemma is to broaden the consideration of what determines the intellectual performance of adults. That is, Gc, as operationally assessed by Cattell, Horn, and others, is just a small portion of the knowledge that adults possess. Intelligence theory has simply been too bound by a convention that avoids testing of information that is not assumed a priori to be generally encountered by nearly all examinees within a dominant culture. As such, psychometric study of the knowledge structures of adults simply has not been done in any type of organized or comprehensive fashion.

A REVOLUTIONARY APPROACH

What is needed for an informed perspective on adult intelligence are three things: (a) a substantial effort devoted to developing a taxonomic representation of knowledge; (b) a battery of assessment instruments that allows wide sampling of the breadth and depth of adult knowledge; (c) new statistical and methodological tools to summarize data from sparse matrices in a fashion that can lead to prediction of relevant criteria. Each of these is briefly discussed next.

Taxonomies of Knowledge

Developing a taxonomy of knowledge is admittedly a subjective enterprise. For example, Adler's (1974) taxonomy of knowledge used as the *Propædia* for the *Encyclopædia Britannica* (*EB*), see Fig. 7.2, has provisions for characterizing many types of declarative knowledge (Adler's taxonomy and the *EB* are primarily fact knowledge) but very little procedural knowledge. An adequate taxonomy of knowledge would certainly need to consider all of Adler's categories. Nonetheless, it is important to keep in mind that not all knowledge is intellectual in content (especially within a particular cultural context, see, for exam-

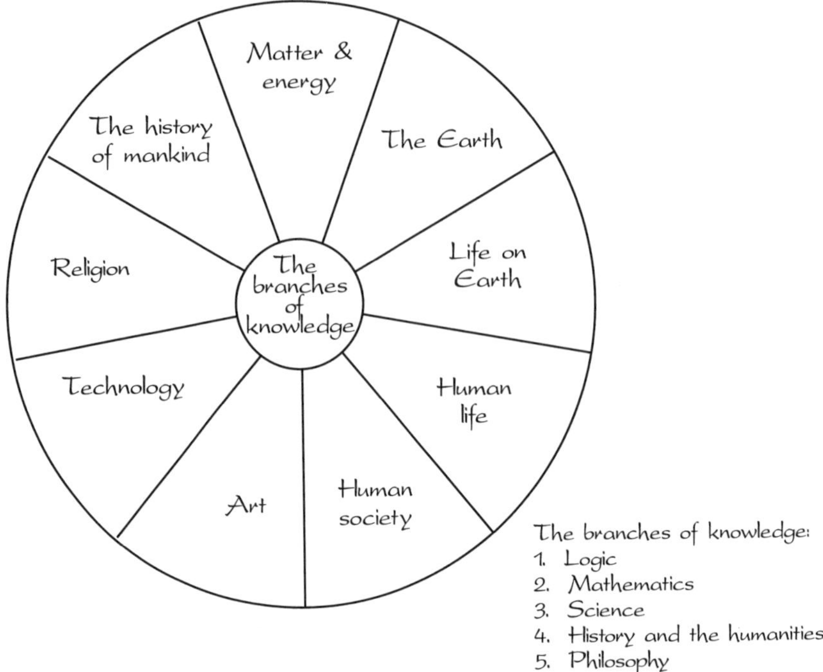

FIG. 7.2 Adler's (1974) wheel of knowledge. Copyright © 1974 by Encyclopædia Britannica, Inc. Reprinted by permission.

ple, Learned and Wood [1938] for an analysis of college student knowledge). For particular intents and purposes, wide domains of knowledge might be considered to be nonintellectual (e.g., sports knowledge may only be relevant to specific avocational situations unless the individual is employed in a sports related occupation).

A more complete taxonomy of intellectual knowledge would include various types of procedural knowledge (e.g., cooking knowledge is primarily procedural, as are many aspects of dance, music, mechanical knowledge, and so on). For an example, see Vernon's depiction of educational abilities in Fig. 7.3. In addition, one might include the kinds of categories that Gardner (1985) considered to be aspects of intelligence, such as interpersonal and intrapersonal knowledge. There is no a priori reason that prevents construction of psychometrically defensible tests for such knowledge types. Similarly, Sternberg's (1990) *tacit knowledge* or *practical intelligence* categories, and Schmidt and Hunter's (1993) *job knowledge* category may be encompassed within a full taxonomy of intellectual knowledge. Note, however, that these various investigators have only scratched the surface of the entire domain of knowledge.

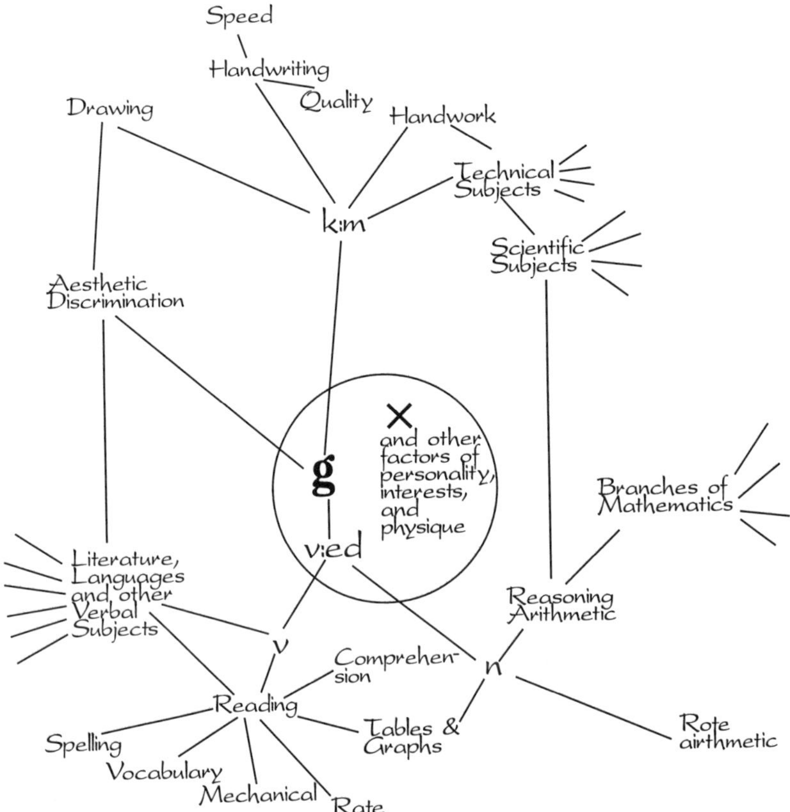

FIG. 7.3 Reprinted from Vernon (1950, p. 47) "Fig. 3. Diagram of the structure of educational abilities." g = general ability; v:ed = Verbal:Educational; k:m = practical:mechanical; v = verbal; **X** = industriousness (including personality and interests). Copyright © 1950 by John Wiley & Sons. Reprinted by permission.

Test Batteries

Given a large taxonomy of knowledge, and the likelihood of a sparse response matrix from typical examinees, a battery of tests must be wide ranging and adaptive. By adaptive, I am referring to the selection of both tests and items in tests. For example, a test procedure should be able to advance to high levels of expertise quickly, or, conversely, abandon a content area when the examinee is unfamiliar with all but the most basic knowledge in a domain. Ideally, examinees would be faced with a series of tests. For each test, minimal familiarity with test content will lead to further probing to achieve depth of knowledge. Adaptation is necessary to bring the testing process into a time frame that is minimally acceptable to the examinee. For many academic domains, knowledge is at least partially linear (e.g., mathematics knowledge typically proceeds from addition and subtraction, to algebra, to calculus before splitting to higher levels of specific types of expertise, such as number theory, topology, and so on). Many nonacademic, or avocational, domains, such as knowledge about music or art, would need to be sampled broadly rather than in linear order. Tests need not be comprehensive but must provide a sample across wide levels of expertise and breadth in order to prevent ceiling effects or insufficient sampling.

For initial study of knowledge structures, it will not be feasible to ascertain fine distinctions of expertise for particular domains. The goal for this program would be analogically similar to an astronomical task of mapping the stars that are visible to the unaided eye (a task that can be accomplished without an expensive telescope), instead of deriving a detailed map of the galaxy (which requires dedication of sophisticated telescopes).

For the academic disciplines (e.g., physical and social sciences, math), a wide range of achievement tests already exist to provide sources of assessment, from elementary to postsecondary levels of education. Also, some occupational and certification tests may provide the foundation for several different domains. However, outside the academic and some occupational disciplines, it will be more difficult to cull existing tests and probably necessary to create new ones.

Methodological Issues

A clearly anticipated problem with using the proposed approach is that, for any pair of individuals, there may be relatively little overlap between knowledge-structure profiles. Generally, people know very little about very many knowledge types but a great deal about a few. Person A may know much about music and art but relatively little about science and technology. Person B may have the opposite profile. It even may not be possible to generate something resembling a general composite score for such tests. On the other hand, it may be feasible to consider profile similarity, or depth–breadth scores from specific knowledge types for predicting particular criteria, such as performance in a given occupation. The individual with high degree of knowledge of science and the individual with high degree of knowledge of art both may be highly intelligent. One would hope that evaluation of individual differences in knowledge can be normed in such a way that allows reference beyond a particular occupational or avocational group.

PERSONALITY, MOTIVATION, INTERESTS, AND ADULT INTELLIGENCE

Some of the more perplexing findings in the literature are the small correlations between adult intelligence and measures of personality, motivation, and interests (Ackerman & Heggestad, in press). Recent investigations, though, suggest how motivation affects the development of expertise (Ericsson et al., 1993). Older literature similarly suggests that interests are indeed related to success in military aviation occupations (for a discussion, see Ackerman & Humphreys, 1991). Also, the personality constructs of typical intellectual engagement and openness to experience have been shown to be more closely associated with measures of crystallized intelligence than fluid intelligence in adults (Ackerman, 1994, Ackerman & Goff, 1994; Goff & Ackerman, 1992). Each of these findings suggests that an adult intelligence measure that includes a substantial sampling of knowledge structures will also be more highly correlated with such noncognitive individual differences.

PREDICTING INDIVIDUAL DIFFERENCES IN ADULT SKILL DEVELOPMENT AND MAINTENANCE

Aside from generating a taxonomy of adult declarative and procedural knowledge, what can be done for predicting real-world criteria from individual differences in adult intellect? Over the past few years, work in our laboratory has focused on generating several measures that appear to tap into these important determinants of skilled performance. For example, self-report ratings of interests and self concept and self-ratings of ability show substantial validity in predicting individual differences in performance for adult skill acquisition tasks, even though these tasks are relatively knowledge-impoverished (i.e., those tasks for which most information necessary to perform the task is provided by the researcher); see for example, Ackerman, Kanfer, and Goff (1995) and Rolfhus and Ackerman (1996). We believe that extensions of this work will provide useful indexes of an individual's repertoire of declarative and procedural knowledge, that can, in turn, be validated by a sampling of objective tests. Fundamentally, prediction of individual differences in performance on real-world tasks, where substantial previous experience is involved, may ultimately come down to knowledge tests that are tailored for the particular skills.[2] Additional assessment of motiva-

[2]It seems odd to come to this conclusion only in the 1990s, given that this is an essentially analogous position to that advocated by Thorndike and Woodworth (1901) in their classic learning and transfer studies.

tional variables, interests and personality variables (e.g., see Ackerman, 1994; Ericsson et al., 1993; Goff & Ackerman, 1992) may provide incremental validity for predictions of life-long skill acquisition and maintenance.

CURRENT INVESTIGATIONS

Our first attempt to understand the nature of individual differences in adult knowledge structures was coarse, in that we depended on self-report estimates of knowledge from college students, and focused mainly on academic sources of knowledge. However, the results from these first studies were illuminating, in the way that knowledge, abilities, interests and personality traits related to each other. A full description of this work is presented in Rolfhus and Ackerman (1996), but a brief overview of the results is informative.

First of all, Rolfhus and Ackerman administered 32 knowledge scales, ranging from art history (e.g., "Distinctions between representational, abstract, and nonrepresentational art") to physics (e.g., "The differences between kinetic and potential energy"). These scales were administered to 203 undergraduate students along with a series of traditional measures of ability, personality, and interests.

By correlating knowledge scale scores with ability composites, it was possible to establish clear patterns of knowledge-ability constellations, that is, domains in which high levels of one type of ability correspond to a high degree of knowledge. By graphing the magnitude of correlation between the ability composites and the score on each knowledge scale, it is possible to see the patterns graphically. Figure 7.4 shows the correlations of the knowledge scales with spatial and verbal ability composites. For example, substantial correlations were found between spatial ability and engineering, calculus, geometry, and physics knowledge scales, whereas the same knowledge scales showed low correlations with verbal ability. Knowledge of literature and knowledge of philosophy, conversely, showed modest correlations with verbal ability, but essentially zero correlations with spatial ability.

Substantial correlations were found between knowledge scales and measures of vocational interests. For example, *Realistic* interests showed high correlations with engineering, physics, and earth science knowledge scales; *Investigative* interests with biology, physics, and chemistry scales; *Artistic* interests with music, poetry, and theater scales; *Social* interests with sociology, education, and psychology scales; *Enterprising* interests with economics, political science, and

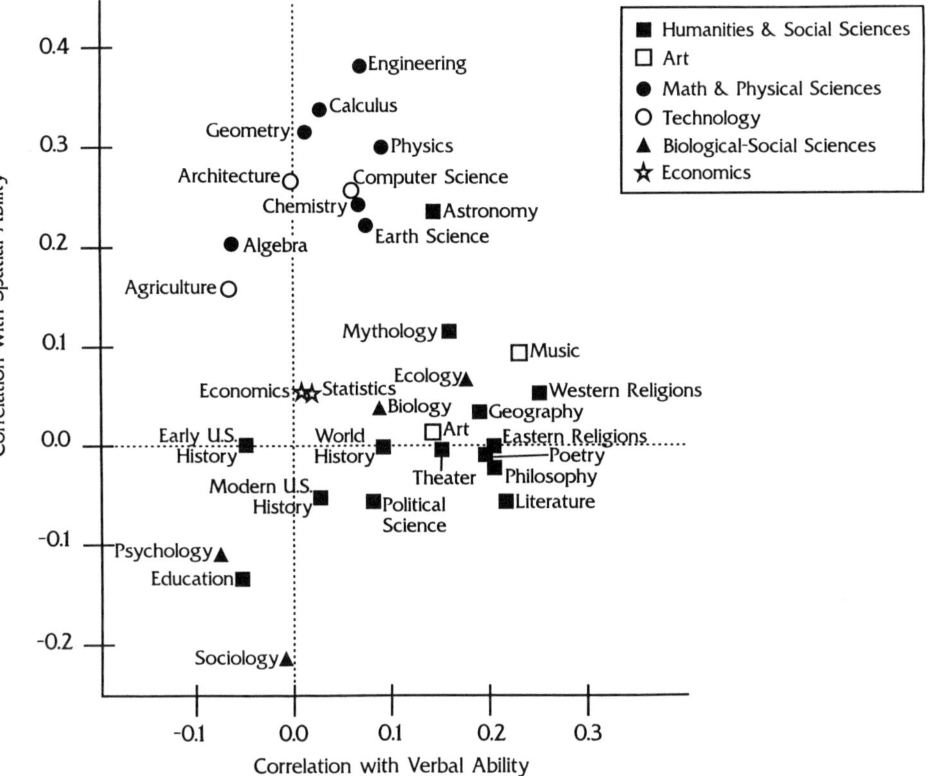

FIG. 7.4 Knowledge scale correlations with spatial ability composite plotted against knowledge scale correlations with verbal ability composite. Symbols indicate knowledge cluster (thematic domain) membership. From Rolfhus and Ackerman (1996, Fig. 1.) Copyright © 1996 by the American Psychological Association. Reprinted by permission.

sociology scales; and *Conventional* interests with economics, statistics, and geometry.

By linking standard measures of ability with interest and personality measures, it is possible to more fully specify a developmental theory of adult intellect—in which various trait sources (cognitive, personality, and motivational) interact to produce increments in domain knowledge. The results of the Rolfhus and Ackerman (1996) study, for example, suggest that there are correlations among content abilities (e.g., spatial, verbal, mathematical), interest in an area, and (at least self-reports of) knowledge about an area. For the future, we are developing objective tests of knowledge, both academic and avocational, which we will use in the study of adult aging.

CONCLUSION

The *Zeitgeist* for intelligence testing this century has focused on the nature of intellect for children and adolescents. Comprehensive study of adult intelligence requires a fundamental shift in orientation away from knowledge-impoverished abilities and toward knowledge-rich domains of cognitive pursuits (Ackerman, 1996b). The proposed perspective requires the study and evaluation of numerous sources of different areas of knowledge and expertise, from science to literature, and from art to current affairs. The cost of such research is substantial, requiring nothing less than development of a taxonomy of human intellectual knowledge, and development of tests for assessment of individual differences in the depth and breadth of knowledge sources. The payoff, it is proposed, is equally substantial. A successful achievement here would be a new perspective on adult intelligence that will contribute to practical applications (e.g., prediction of occupational success), to scientific study (e.g., assessment of changes in intellectual functioning over the life span), and to the integration of personality, motivation, and interest constructs in the context of the development and expression of adult intellect.

ACKNOWLEDGMENTS

Preparation of this chapter was supported by a grant from the U.S. Air Force Office of Scientific Research "*Cognitive/Self-Regulatory Aptitudes and Instructional Methods for Complex Skill Learning*" to Phillip L. Ackerman and Ruth Kanfer (F49620-93-1-0206). The opinions represented here are the author's and do not necessary reflect those of the sponsoring institution. I wish to acknowledge insightful discussions and correspondence with Lee J. Cronbach, John B. Carroll, and Frank L. Schmidt regarding the issues presented in this chapter.

REFERENCES

Ackerman, P. L. (1994). Intelligence, attention, and learning: Maximal and typical performance. In D. K. Detterman (Ed.) *Current topics in human intelligence. Vol. 4: Theories of intelligence* (pp. 1–27). Norwood, NJ: Ablex.

Ackerman, P. L. (1996a). Knowledge structures: Successive glimpses of an elusive theory of adult intelligence. In D. K. Detterman (Ed.), *Current topics in human intelligence*. (Vol. 5. pp. 105–111). Norwood, NJ: Ablex.

Ackerman, P. L. (1996b). A theory of adult intelligence development: process, personality, interests, and knowledge. *Intelligence, 22,* 229–259.

Ackerman, P. L., & Goff, M. (1994). Typical intellectual engagement and personality: Reply to Rocklin (1994). *Journal of Educational Psychology, 86,* 150–153.

Ackerman, P. L., & Heggestad, E. D. (in press). Intelligence, personality, and interests: Evidence for overlapping traits. *Psychological Bulletin.*

Ackerman, P. L., & Humphreys, L. G. (1991). Individual differences theory in industrial and organizational psychology. In M. D. Dunnette & L. M. Hough (Eds.), *Handbook of industrial and organizational psychology* (Vol. 1, pp. 223–282). Palo Alto, CA: Consulting Psychologists Press.

Ackerman, P. L., Kanfer, R., & Goff, M. (1995). Cognitive and noncognitive determinants and consequences of complex skill acquisition. *Journal of Experimental Psychology: Applied, 1,* 270–304.

Adler, M. (1974). The circle of learning. In *Encyclopædia Britannica-Propaedia* (pp. 5–7). Chicago: Encyclopdia Britannica, Inc.

Anastasi, A. (1982). *Psychological testing* (5th ed.). New York: Macmillan.

Baltes, P. B., & Schaie, K. W. (1976). On the plasticity of intelligence in adulthood and old age: Where Horn and Donaldson fail. *American Psychologist, 31,* 720–725.

Baltes, P. B., & Staudinger, U. M. (1993). The search for a psychology of wisdom. *Current Directions in Psychological Science, 2,* 75–80.

Binet, A., & Simon, T. (1961a). The development of intelligence in the child (Elizabeth S. Kite, Trans.). In J. J. Jenkins & D. G. Paterson (Eds.), *Studies of individual differences: The search for intelligence* (pp. 96–111). New York: Appleton-Century-Crofts. (Original work published in 1908)

Binet, A., & Simon, T. (1961b). New methods for the diagnosis of the intellectual level of subnormals (Elizabeth S. Kite, Trans.). In J. J. Jenkins & D. G. Paterson (Eds.), *Studies of individual differences: The search for intelligence* (pp. 90–96). New York: Appleton-Century-Crofts. (Original work published in 1905)

Binet, A., & Simon, T. (1961c). Upon the necessity of establishing a scientific diagnosis of inferior states of intelligence (Elizabeth S. Kite, Trans.). In J. J. Jenkins & D. G. Paterson (Eds.), *Studies of individual differences: The search for intelligence* (pp. 81–90). New York: Appleton-Century-Crofts. (Original work published in 1905)

Boring, E. G. (1961). Intelligence as the tests measure it. In J. J. Jenkins & D. G. Paterson (Eds.), *Studies in individual differences: The search for intelligence* (pp. 210–214). New York: Appleton-Century-Crofts. (Original work published 1923)

Cattell, R. B. (1987). *Intelligence: Its structure, growth, and action.* Amsterdam: North-Holland. (Original work published 1971)

Chase, W. G., & Simon, H. A. (1973). The mind's eye in chess. In W. G. Chase (Ed.), *Visual information processing* (pp. 215–281). San Diego, CA: Academic Press.

Chi, M. T. H., Glaser, R., & Rees, E. (1982). Expertise in problem solving. In R. J. Sternberg (Ed.), *Advances in the psychology of human intelligence* (Vol. 1, pp. 7–76). Hillsdale, NJ: Lawrence Erlbaum Associates.

Conrad, L., Trismen, D., & Miller, R. (Eds.), (1977). *Graduate record examinations technical manual.* Princeton, NJ: Educational Testing Service.

Creager, J. A., & Harmon, L. R. (1966). *On-the-job validation of selection variables.* Washington, DC: Office of Scientific Personnel, National Academy of Sciences—National Research Council.

Ericsson, K. A., Krampe, R. T., & Tesch-Römer, C. (1993). The role of deliberate practice in the acquisition of expert performance. *Psychological Review, 100,* 363–406.

Gardner, H. (1985). *Frames of mind: The theory of multiple intelligences.* New York: Basic Books.

Glaser, R. (1991). Intelligence as an expression of acquired knowledge. In H. A. H. Rowe (Ed.), *Intelligence: Reconceptualization and measurement* (pp. 47–56). Hillsdale, NJ: Lawrence Erlbaum Associates.

Goff, M., & Ackerman, P. L. (1992). Personality–intelligence relations: Assessing typical intellectual engagement. *Journal of Educational Psychology, 84*, 537–552.

Hertzog, C., & Schaie, K. W. (1988). Stability and change in adult intelligence: 2. Simultaneous analysis of longitudinal means and covariance structures. *Psychology and Aging, 3*, 122–130.

Horn, J. L. (1965). Fluid and crystallized intelligence: A factor analytic study of the structure among primary mental abilities. Doctoral dissertation, University of Illinois [no. 65-7113]. Ann Arbor, MI: University Microfilms, Inc.

Horn, J. L. (1968). Organization of abilities and the development of intelligence. *Psychological Review, 75*, 242–259.

Horn, J. L., & Cattell, R. B. (1966). Refinement and test of the theory of fluid and crystallized general intelligences. *Journal of Educational Psychology, 57*, 253–270.

Horn, J. L., & Donaldson, G. (1976). On the myth of intellectual decline in adulthood. *American Psychologist, 31*, 701–719.

Horn, J. L., & Donaldson, G. (1977). Faith is not enough: A response to the Baltes-Schaie claim that intelligence does not wane. *American Psychologist, 32*, 369–373.

Hunter, J. E. (1983). A causal analysis of cognitive ability, job knowledge, job performance, and supervisor ratings. In F. Landy, S. Zedeck, & J. Cleveland (Eds.), *Performance measurement and theory* (pp. 257–266). Hillsdale, NJ: Lawrence Erlbaum Associates.

Learned, W. S., & Wood, B. D. (1938). *The student and his knowledge: A report to the Carnegie Foundation for the Advancement of Teaching* (Bulletin No. 29). New York: Carnegie Foundation.

Lenat, D. B., & Guha, R. V. (1990). *Building large knowledge-based systems: Representation and inference in the Cyc project*. Reading, MA: Addison-Wesley.

Lin, P. C., & Humphreys, L. G. (1977). Predictions of academic performance in graduate and professional school. *Applied Psychological Measurement, 1*, 249–257.

Rolfhus, E. L., & Ackerman, P. L. (1996). Self-report knowledge: At the crossroads of ability, interest, and personality. *Journal of Educational Psychology, 88*, 174–188.

Schaie, K. W., & Strother, C. R. (1968). A cross-sequential study of age changes in cognitive behavior. *Psychological Bulletin, 70*, 671–680.

Schmidt, F. L., & Hunter, J. E. (1993). Tacit knowledge, practical intelligence, general mental ability, and job knowledge. *Current Directions in Psychological Science, 2*, 8–9.

Stern, W. (1914). *The psychological methods of testing intelligence* (Guy Montrose Whipple, Trans.). Baltimore: Warwick & York. (Original work published 1912)

Sternberg, R. J. (1990). *Metaphors of mind: Conceptions of the nature of intelligence*. Cambridge: Cambridge University Press.

Sternberg, R. J., & Wagner, R. K. (1989). Individual differences in practical knowledge and its application. In P. L. Ackerman, R. J. Sternberg, & R. Glaser (Eds.). *Learning and individual differences: Advances in theory and research* (pp. 255–278). New York: W. H. Freeman.

Sternberg, R. J., & Wagner, R. K. (1993). The g-ocentric view of intelligence and job performance is wrong. *Current Directions in Psychological Science, 2*, 1–4.

Terman, L. M., & Merrill, M. A. (1937). *Measuring intelligence*. Boston: Houghton Mifflin.

Thorndike, E. L., & Woodworth, R. S. (1901). The influence of improvement in one mental function upon the efficiency of other functions. *Psychological Review, 8*, 247–262.

Thurstone, L. L. (1938). Primary mental abilities. *Psychometric Monographs, 1*, 1–121.

Vernon, P. E. (1950). *The structure of human abilities*. New York: John Wiley & Sons.

Wechsler, D. (1939). *The measurement of adult intelligence*. Baltimore: Williams & Wilkins.

Willinham, W. W. (1974) Predicting success in graduate education. *Science, 183*, 273–278.

CHAPTER 8

The Effects of Display Layout on Keeping Track of Visual–Spatial Information

Mark C. Detweiler
Stephen M. Hess
Pennsylvania State University

R. Darin Ellis
Wayne State University

Broadly conceived, working memory is associated with the cognitive structures and processes involved in temporarily storing and manipulating information as different types of cognitive tasks are performed (see Baddeley, 1986; Baddeley & Hitch, 1994; Schneider & Detweiler, 1987). Since the 1980s considerable progress has been made at both conceptualizing the role of working memory in development and learning and in investigating numerous age-related differences that emerge across a wide range of tasks (see, e.g., Salthouse, 1990, 1994). At one end of the developmental continuum, working-memory capacity has been reported to increase with age (e.g., Case, Kurland, & Goldberg, 1982; Chi, 1976, 1978), whereas, at the other end, working-memory capacity and/or efficiency has been reported to decrease with age (e.g., Gick, Craik, & Morris, 1988; Morris, Gick, & Craik, 1988; Salthouse, 1990; Salthouse & Babcock, 1991).

The majority of measures used to assess age differences in working memory, for example, measures of spans of running memory, reading, listening, and computation, have revealed that younger adults tend to perform better on these tasks than older adults (Dobbs & Rule, 1989; Salthouse, 1990). Despite the number of methodologies for cataloging age-related differences, there is still considerable question about what factors are responsible for them. For example, cases have been made for decreasing storage capacity (e.g., Inman & Parkinson, 1983), declining processing resources or processing efficiency (Gick et al., 1988; Morris et al., 1988), and reduced availability or efficiency of control processes

(Dobbs & Rule, 1989; Rabbitt, 1981; Van der Linden, Brédart, & Beerten, 1994).

This chapter has two primary goals. The first goal is to explore age-related differences with a more complex task than traditionally used to measure working memory, thereby tapping a range of processing and storage loads. The second and more applied goal is related to our belief that many tasks currently require operators to perform at or near their working-memory limits. We believe such tasks can be redesigned to reduce working-memory demands. Thus these experiments represent attempts to further understand the types of external support that can help humans maintain intermediate results for later processing. Specifically, they explore how information display and layout can shape performance as a function of processing load and begin to investigate which types of displays can help operators monitor dynamically changing information. Before describing the task we designed to support these goals, we consider earlier work that attempted to assess dynamic aspects of working memory.

Kirchner (1958) was one of the first to investigate age-related differences in running memory by having young (18–24 years) and older (60–84 years) adults view either a series of 6 or 12 randomly presented lights at the rate of one light every 1.5 seconds. The participants' task was to press keys corresponding to the spatial locations of the lights under several conditions. In the zero-back condition, they pressed the key directly below each light as it appeared. In the one-back condition, they pressed the key corresponding to the light one back in the series, i.e., the light that had just been extinguished. In addition, participants also responded to lights two- and three-back in the series—placing increasingly greater demands on working memory. Both younger and older adults performed about equally well in the zero-back condition. However, in the one-back condition the younger adults performed about as well as they did in the zero-back condition, whereas the older adults' accuracy dropped close to 17% in total correct responses. In the two-back condition the younger adults continued to perform well, whereas the older adults' performance deteriorated dramatically—averaging fewer than half the number of correct responses they achieved in the one-back condition. Interestingly, only 3 of the 20 older adults were able to perform the three-back version at all. Although the younger adults were able to perform the three-back version, their performance dropped precipitously. Kirchner argued that motor performance played only a minor role in the older adults' poorer performance, and suggested that limitations in central-organizing (control) processes were more likely. In Kirchner's view, these central processes orchestrate the continual acts of putting items into and taking them out of temporary storage, and he speculated that these processes may slow down with age.

Yntema and his associates (Yntema & Mueser, 1960, 1962; Yntema & Schulman, 1967) were also interested in running memory but studied it within a "keeping-track" paradigm. Yntema and Mueser (1960, 1962) had participants keep track of values of several attributes (1 of 4 unique values of shape, direction, food, mark, animal, number, weather, and color) of one object (from the letters, D, H, K, L, N, W, X, or Z), or one attribute (e.g., colors with the unique values red, yellow, green, or blue of several objects, e.g., D, N, Z). This design allowed Yntema and Mueser to independently vary the number of variables participants had to keep track of, and how the attributes and objects were mapped to one another. In the one–many condition participants kept track of the same attribute of different numbers of objects (2, 3, 4, 6, and 8); in the many–one condition they kept track of different numbers of attributes (2, 3, 4, 6, and 8) of one object. In both conditions, participants kept track of auditorily presented values of attributes so they could respond with an attribute's most recent value when later questioned about it. The task was self-paced, and an attribute–object value was only available when it was updated and never when a question was asked about its status. In addition, participants did not receive feedback about their response accuracy.

Yntema and Mueser (1960, 1962) found that the percentage of questions answered correctly decreased as the number of variables whose values had to be remembered increased. Moreover, accuracy was lower when participants kept track of the same single attribute of different objects (one–many condition), rather than when they kept track of different attributes of the same object (many–one condition). Part of the reason for the decrease in accuracy can be attributed to the fact that as the number of variables increases, the mean number of updates and questions that intervene between when an update occurs and when a question is asked about it increases. Yntema and Mueser called this delay the *response lag*. Generally, as the number of intervening items increased, so did the probability that participants were not able to correctly recall previously updated values. In summary, despite the fact that participants had to keep track of the same number of items, keeping track of one object with several attributes imposed a markedly smaller load on working memory than keeping track of combinations of multiple objects and attributes, resulting in greater accuracy.

More recently, Hess, Detweiler, and Ellis (1994) used a keeping-track task similar to Yntema and Mueser's to investigate the effectiveness of using two different types of displays to present rapidly changing information. In one condition, participants kept track of several attributes of one object, or one attribute of several objects. However, the attribute values were presented in a grid of five columns of attributes by five rows of objects. As new information appeared to be updated or a question was asked about an attribute–object value, either the value or question was displayed at the intersection of the appropriate attribute column and object row. That is, each value to be remembered appeared in a unique spatial location. Thus the grid provided additional spatial information participants could use to help them keep track of the values. In a second condition, participants saw the same attribute–object information appear in two windows at the center of the display screen. The object always appeared in the window at the left with its attribute in the window on the right. In this case no unique spatial information was available in the display to help them keep track of the values.

Unlike Yntema and Mueser's (1960, 1962) experiments, in which different values were associated with each attribute, for example, red, yellow, green, and blue for colors, or up, down, right, and left for directions, Hess et al. had participants keep track of the same values (digits 1–4) representing four different states of each attribute at a computer-paced rate. Under these conditions, Hess et al. failed to find the mapping effect reported by Yntema and Mueser. However, they showed that the type of screen layout used to support the keeping-track task had a large effect on how accurately and quickly participants performed the task, with participants using the grid layout performing much better than participants using the window layout. Hess et al. found that the type of screen layout used interacted with the delay between the times when a value was updated and when a question was asked about its status, as well as the number of variables being monitored. Overall, this experiment suggested that the grid layout provided unique spatial information that was beneficial in helping participants keep track of the rapidly changing information. This benefit might have come from the grid's role in supporting control processes needed to minimize interference in working-memory processes and stores, or from the additional spatial cues provided at encoding and retrieval. If the former were true, then one might expect spatial information to be a useful source of support for older adults by assisting them in initiating and coordinating control processes in keeping-track tasks.

EXPERIMENTAL OVERVIEW

This chapter describes two experiments designed to address questions about the relative effectiveness of alternative information displays to support younger and older adults' performance in keeping track of dynamically changing information. Moreover, it seeks to explore potential age differences that emerge as rapidly changing information must be encoded and retrieved. Several characteristics of the keeping-track task make it an excellent testbed for exploring age-related differences in memory performance. First, the keeping-track task requires participants to simultaneously process new information while they hold some of the outcomes of previous processing in working memory for later use—thus requiring both control processes and storage resources to be used. Second, the keeping-track task allows several different kinds of working-memory load to be explored. For example, pairing the mapping manipulation (many–one and one–many) with increasing numbers of to-be-updated attribute-object values has the potential of uncovering differential age effects of load across a range of working-memory loads. Finally, having different lengths of delay, that is, different response lags, between when a value is updated and when a question is asked about its value creates opportunities to assess potential differences in the effects of interference on younger and older adults. In addition having different lags also provides means of raising questions about the kinds of control processes required to encode and maintain the attribute values.

As in the Hess et al. (1994) study, we were explicitly interested in assessing the value of spatial-location information to support keeping-track performance. In these experiments we introduced differences in the kinds of materials participants kept track of, moving from highly verbal to visuospatial items. Specifically, because nearly all previous work with keeping-track tasks had used materials that placed large demands on the central executive and verbal working-memory subsystems, corresponding to Baddeley and Hitch's (1994) phonological loop, we attempted to create materials that were not inherently verbal or countable. Thus we hoped to shift demands to the visuospatial working-memory subsystem, corresponding to Baddeley and Hitch's (1994) visuospatial sketchpad. Further, each attribute category had four unique visuospatially represented states (see Fig. 8.2), and each category had its own set of four response keys.

In this study, both younger and older adults kept track of several attributes of one object, or one attribute of several objects, and periodically reported the current value of an attribute. These attribute–object values were presented in two different display formats. As shown at the top of Fig. 8.1, every attribute–object combination in the grid-screen condition was presented in a unique spatial location. Thus, participants in this condition had information about spatial location available to help support their performance. Alternatively, as shown at the bottom of Fig. 8.1, participants in the window-screen condition

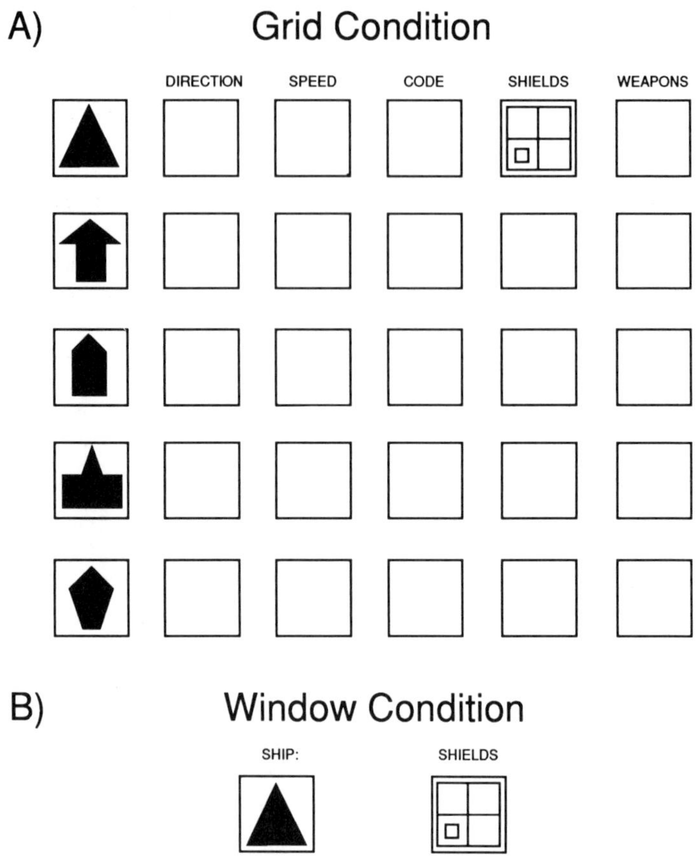

FIG. 8.1 (A) Example of the screen layout used in the grid condition. (B) Example of the screen layout used in the window condition. Both portions of the figure show how each display might appear as a value for the shields attribute is updated for one of the five alien ships.

saw the attribute–object information appear in a pair of windows at the center of the display screen. Here unique information about spatial location was not available as participants attempted to keep track of the various attribute–object pairings.

Based on our earlier work (Hess, Detweiler, & Ellis, 1994), we predicted that we would find significant differences between the two types of screen layouts, with the Grid layout supporting performance much better than the window layout. We expected this difference because participants using the grid should be able to take advantage of the additional spatial-location information to support control processes and/or to serve as additional encoding and retrieval cues not available in the window condition. We felt this benefit might be most pronounced for older adults, particularly if the additional spatial information provided by the grid could help them to initiate and maintain control processes needed to cope with the demands of continuously updating values. Further, we expected to see the same types of outcomes Yntema and Mueser (1960, 1962) reported, particularly because we insured that the values of the different attributes were very distinct from each other, just as Yntema and Mueser had done. Specifically, we expected participants to keep track of: (a) several attributes of one object better than one attribute of several different objects; (b) small numbers of variables better than larger numbers of variables; and (c) values with small numbers of intervening events better than larger ones.

EXPERIMENT 1

Method

Participants. Forty-three undergraduates were recruited from introductory psychology courses at The Pennsylvania State University, and these students participated in exchange for course credit. Three participants were excluded from analysis because they failed to follow instructions, leaving 20 in each screen condition. Participants served in one 50- to 60-minute session.

Equipment. Displays were shown on IBM-compatible microcomputers equipped with color VGA monitors set to emulate EGA. The Micro Experimental Laboratory (MEL) software (Schneider, 1988) was used to display stimuli, control timing, and collect responses.

Design, Procedure, and Materials. A 2 × 2 × 4 mixed-factorial design was used. *Screen Type* (grid or window) was the between-participants factor, and the kind of *Mapping* of attributes to objects (one-to-many or many-to-one), and *Number of Variables* (2, 3, 4, or 5) were the repeated factors. Participants were randomly assigned to one of the screen layout conditions, and completed eight blocks of trials created by crossing the mapping and number of variables factors. Thus, each block consisted of a randomly selected combination of 2, 3, 4, or 5 variables with a mapping of one attribute to many ships or many attributes to one ship. Block order was randomized for each participant, and rest breaks were provided between blocks. Self-paced instructions were presented on the computer in the form of a cover story explaining that the participant would act as a weapons officer defending a space station against alien attack. The instructions introduced the participant's particular screen layout (grid or window), together with icons of the alien ships (see Fig. 8.1) and examples of their attributes.

Figure 8.2 illustrates the five attributes employed (direction, speed, code, shields, and weapons), and the four values of each as they appeared on the keys used to enter responses. In contrast to Figs. 8.1 and 8.2, all five ship icons appeared in colors chosen to insure easy visibility and discriminability on the computer screen. Specifically, the ships were white against a black background, as was each line used to create the set of five attributes and their values. In addition, the small squares indicating direction were red, the bars indicating speed were red, the boxes indicating code status were medium blue, the small squares indicating shield status were dark blue, and the circle, triangle, square, and diamonds indicating weapons status were purple.

Attribute values were updated 80 times in each block of trials, and questions were posed about the most recent status of 20 values. To insure that questions were evenly distributed across the session, two questions were placed among each set of ten updates, with the constraint that no two questions ever appeared consecutively, that is, they did not appear consecutively within or between the groups of 10 updates. Participants placed their hands on two prepared hand prints at each end of the keyboard as attribute values were updated to prevent them from using their hands as external memory aids over the response keys. When a question appeared on the screen, participants were instructed to move one of their hands from the hand prints, and to enter the most recently presented value of the attribute needed to

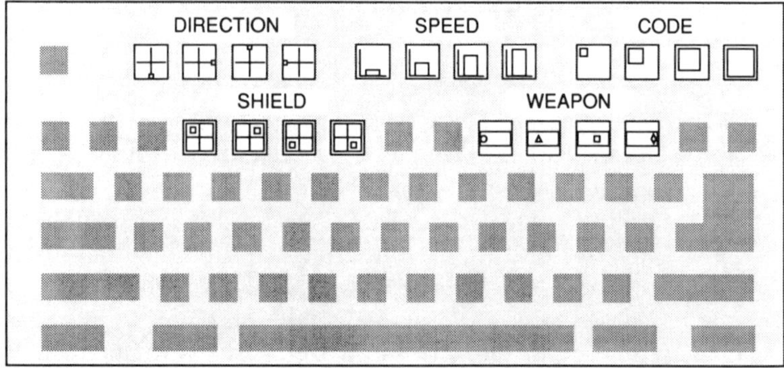

FIG. 8.2 Example of the 5 ship attributes and their 4 values as they appeared on the keyboard. When questioned about the status of an attribute, the participant pressed one of the 20 keys illustrated in the figure to enter his or her answer.

fire upon the enemy ship by pressing the appropriate key (see Fig. 8.2). Starting values for the attributes presented in each block were chosen randomly and displayed in addition to the 80 updated values and 20 questions.

When attribute values were updated, the following sequence of events occurred: (a) the box representing the attribute–ship combination to be updated turned black, (b) an icon representing the value of the attribute to be updated appeared centered in the box 800 msec later and remained on the screen for 1000 msec before the box returned to its prior "closed" state, and (c) 800 msec later the next update or question sequence began. On question trials, the box corresponding to the requested attribute-ship value turned red with a yellow question mark in its center. Participants had 10 seconds to respond. If they responded correctly, a picture of an exploding alien ship appeared on the screen; if they responded incorrectly, a picture of crosshairs in empty space appeared.

Grid Condition. As shown in Fig. 8.1, ships and attribute values were presented in a 5 row × 6 column grid of 2.54 cm^2 boxes, with rows spaced 0.64 cm and columns 1.27 cm apart. The leftmost column of the grid contained icons of five alien space ships, one in each box. The five columns to the right of the ships consisted of empty boxes with a heading at the top of each row, denoting which attribute would appear under it. The five attributes corresponded to each ship's: direction, speed, code status, shield status, and weapons status described in the cover story. Therefore, the Grid screen provided a unique spatial location for each attribute value that could be updated across the session.

Window Condition. As shown in Fig. 8.1, ships and attribute values were presented in two 2.54 cm^2 windows located in the center of the screen approximately 6.35 cm apart. The same attribute and ship information was presented as described for the Grid screen, except that it appeared only in these two windows. When attribute values were updated, the ship appeared in the left-hand window while the heading indicating the attribute being updated appeared over the right-hand window with the new value inside the window. When participants monitored many attributes of one ship, the ship presented in the window on the left never changed, and the window on the right displayed all attribute values. When participants monitored one attribute of many ships, the heading over the right-hand window remained the same while the alien ships and their corresponding attribute values changed.

Results and Discussion

In addition to exploring the effects of the Mapping and Number of Variables factors, previous keeping-track research has also examined the effect of the number of intervening events that occur between when an attribute-object value is displayed and when a question is asked about the status of that value (e.g., Yntema & Mueser, 1960, 1962). In most experimental designs of this type, the size of a "report lag" is constrained by the number of variables one must keep track of. As the number of variables increases, the mean number of events that can occur between an update and a question also increases. Because we wanted to treat both report lag and the number of variables monitored as factors in one analysis of variance (ANOVA), we devised a method to represent lag size in three groups (described below). Thus the full model for all analyses reported below was a four-way 2 (screen type) × 2 (mapping) × 4 (number of variables) × 3 (lag size) mixed factorial, with screen type as the between-participant factor.

Here we want to point out that the lag size groups do not directly represent the number of intervening events between an update and a question. Rather, they represent groups of report lags constructed to meet two criteria: the mean values of report lag within a group had to be approximately equal across levels of number of variables, and the proportion of total observations in each group had to be approximately equal across levels of number of variables. We created these lag size groups by using only report lags of 10 or smaller, and dividing them into three groups. This constraint excluded less than 15% of the total observations, and insured that the largest lag group did not include extreme and infrequent lags. The composition of these groups, in terms of the number of intervening events that occurred between an update and a question, was identical for all levels of number of variables. The small-lag group contained observations with report lags of 1, the medium-lag group with lags of 2 or 3, and the large-lag groups with lags between 4 and 10. Mean accuracies and response times were calculated for each experimental cell, by subject, and all analyses were conducted on these mean data.

Accuracy. The overall mean proportion of correct responses was .82 in the grid condition and .74 in the window condition. An ANOVA conducted on the mean proportion correct revealed reliable main effects of screen type, $F(1, 38) = 5.11, p < .03, MS_e = .3257$, mapping, $F(1, 38) = 8.52, p < .01, MS_e = .0510$, number of variables, $F(3, 114) = 33.16, p < .00$ $MS_e = .0413$, and lag size, $F(2, 76) = 83.44, p < .00$, $MS_e = .0651$. Participants' superior performance in the grid screen condition suggests that the availability of spatial cues was beneficial at encoding, retrieval or both. The main effects of lag size and number of variables were also in the expected direction: The mean proportion correct declined as the number of variables increased and as lag size increased. Further analyses revealed a significant Number of Variables × Lag Size interaction, $F(6, 228) = 3.31$, $p < .00$, $MS_e = .0288$. This interaction suggests that the combined load imposed by these variables had a significant effect on performance that was most evident at high levels of both variables.

Figure 8.3A shows the mean proportion correct for the three levels of lag size across levels of number of variables. First, notice that performance declines as the number of variables increases, especially with large lags. Lag size also interacted significantly with screen type, such that the difference between performance in the grid and window conditions was smaller for the small Lag group relative to the other two groups $F(2, 76) = 3.01$, $p < .06$, $MS_e = .0651$. Given that the small-lag group contained only lags of 1, and the apparent lack of an increasing separation in performance across all three levels of lag size, this interaction offers only weak support for the notion that the benefits of spatial support were apparent at higher levels of working-memory load.

Analyses also revealed significant interactions between the mapping factor and the screen type, $F(1, 38) = 8.18$, $p < .01$, $MS_e = .0510$, number of variables, $F(3, 114) = 3.14$, $p < .03$, $MS_e = .0481$, and lag size factors, $F(2, 76) = .06$, $p < 2.94$, $MS_e = .0303$. Viewed together, these interactions suggest that keeping track of one attribute of many objects is more difficult than keeping track of many attributes of one object when the load on working memory is greatest. When spatial-location information was unavailable in the window screen condition, the mapping effect was present, but when it was available in the grid screen condition the mapping effect was absent. Further, the mapping effect for the window screen condition increased as the number of variables to be remembered and lag size increased. Figures 8.4A and 8.5A show the mean proportion correct for each screen type by mapping condition across levels of lag size and number of variables respectively. These results are strikingly similar, in that both reveal the increasing mapping effect in the window screen condition, but not in the grid screen condition. Thus, it appears that the grid layout provided valuable support not present in the window layout that could be used to offset the demands imposed by higher variable loads and longer lags between when a value was updated and when a question was asked about it.

Reaction Time. The reaction time (RT) data reflect the average amount of time (in msec) that elapsed between the onset of a red

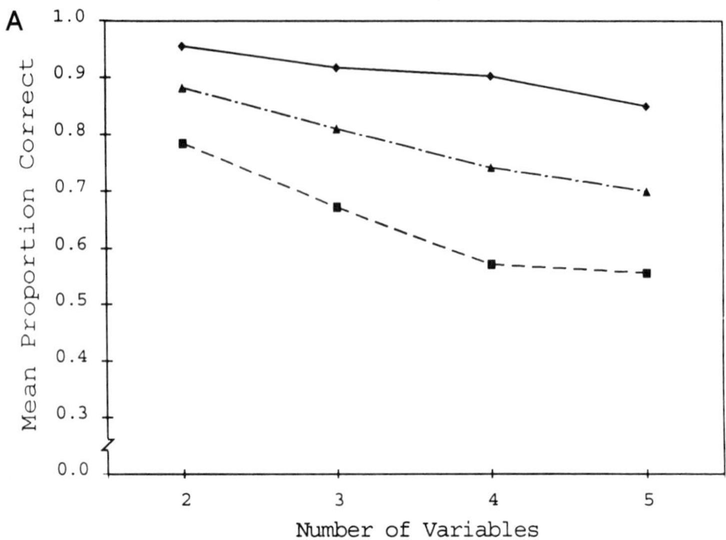

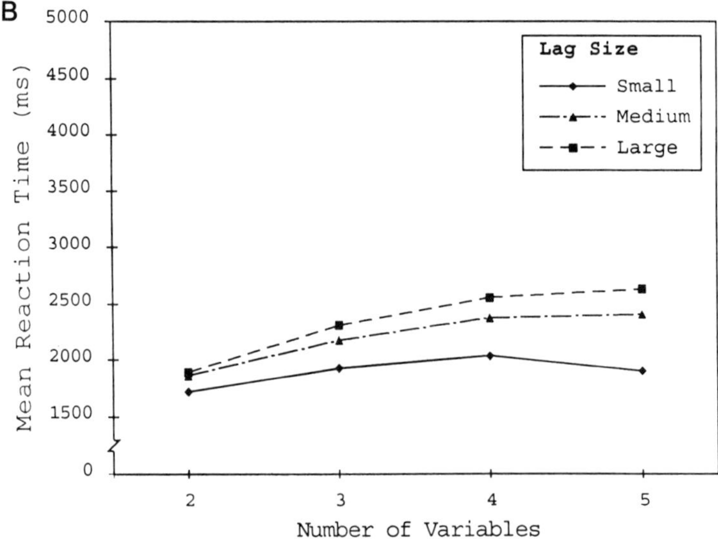

FIG. 8.3 A. Mean proportion correct for small, medium, and large Lags across levels of the Number of Variables. B. Mean RT for small, medium, and large Lags across levels of the Number of Variables participants were required to update, Experiment 1.

question box and when a correct response was entered. The overall mean RT for correct responses was 2159 msec in the grid condition and 2143 msec in the window condition. An overall ANOVA conducted on mean RTs revealed reliable main effects of mapping, $F(1, 38) = 53.06$,

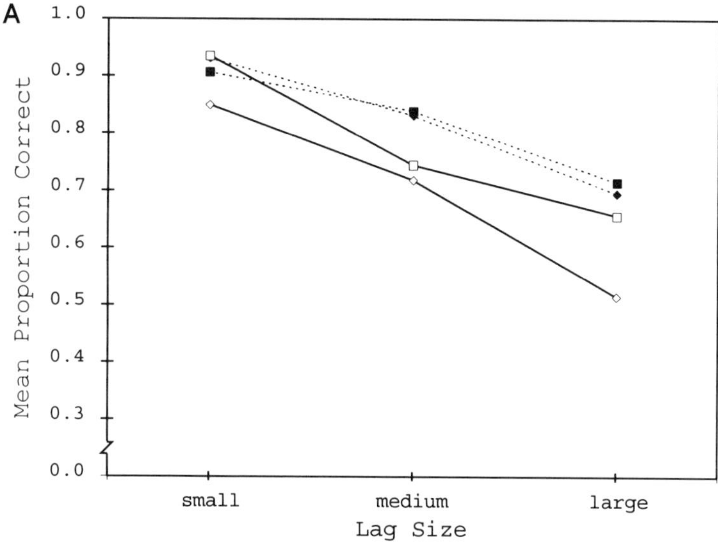

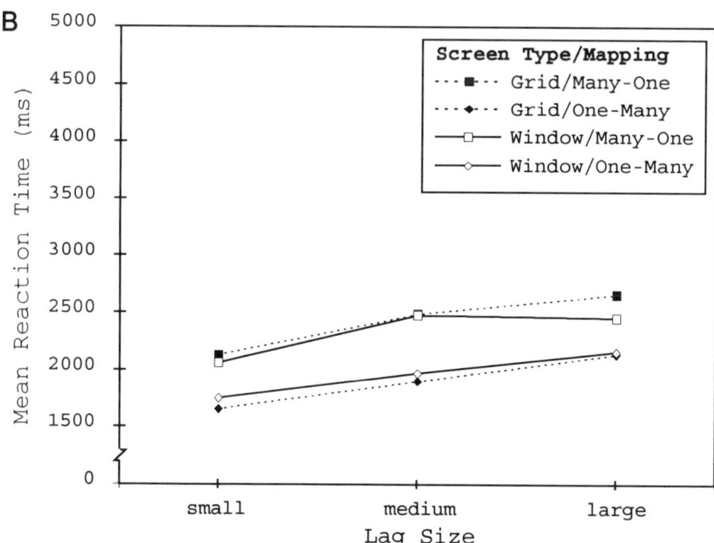

FIG. 8.4 A. Mean proportion correct for the grid and window layouts by mapping condition for small, medium, and large lags. B. Mean RT for the grid and window layouts by mapping condition for small, medium, and large lags, Experiment 1.

$p < .00$, $MS_e = 913902.20$, number of variables, $F(3, 114) = 25.07$, $p < .00$, $MS_e = 514385.57$, and lag size, $F(2, 76) = 52.21$, $p < .00$, $MS_e = 327508.26$. Number of variables and lag size behaved as expected: As each increased, the mean time to respond also increased. Further, as

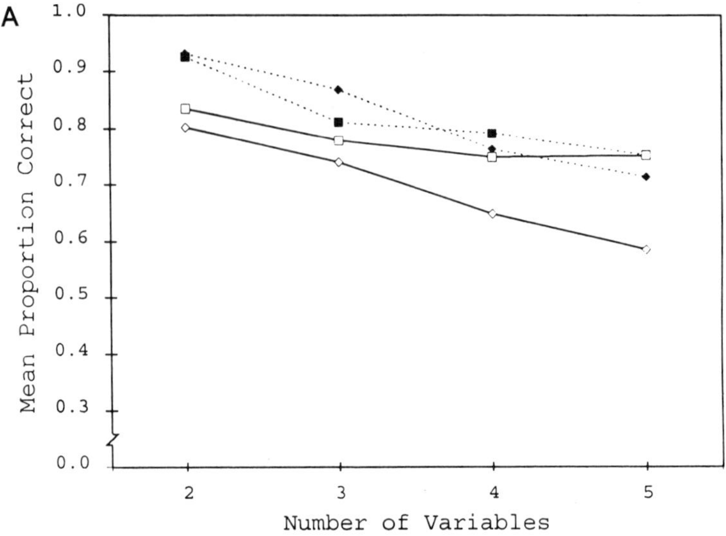

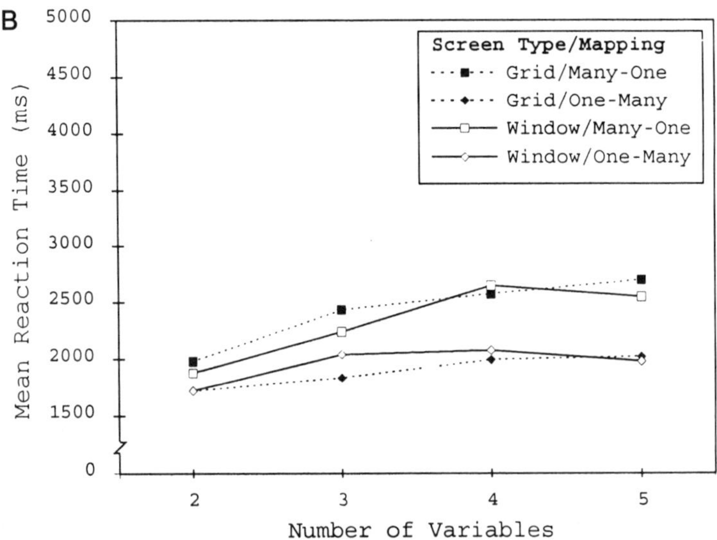

FIG. 8.5 A. Mean proportion correct for the grid and window layouts by mapping condition across levels of the number of variables. B. Mean RT for the grid and window layouts by mapping condition across levels of the number of variables, Experiment 1.

found in the accuracy results, there was a significant Number of Variables × Lag Size interaction, $F(6, 228) = 5.60$, $p < .00$, $MS_e = 203878.23$. Figure 8.3B presents the mean RT for each lag size across levels of number of variables. This graph complements the accuracy data by showing an orderly change in performance across this combination of variables. However, notice that the mapping effect present in the RT data is markedly more pronounced than that found in the accuracy data. Further, there was no main effect of screen type, and screen type did not interact with any other variable; thus, the mapping effect in RT was present regardless of screen type.

Further analyses revealed a significant Mapping × Number of Variables interaction, $F(3, 114) = 3.20$, $p < .03$, $MS_e = 641505.45$. Participants responded to questions about one attribute of many ships faster than they responded to questions about one of many attributes of one ship, regardless of the number of variables. This difference increased, however, as the number of variables increased. Notice that these data stand in contrast to the accuracy data and suggest that some type of speed-accuracy tradeoff may have occurred. Figures 8.4B and 8.5B show the mean RT for each screen type by mapping condition across levels of lag size and number of variables respectively. These figures show a clear RT advantage of the one-to-many mapping. Also, when compared to the accuracy graphs showing the same combinations of variables (Figs. 8.4A and 8.5A), it is striking that the mapping variable exerted such a dominant effect on RT, while the screen type effects which dominated the accuracy data seemed to be absent. The four-way Screen Type × Mapping × Number of Variables × Lag Size interaction was also significant, $F(6, 228) = 2.19$, $p < .05$, $MS_e = 219510.27$. This complex interaction is probably due to differences between the grid and window conditions (between-participants factors) at some combinations of lag size and number of variables. These fluctuations are probably best attributed to random between-groups variation in the data.

In summary, Experiment 1 showed a substantial benefit in accuracy when the attribute–ship values were presented at separate spatial locations in the grid condition, as opposed to when they were presented in two locations in the window condition. Thus, although both the grid and window layouts required participants to keep track of the same types of attribute–ship values, the grid layout served an important role in elevating accuracy. Further, in contrast to Yntema and Mueser's (1960, 1962) results, the benefit of mapping many attributes to one ship over one attribute to many ships, emerged only in the window condition. Therefore, having the grid locations available at time of encoding and retrieval seems to have eliminated the mapping effect. However, when the grid locations were not available, the mapping effect was present. With respect to working-memory load, as participants had to keep track of more values, their abilities to correctly recall those values declined. Accuracy also declined as the number of intervening events increased between when an attribute-ship value was updated and when a question was asked about that value.

The foregoing benefits of using additional spatial support, and declines in performance with increasing working-memory load, need to be qualified in terms of how quickly participants responded when they answered correctly. First, although no mapping effect was found in the accuracy data, a strong mapping effect did emerge in the RT data. Regardless of whether participants used grid or window layouts, they responded substantially faster when one attribute was paired with many ships than when many attributes were paired with one ship. Further, although participants generally took more time to respond as the number of variables increased, the magnitudes of these RT costs were markedly greater for the many–one mappings, regardless of whether participants used the grid or window layouts. Finally, on the whole, it took participants more time to respond with the correct answer as the number of intervening events increased between when an attribute-ship value was updated and when a question was asked about that value.

EXPERIMENT 2

Experiment 2 examined the types of age-related deficits reflected in older participants' abilities to keep track of dynamically changing visual–spatial information. The keeping-track task provides an excellent means of exploring potential age differences for several reasons. First, this task requires participants to simultaneously process incoming information and hold some of the products of prior processing in working memory for later use. Second, unlike some working-memory tasks, the keeping-track task is well suited for exploring different kinds of storage and processing loads. Third, grouping the number of intervening events into small, medium, and large lags also offers an opportunity to explore how length of delay and intervening-processing demands between when a value is updated and when a question is asked about that value influence performance. Finally, the screen type manipulation offers an excellent means of addressing how effective these differences in display layout are in supporting working memory under different loads.

As predicted in Experiment 1, we expected participants in the grid condition to perform better than participants in the window condition, because they should have been able to use the spatial-location information to help them keep track. According to the environmental-support hypothesis (Craik, 1986), older adults who have experienced age-related declines in processing resources may find tasks that impose effortful, self-initiating encoding and retrieval processes particularly difficult. Thus, if the tasks can be re-engineered to reduce the load on encoding and retrieval processes, for example, by providing environmental or contextual support, then this should be reflected in increases in accuracy. Therefore, in contrast to Experiment 1, we predicted that the spatial support provided by the grid layout might be even more important for the older adults, and that the differences between the two groups might be even greater in Experiment 2. As in Experiment 1, we also predicted that the older adults would: (a) keep track of several attributes of one object better than one attribute of several different objects; (b) perform better with small Numbers of Variables than with larger numbers; and (c) perform better with small numbers of intervening events than larger ones.

Method

Participants. Forty healthy older adults were recruited from a pool of volunteers from the greater Detroit area and paid for their participation in the study. Three participants were unable to complete the task, and data from 3 others were lost due to computer error. Of the remaining participants, 18 were randomly assigned to the grid condition and 16 to the window condition (M = 71 years; SD = 6.6 years; range = 62–82 years), and none reported having difficulty reading the characters displayed on the computer screen. Participants took approximately 70 minutes to complete the tasks.

Design, Procedure, and Materials. All procedures, materials, and equipment were the same as used in Experiment 1, except older adults performed the tasks rather than college students, and older adults took more time to complete the tasks.

Results and Discussion

The data and ANOVA analyses for the older adults' data were treated in the same way as described in the Results section of Experiment 1. The full ANOVA model was a 2 (screen type) × 2 (mapping) × 4 (number of variables) × 3 (lag size) mixed factorial. Selected results of a combined ANOVA of Experiments 1 and 2, treating age as a variable, are included at the end of this section.

Accuracy. The overall mean proportion of correct responses was .50 in the grid condition and .37 in the window condition. An ANOVA conducted on the mean proportion correct revealed reliable main effects of screen type, $F(1, 31) = 9.60$, $p < .00$, $MS_e = .3149$, mapping, $F(1, 31) = 7.51$, $p < .01$, $MS_e = .1224$, number of variables, $F(3, 93)$

$= 3.39, p < .02\ MS_e = .0470$, and lag size, $F(2, 62) = 124.94, p < .00, MS_e = .1056$. As in Experiment 1, participants performed best in the grid screen condition, suggesting that the availability of spatial information was beneficial at encoding, retrieval or both. Similarly, accuracy decreased as both the number of variables monitored and the lag size increased. This pattern is consistent with the results of Experiment 1 and previous research. Interestingly, however, the decline in performance between the small and medium lag sizes was larger than that between the medium and large lag sizes. Unlike the results of Experiment 1, the older adults' performance was extremely sensitive to interference from intervening events between when a value was updated and when a question was asked about that value.

Figure 8.6A displays the mean proportion correct for each lag size by number of variables factor. First, notice the nearly flat performance on the medium and large lag size groups across number of variables. This pattern suggests that the older adults performed near floor when lags greater than one occurred between when a value was updated and when a question was asked about that value. A marginally significant Lag Size × Screen-Type interaction also appeared, $F(2, 62) = 2.54, p < .09, MS_e = .1056$. Figure 8.7A shows the mean proportion correct for each lag size by screen type by mapping factors. In contrast to the results of Experiment 1, this interaction seems to stem from a small benefit of the grid screen at the largest lag size. Recall that in Experiment 1, accuracy was very high for the smallest lag group, and there was little difference between screen types; however, for the older adults a clear stratification appeared in the screen type and mapping means at the smallest lag size. This pattern is further supported by a marginally significant Mapping × Lag Size interaction, $F(2, 62) = 2.96, p < .06, MS_e = .0524$. Although these two interactions do not meet the generally accepted 5% level of significance, they suggest that the older adult performance is near floor at large lag sizes which the additional spatial support does not seem to mitigate.

The main effect of mapping was in the opposite direction for the older adults relative to the young adults in Experiment 1. Figure 8.8A shows the mean proportion correct for each screen type by mapping by number of variables factors. This graph clearly shows that regardless of screen type, the older adults performed best when the values to be remembered were one attribute of many ships. This result stands in strong contrast to the younger adults' performance, which was best when they kept track of multiple attributes of a single object in the window condition but unclear in the grid condition. The Mapping × Number of Variables interaction suggested by this graph was not significant, $p > .1$, although the pattern of means seems to indicate that this mapping effect was especially robust when participants

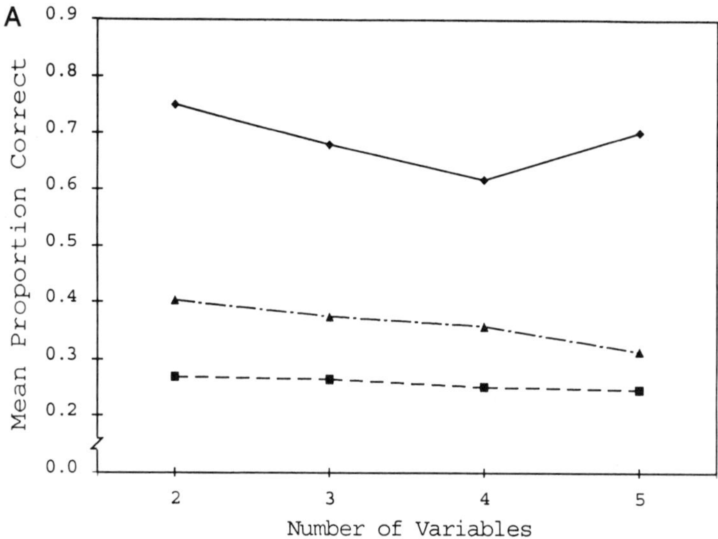

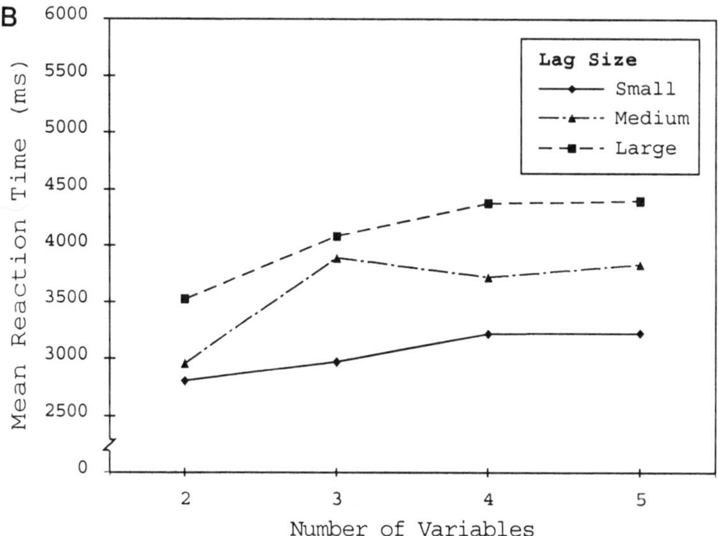

FIG. 8.6 A. Mean proportion correct for small, medium, and large lags across levels of the number of variables participants were required to update. B. Mean RT for small, medium, and large lags across levels of the number of variables, Experiment 2.

updated more than two values. This mapping reversal may be attributable to the fact that participants had to select one of four possible keys (one bank of four keys) in the one-attribute condition, regardless of the number of variables, while in the many-attributes case they had

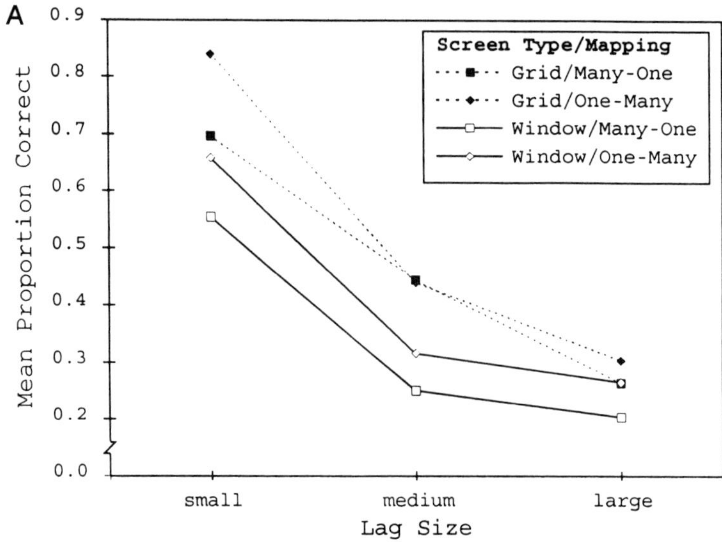

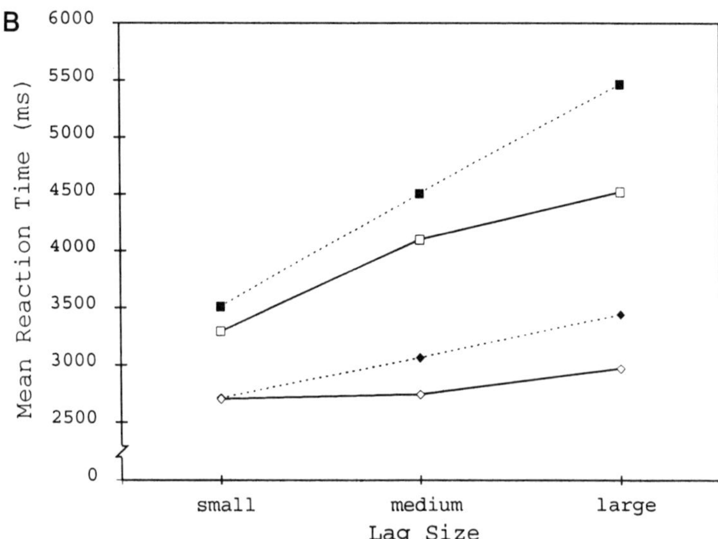

FIG. 8.7 A. Mean proportion correct for the grid and window layouts by mapping condition for small, medium, and large lags. B. Mean RT for the grid and window layouts by mapping condition for small, medium, and large lags, Experiment 2.

to select one key from as many as 20 keys (five banks of four keys). Part of the working-memory load associated with keeping track of the correct values involved keeping track of the appropriate response spaces. If the older adults had trouble remembering and controlling the

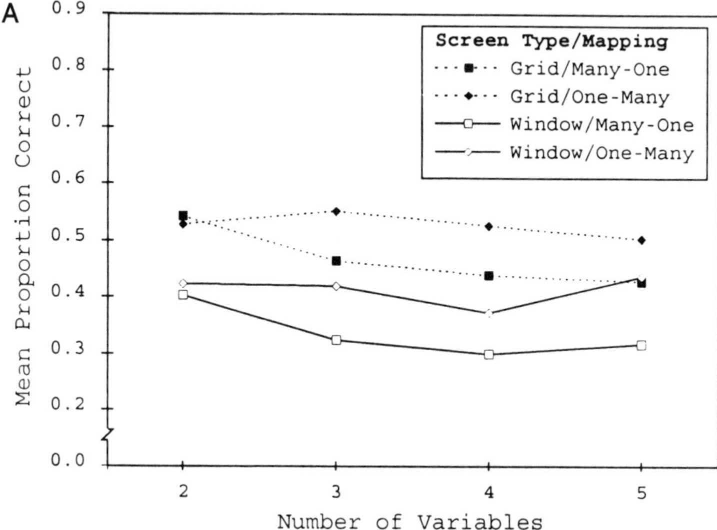

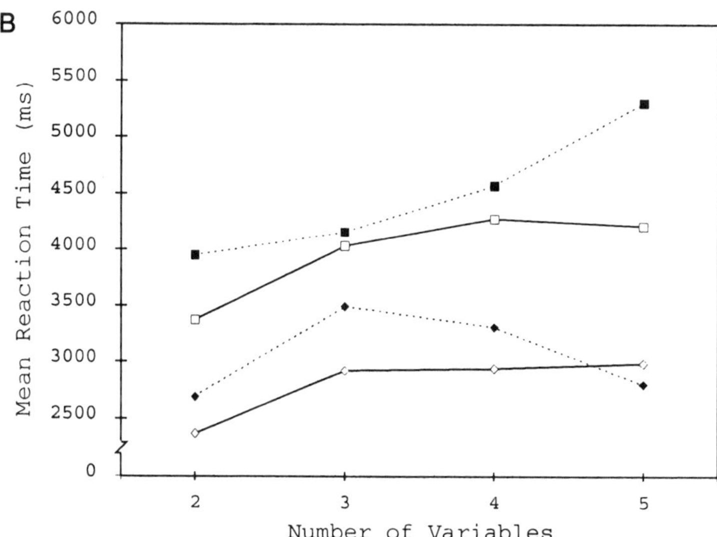

FIG. 8.8 A. Mean proportion correct for the grid and window layouts by mapping condition across levels of the number of variables. B. Mean RT for the grid and window layouts by Mapping condition across levels of the number of variables, Experiment 2.

response portion of the task, this pattern of results might reflect such difficulties, even if remembering multiple attributes of a single object were an easier task—based on the chunking explanation offered by Yntema and Mueser (1960, 1962).

Reaction Time. The overall mean time to respond to questions in the grid condition was 3783 msec and 3387 msec in the window condition. An overall ANOVA conducted on the mean RTs revealed reliable main effects of mapping, $F(1, 31) = 102.51$, $p < .00$, MS_e = 3229075.70, number of variables, $F(3, 93) = 13.72$, $p < .00$, MS_e = 1600898.07, and lag size, $F(2, 62) = 54.44$, $p < .00$, MS_e = 1315851.61. As expected, as the number of variables and lag size increased, the mean time to respond also increased. Figure 8.6B shows the mean RT for each lag size by number of variables factor. The interaction suggested between these variables was not significant, $p > .1$, however, a significant Number of Variables × Lag Size × Screen Type interaction, $F(6, 186) = 3.08$, $p < .01$, $MS_e = 1245578.19$ did occur. As in Experiment 1, the effects of lag size were most evident when participants monitored more than two variables. The Lag Size × Screen Type interaction was also significant, $F(2, 62) = 25.67$, $p < .02$, $MS_e = 1315815.61$.

Figure 8.7B presents the mean RT for each lag size by screen type by mapping factor combination. In both the grid and window conditions, the time to respond increased as the lag size increased between when a value was updated and when a question was asked about that value, however, a slight speed–accuracy tradeoff seems to have occurred, such that the time to respond to many attributes of one object was greatest in the grid condition. The pattern of RTs shown in Figure 8.7B provides important clues about the nature of the older adults' retrieval processes with the different screen types and mapping conditions. Recall that the younger adults' RTs also revealed a striking separation between the many–one and one–many mappings (Figure 8.4B); however, there was only a small cost of increasing lag size for both Mapping conditions. In contrast, the older adults' RTs not only revealed a striking separation between the two types of mappings, but more interestingly, revealed substantial increases in mean time to respond as lag size increased. In addition, it is likely that because the many attributes portion of the grid screen condition had such high RTs, this condition is responsible for the Lag Size × Screen Type interaction.

Further analyses revealed significant Mapping × Number of Variables, $F(3, 93) = 5.73$, $p < .00$, $MS_e = 1486806.87$, and Mapping × Lag Size interactions, $F(2, 62) = 25.67$, $p < .00$, $MS_e = 794619.03$. The three-way Mapping × Number-of-Variables × Screen-Type interaction, $F(3, 93) = 4.57$, $p < .01$, $MS_e = 1486806.87$ was also significant. Figure 8.8B shows the mean RT for the number of variables by screen type by mapping factors. Notice that across both lag size (Fig. 8.7B) and number of variables (Fig. 8.8B), the increase in RT was steeper for the many–one mappings than the one–many mappings. This pattern was especially evident in the grid screen condition shown in Fig. 8.8B, resulting in the three-way interaction noted above. Perhaps the most notable feature of these data, and consistent with Experiment 1, is the contrast between the RT and accuracy results. As reflected in Figs. 8.8A and 8.8B, the effect of screen type is evident in the accuracy results, and the effect of mapping is evident in the RT results.

In summary, the results of Experiment 2 were largely consistent with those of Experiment 1 with a few notable exceptions. As did the young adults in Experiment 1, the older adults benefited from the presence of spatial support in the grid screen and suffered as the number of variables and lag size increased. Interestingly, however, the older adults' accuracy was highest when they responded to questions about one attribute of many objects, regardless of screen type. The younger adults' results showed a complex interaction in which a mapping effect appeared only in the window condition, and this was in the opposite direction of the effect found in the older adults' results.

COMBINED ANALYSIS OF YOUNGER AND OLDER ADULTS' PERFORMANCE

Due to the complexity of the combined ANOVA model results, particularly higher-order interactions, and the statistical problems inherent in comparing two groups known to differ in variance, here we report only results that have a direct impact on our informal comparison of Experiments 1 and 2. The full model used in this analysis was a 2 (age) × 2 (screen type) × 2 (mapping) × 4 (number of variables) mixed factorial. Overall mean proportion correct and overall mean time to respond were computed in separate analyses.

Overall main effects of age were evident in both accuracy, $F(1, 69) = 158.20$, $p < .00$, $MS_e = .3208$, and RT $F(1, 69) = 138.34$, $p < .00$, $MS_e = 6449294.42$. As suggested in the individual analyses, a significant Mapping × Age interaction appeared in accuracy, $F(1, 69) = 16.00$, $p < .00$, $MS_e = .0831$, but the main effect of mapping did not appear ($p > .35$). This failure to find a mapping main effect was due to the alternation of effects of each mapping condition for the younger and older adults. Therefore, this pattern is consistent with the suggested mapping reversal discussed in the previous section. Interestingly, a robust mapping main effect did appear in the RT data, $F(1, 69) = 168.60$, $p < .00$, $MS_e = 1954052.61$. Thus, the reversal seen in accuracy was absent in RT. Further, strong effects of number of variables and lag size were present for both the younger and older adults, as found in the individual analyses. The presence of a Number of Variables × Age interaction in accuracy, $F(3, 207) = 6.29$, $p < .00$, $MS_e = .0438$, and interactions between lag size and age in both accuracy, $F(2, 138) = 20.30$, $p < .00$, $MS_e = .0833$, and RT, $F(2, 138) = 16.48$, $p < .00$, $MS_e = 771530.40$, corroborate the suggestion that overall working-memory load had large consequences for the older adults' performance.

GENERAL DISCUSSION

The primary goals of this study were to explore sources of age-related decrements in working memory and to assess the relative value of using unique versus the same spatial locations to support keeping track of updated information. We predicted that if working-memory abilities decline with age, then age-related differences should be reflected in both how accurately and quickly older adults could keep track of rapidly changing information relative to younger adults. Further, we expected the grid layout to support both younger and older adults' performance better than the window layout and differences between the two layouts to become greater as the load on working memory increased.

Experiments 1 and 2 showed that accuracy was better in the grid condition than in the window condition. Although all participants kept track of the same types of attribute–ship values, the unique spatial locations in the grid condition provided environmental or contextual support that assisted them in encoding and/or retrieving the attribute–ship values better than when the same two locations were reused in the Window condition, for both younger and older adults. Further, consistent with Yntema and Mueser's (1960, 1962) findings, participants kept track of attribute values with small numbers of intervening events better than larger ones, and small numbers of variables better than larger ones. As expected, the older adults were less accurate and required more time to respond than the younger adults. In addition, several other age-related differences are worth considering. Although these differences are subtle, given the overall consistency in the patterns of results, they may be best explained as reflecting decrements in the older adults' abilities to use working-memory control processes to create and maintain goals and plans needed to successfully keep track of the dynamically changing information.

As Kirchner (1958), Craik (1986), Dobbs and Rule (1989) and others have all suggested, older adults tend to have more difficulty than younger adults when tasks involve sizable investments in encoding effort and/or require much information to be actively held and manipulated in working memory. The keeping-track task requires just these sorts of investments, and we believe demanding control processes (see Rabbitt, 1981; Shallice, 1994) are needed to successfully encode and retrieve the dynamically changing information. For example, control processes are involved in encoding and updating presented attributes, rehearsing and maintaining the most recent values of those attributes, and selecting the correct response given the status and mapping of attributes to objects. Moreover, in a task this complex, it is especially crucial that participants be able to maintain a balance in how they interleave multiple goals to accomplish the overall task, that is, participants must balance how they actively attend to, encode, and rehearse relevant information while coordinating the links between incoming information and the attributes and objects to which that information is linked. Also, when a participant sees a new attribute value to be updated, he or she must update the new value without disturbing any of the other current attribute values; for example, if the speed of a ship changes, he or she may have to update that value while maintaining the current values of its weapons and code status. Thus some of the coordinative effort involves creating and maintaining links between environmental inputs, for example, spatial location and/or the name of the attribute and the mental representations of the attribute values held in working memory.

Additional coordinative effort is required to intermittently rehearse unchanged attribute values in the face of dynamically changing information, and to select responses based on environmentally cued information. Participants must be able to create and maintain a continuous stream of goals or plans. Presumably participants will not perform this task well if they can not effectively encode, rehearse, and maintain links between the representations held in working memory and their environmental counterparts (cues and response keys) across the duration of a block. If these processes are successfully executed, then participants should be able to keep track of changing information with little cost to the represented information which does not change, that is, other represented information that is not involved in the current update or question. If participants cannot maintain multiple goals in succession, or if executing one goal, for example, encoding a new value interferes with or fails to cue other goals, for example, rehearsing other values, then one would expect problems in keeping track of values beyond a lag of one. To illustrate, recall that younger and older adults' accuracies differed as a function of lag size (see Figs. 8.3A and 8.6A). Younger adults showed a gradual decrease in accuracy as lag size increased, while older adults showed an abrupt decrease in accuracy when Lag Size was greater than one. This pattern of results might be expected if older adults had difficulty maintaining old information while simultaneously updating a current attribute value.

Other interpretations of these data are also possible. For instance, older adults may have been able to initiate, maintain, and interleave a series of encoding, rehearsal, and response operations, but were more likely to suffer the effects of proactive interference. Although this interpretation is plausible, we feel this is an unlikely explanation for the observed decrements; if it were true, the older adults' performance would have been best in the many–one mapping condition in which each attribute had a unique set of four states. Thus, interference should have been least relative to the one–many condition in which every value to be remembered was drawn from the same set of four states. This was not the case. Thus we suggest that the older adults' poorer performance at lag values greater than one was driven largely by reduced abilities to acquire, maintain, and/or execute the control processes needed to keep track of the dynamically changing information. Further, we believe the different patterns of responses to the mapping manipulation found for the two age groups reflect deficits in the older adults' abilities to maintain the appropriate links between represented information and the response space. In the many–one mapping conditions, participants had to maintain links between represented information and between 8–20 keys on the keyboard, whereas in the one–many mapping condition, participants only had to maintain links with one bank of four keys. We propose that older adults had more difficulty maintaining these links than did the younger adults.

Many tasks performed in the workplace and home exhibit characteristics similar to those found in the keeping-track experiments. For example, younger and older adults must routinely use working-memory control processes to: encode information into and retrieve it from working memory over different temporal intervals; coordinate the contents of working memory with other information from long-term memory or the task environment, and schedule mental activities (e.g., encoding, rehearsing, and initiating responses) to minimize interference among contents held in working memory. Recently there has been a growing appreciation of the limited nature of control processes, as well as concern with developing techniques to help offset their limitations. For example, Sweller (1993) has reviewed compelling evidence that providing worked examples and minimizing the extent to which learners must divide their attention can significantly reduce cognitive load and promote more effective learning. Zhang and Norman (1994) also reported that participants benefited from opportunities to use the physical environment to off load working-memory demands, resulting in dramatic effects in their abilities to solve problems and reduce errors. Similarly, Ballard, Hayhoe, and Pelz (1995) found that when participants were allowed to choose their own task parameters in an everyday hand–eye task, they used eye movements to defer gathering task relevant information until just before it was needed—in efforts to minimize their working-memory load.

Although it may not be possible to offset or eliminate all of the factors that place excessive demands on control processes and contribute to working-memory load, we believe it is possible and desirable to redesign many existing displays and task environments to support working memory. We also believe that as information and display designers learn more about how to distribute processing demands in the physical world, both younger and older adults will benefit. Although the importance of consistency has been stressed in discussions of age-related research (see Fisk & Rogers, 1991), much additional work is still needed to understand how to take advantage of various consistencies to support control processes, in addition to fostering the acquisition of automatic processes. The foregoing experiments show that changes in spatial layout can have significant consequences for how accurately and quickly changing values can be monitored and updated—for both older and younger adults. Moreover, we believe many other types of consistencies can be used to lessen the burden on limited control processes and working memory. Consistencies that could offset placekeeping demands, both at encoding and retrieval, seem particularly worth exploring. For example, presenting items in a consistent order would provide a predictable structure for the information to be remembered. And having all of changing information constantly available on the display would provide many more opportunities for performers to encode and rehearse the changing values.

REFERENCES

Baddeley, A. (1986). *Working memory*. New York: Oxford University Press.

Baddeley, A. D., & Hitch, G. (1994). Developments in the concept of working memory. *Neuropsychology, 8*, 485–493.

Ballard, D. H., Hayhoe, M. M., & Pelz, J. B. (1995). Memory representations in natural tasks. *Journal of Cognitive Neuroscience, 7*, 66–80.

Case, R., Kurland, D. M., & Goldberg, J. (1982). Operational efficiency and the growth of short-term memory span. *Journal of Experimental Psychology, 28*, 386–404.

Chi, M. T. H. (1976). Short-term memory limitations in children: Capacity or processing deficits? *Memory & Cognition, 4*, 559–572.

Chi, M. T. H. (1978). Knowledge structures and memory development. In R. Siegler (Ed.), *Children's thinking: What develops?* (pp. 73–96). Hillsdale, NJ: Lawrence Erlbaum Associates.

Craik, F. I. M. (1986). A functional account of age differences in memory. In F. Klix & H. Hagendorf (Eds.), *Human memory and cognitive capabilities: Mechanisms and performances* (pp. 409–422). New York: Elsevier.

Dobbs, A. R., & Rule, B. G. (1989). Adult age differences in working memory. *Psychology and Aging, 4,* 500–503.

Fisk, A. D., & Rogers, W. A. (1991). Development of skilled performance: An age-related perspective. In D. Damos (Ed.), *Multiple-task performance* (pp. 415–443). Bristol, PA: Taylor & Francis.

Gick, M. L., Craik, F. I. M., & Morris, N. (1988). Task complexity and age differences in working memory. *Memory & Cognition, 16,* 353–361.

Hess, S. M., Detweiler, M. C., & Ellis, R. D. (1994). The effects of display layout on monitoring and updating system states. In *Proceedings of the Human Factors and Ergonomics Society—38th annual meeting* (pp. 1336–1340). Santa Monica, CA: The Human Factors and Ergonomics Society.

Inman, V. W., & Parkinson, S. R. (1983). Differences in Brown-Peterson recall as a function of age and retention interval. *Journal of Gerontology, 8,* 58–64.

Kirchner, W. K. (1958). Age differences in short-term retention of rapidly changing information. *Journal of Experimental Psychology, 55,* 352–358.

Morris, N., Gick, M. L., & Craik, F. I. M. (1988). Processing resources and age differences in working memory. *Memory & Cognition, 16,* 362–366.

Rabbitt, P. (1981). Human ageing and disturbances of memory control processes underlying "intelligent" performance of some cognitive tasks. In M. P. Friedman, J. P. Das, & N. O'Connor (Eds.), *Intelligence and learning* (pp. 427–439). New York: Plenum Press.

Salthouse, T. (1990). Working memory as a processing resource in cognitive aging. *Developmental Review, 10,* 101–124.

Salthouse, T. (1994). The aging of working memory. *Neuropsychology, 8,* 535–543.

Salthouse, T., & Babcock, R. L. (1991). Decomposing adult age differences in working memory. *Developmental Psychology, 27,* 763–776.

Schneider, W. (1988). Micro Experimental Laboratory: An integrated system for IBM PC compatibles. *Behaviour Research Methods, Instruments, and Computers, 20,* 206–217.

Schneider, W., & Detweiler, M. (1987). A connectionist/control architecture for working memory. In G. H. Bower (Ed.), *The psychology of learning and motivation* (Vol. 21, pp. 53–119). San Diego, CA: Academic Press.

Shallice, T. (1994). Multiple levels of control processes. In C. Umiltà & M. Moscovitch (Eds.), *Attention and performance XV: Conscious and nonconscious information processing* (pp. 395–420). Cambridge, MA: MIT Press.

Sweller, J. (1993). Some cognitive processes and their consequences for the organisation and presentation of information. *Australian Journal of Psychology, 45,* 1–8.

Van der Linden, M., Brédart, S., & Beerten, A. (1994). Age-related differences in updating working memory. *British Journal of Psychology, 85,* 145–152.

Yntema, D. B., & Mueser, G. E. (1960). Remembering the present states of a number of variables. *Journal of Experimental Psychology, 60,* 18–22.

Yntema, D. B., & Mueser, G. E. (1962). Keeping track of variables that have few or many states. *Journal of Experimental Psychology, 63,* 391–395.

Yntema, D. B., & Schulman, G. M. (1967). Response selection in keeping track of several things at once. *Acta Psychologica, 27,* 316–324.

Zhang, J., & Norman, D. A. (1994). Representations in distributed cognitive tasks. *Cognitive Science, 18,* 87–122.

CHAPTER 9

Assessing Age-Related Differences in the Long-Term Retention of Skills

Wendy A. Rogers
University of Georgia

Consider a retired couple taking up golf at age 60. They may spend the summer and fall months developing golf skills. What will happen to those skills after the winter months, during which time they are unable to play? Would the older golfers' abilities decline more than younger golfers' would in a similar situation? How much practice should individuals engage in during those winter months to maintain their skill levels? Will there be a need for extensive retraining in the spring or will the previous skill levels be immediately reinstated? Will the level of decline vary as a function of how skilled they were to begin with? These are questions for which we do not currently have answers.

Although the preceding example involves the popular sport of golf, the issues are similar for a wide range of skill domains (e.g., learning to drive, performing cardiopulmonary resuscitation, using different types of computer software, programming a videocassette recorder, and administering an insulin injection). An older individual may be taught all these skills even though he or she may not use them for some time—days, months, or even years. Whereas the consequences of forgetting some of these skills are minor, in other cases the consequences may be life-threatening.

Our understanding of age-related differences in skill retention stems primarily from studies focused on how skills acquired at a young age are retained into old age. For example, skilled typists in their 60s and 70s can type as quickly and as accurately as skilled typists in their 30s and 40s (Bosman, 1993; Salthouse, 1984). Similarly, highly rated chess players can maintain their skill levels at least into their 60s (Charness

& Bosman, 1990). However, there has been limited research on the degree to which older adults can acquire *new* skills and retain those capabilities across time.

The purpose of the present chapter is to review the current literature on age-related differences in the retention of skills. The ultimate goal is to describe the current state of awareness about age-related differences in the retention of skills and to elucidate the areas in which knowledge and research are lacking. An aim of this chapter is to provide an impetus for future research in the area of skill retention and aging. As will become clear, there is a paucity of research in this area. The data that are available are drawn from laboratory tasks, primarily for pragmatic reasons. For an individual to achieve expertise in a variety of real-world tasks may require as long as 10 years (Ericcson & Charness, 1994), thus making it difficult for researchers to study skill acquisition and retention over periods of disuse. Consequently, researchers have focused on the acquisition of skill for more constrained tasks and the subsequent retention of such skills. It is important to remember that the principles derived from laboratory studies of skill are applicable to real-world skilled behaviors (Schneider, 1985). Moreover, laboratory tasks such as memory for items, visual search, tracking, and so on, are often components of skilled behaviors acquired outside the laboratory. Thus, although it is critical to understand skilled behaviors in their natural contexts, it is equally important to try to understand basic processes and principles through experimental control (Fisk & Kirlik, this volume).

OVERVIEW OF CHAPTER

As the chapter is focused on the retention of skills, it is important to specify what is meant by a "skill." For the present purposes, Adams' (1987) definition will be adopted: "Skills . . . have three defining characteristics . . . 1. Skill is a wide behavioral domain . . . 2. Skill is learned . . . 3. Any behavior that has been called skilled involves combinations of cognitive, perceptual, and motor processes with different weights" (p. 42). Thus, the present focus on the retention of skills encompasses a broad array of different types of acquired aptitudes that vary in terms of their cognitive, perceptual, and motor components.

There has been a limited amount of research conducted on the retention of newly learned skills for older adults. However, there has been much research on the retention of knowledge and skills for younger adults (dating back to Ebbinghaus, 1964; see reviews by

Adams, 1987; Annett, 1979; Hagman & Rose, 1983; Schendel & Hagman, 1991). Consequently, to introduce the topics of concern for the study of retention, some of the relevant research with young adults will be reviewed for each topic, and, when available, research on older adults will be discussed. In many cases, the age-comparative data are based on studies of memory tasks, search–detection tasks, associative learning, and so on; that is, they are based on tasks that may be components of skills rather than on the retention of whole, more complex, skills.

It is important to understand the variables that affect skill acquisition and retention and the degree to which the effects of those variables differ for young and older adults. Variables that affect skill acquisition will not necessarily have the same effect on retention (Brainerd, Kingma, & Howe, 1985; Howe & Hunter, 1986; Schendel & Hagman, 1991). Consequently, knowing that age affects a certain variable that in turn affects skill acquisition may not be informative about age differences in retention. A number of variables have been identified as important for successful retention such as overlearning, spacing of practice, type of information to be retained (e.g., declarative versus procedural; task-specific versus stimulus-specific), type of task being performed (e.g., visual search versus memory search), and feedback (general and augmented). Each of these variables will be discussed in turn.

OVERLEARNING

To determine the factors that improve retention performance, researchers have focused on overlearning (e.g., Goldberg & O'Rourke, 1989; Hagman & Rose, 1983; Jones, 1989). According to Jones (1989), "Overpractice improves retention . . . Overpractice is defined as the amount of additional practice that a subject is given after correct performance has been achieved" (p. 183). Thus, he makes a general claim about the benefits of overpractice on retention performance. One qualification, proposed by Hagman and Rose (1983) concerns the degree to which overpractice will be cost effective. At some point, the benefits no longer outweigh the costs (either financial or temporal), and this point of diminishing returns must be determined to maximize the utility of overtraining.

There are also methodological issues that must be considered when assessing the benefits of overlearning. For example, the criteria for overlearning may be somewhat arbitrary (e.g., when is acquisition complete, how is this information quantified, how can overlearning be defined). According to Druckman and Bjork (1991) such issues make it difficult to make comparisons across studies.

The specific influence of overpractice and its benefits for retention have not been directly assessed for older adults. However, Jones' (1989) method may be a useful approach. Jones estimated the level of overpractice for young naval recruits (aged 19–24 years) by determining when subjects reached asymptote and how many practice trials followed asymptotic performance. He reported that this measure of overpractice correlated significantly with retention performance (across 4–18 months), ranging from .38 to .83 for different video games. It would be informative to determine the degree to which overpractice is predictive of retention level for older adults. In addition, such an approach could be used to determine which (if any) levels of overpractice by older adults yielded retention performance that met a particular goal. For example, if the goal is for individuals to maintain an 80% accuracy level after a retention interval of 6 months, then the particular level of overpractice necessary to achieve this goal could be determined.

SPACING OF PRACTICE

Spacing of practice is a variable that has differential influences on skill acquisition and skill retention (Schendel & Hagman, 1991). Spacing of practice refers to the degree to which practice is "massed" (provided in large chunks) or "distributed" (spread out over time). Massed practice typically yields superior performance at acquisition but distributed practice yields superior retention. However, the qualifying factors surrounding the spacing effects on retention remain to be determined. For example, spaced trials appear to be more beneficial than spaced sessions, and spacing is most effective when it occurs prior to asymptotic performance levels (Hagman & Rose, 1983). In addition, the influence of spacing of practice appears to be more critical for verbal tasks than motor tasks (Schendel & Hagman, 1991).

Fisher (this volume) has provided a direct test of spacing effects for skill acquisition and retention for young and older adults. He found that the block size (number of word pairs to be learned) had different influences on immediate memory tests versus intermediate (2-minute) and long (24-hour) retention tests. As would be predicted, massed practice was better for immediate performance and distributed practice was better for longer retention intervals and this was true for both age groups. Thus, the spacing effects on skill acquisition and retention appear to be the same for young and older adults, at least within this task domain.

FEEDBACK

Schendel and Hagman (1991) discussed several different types of feedback and their effects on the retention of skills. Knowledge of results refers to "externally provided information about the discrepancy between a learner's actual response and the criterion response" (p. 66). Knowledge of results improves skill acquisition but may hinder skill retention. Benefits are often diminished when the feedback is removed.

Response-produced feedback refers to the sights, sounds, and feelings associated with particular movements (e.g., the feel and sound of the keys on a keyboard). This type of feedback has been shown to be beneficial for both the acquisition and retention of motor skills.

Augmented feedback involves providing "extra cues or information that would normally not accompany the task being performed" (Schendel & Hagman, 1991, p. 68). An example of augmented feedback would be to highlight the relevant information in a search task. As with knowledge of results, augmented feedback may improve performance but the benefits diminish when the augmentation is removed.

From an age-related perspective, researchers must consider the degree to which feedback will improve performance but also the degree to which it may help or hinder retention. Older adults do benefit from having knowledge of results and augmented feedback for the initial acquisition of tasks (e.g., Jagacinski, Greenberg, Liao, & Wang, 1993; for a review see Kausler, 1991); however, additional training without the feedback may be necessary to ensure retention of the skills across time. Although response-produced feedback may seem to be ideal for both acquisition and retention, there is some evidence to suggest that relative to younger adults, older adults do not benefit as much from proprioceptive feedback (also reviewed in Kausler, 1991).

The effects of the various feedback types on the acquisition and retention of skills for older adults remain to be determined for older adults. The benefits and potential costs may differ across task domains, skill levels, and individual difference variables such as ability, motivation, and locus of control (Rogers, in press).

ACQUISITION CONTEXT AND INSTRUCTION

Organization of information during learning has been shown to facilitate long-term retention of declarative knowledge memories (e.g., Masson & McDaniel, 1981; McDaniel & Kerwin, 1987; & Wortman, 1975). Such organizational benefits across long-term retention intervals have also been demonstrated for older adults. For example, Hultsch and Dixon (1983) demonstrated that although there were age differences at immediate testing, prose memory for schematically relevant stories did not differ after a 1-week retention interval. The benefits of providing organizational schemas for the long-term retention of both young and older adults should be investigated in more depth to determine whether there are benefits of organization for nonverbal information, what types of organization are most beneficial (e.g., hierarchical, categorical), and so on.

There have been some efforts to determine if particular instructional methods will yield superior levels of retention. For example, Jamieson (1971) investigated young (aged 24–39) and older adults' (aged 51–71) ability to learn binary notation. Jamieson compared discovery learning and programmed instruction wherein rules were provided one step at a time. The young and older adults performed equally well initially. Age differences after the 4-month retention interval were observed but only for the subjects who had received programmed instruction; older adults who learned by the method of discovery retained the information as well as younger adults. Jamieson suggested that the discovery method may have required more active participation on the part of the learner and thus may have improved retention performance for the older adults (there was no difference between programmed instruction and discovery for the younger adults). The importance of active participation during learning deserves further investigation.

Providing young adults with a recall test at the end of the acquisition phase greatly improved their retention of word lists after 4 days (Nelson & Vining, 1978). Thus having the opportunity for retrieval improved subsequent retention of the information (see also Schendel & Hagman, 1991). This variable has not yet been investigated directly for older adults. However, Rogers, Gilbert, and Fisk (1994) discovered that there were no significant age differences in retention after 3 months on an associative learning task that provided multiple recall and recognition tests during acquisition. Thus, interim testing may provide benefits at retention for older adults as has been demonstrated for younger adults.

Along with interim testing, the provision of more opportunities for training yields substantial benefits for older adults. In the context of providing cognitive training for an abstract reasoning task, Willis and Nesselroade (1990) demonstrated that, although the largest benefits were observed for the initial training session, cumulative benefits were observed for additional training sessions after 1- and 5-year intervals. They suggested that such multiphase cognitive training may allow adults in their late seventies to perform as well as adults in their sixties.

TASK-SPECIFIC VERSUS STIMULUS-SPECIFIC RETENTION

Skill acquisition may involve general learning of task procedures as well as specific learning of particular stimuli. For example, learning to play a violin involves learning how to hold the instrument, where to place your fingers, and how to move the bow. In addition, a musician may become skilled at playing particular pieces. Thus, the skill of playing the violin requires general learning as well as stimulus-specific learning.

In the laboratory task of visual search, individuals must learn general information such as how to respond (e.g., which fingers to use and which keys to press), where to look on a computer screen, and what strategies to use to maintain speed and accuracy levels. In addition, they must learn specific stimulus characteristics (e.g., *animal* words are target items and *fruit* words are distractor items). Fisk and his colleagues investigated the retention of visual search skills for young adults (Fisk & Hodge, 1992) and in an age-comparative study (Fisk, Hertzog, Lee, Rogers, & Anderson-Garlach, 1994).

Fisk and Hodge (1992) found impressive levels of retention of a visual search skill for young adults. Less than 8% decline in performance was observed following a 30-day retention interval. Although this level of decline was statistically significant, it is relatively small. Fisk et al. (1994) discovered that both younger (mean age 22) and older adults (mean age 71) were able to retain some level of visual search skill even after a 16-month retention interval. Fisk and Hodge focused on stimulus-specific retention, but Fisk et al. found that the separation of general task-specific retention from stimulus-specific retention was informative about differential age effects. Stimulus-specific retention represents the difference between performance on the trained task at the beginning of retention and at the end of training. Task-specific savings represent the degree to which performance at retention on a comparable visual search task with novel stimuli is better than initial performance at the beginning of training. Young adults showed greater retention of stimulus-specific information, whereas there was no age difference in level of task-specific retention.

It is important to note that visual search skills typically show qualitatively different levels of skill acquisition for young and older adults (e.g., Fisk & Rogers, 1991; Rogers, Fisk, & Hertzog, 1994). Thus, the age differences in stimulus-specific information may reflect age differences in the type of learning reflected in final-level performance. The important point is that conclusions about age-related differences in retention differ depending on the type of retained information that is assessed. Older adults who successfully acquired a general search skill were as likely to retain that information over a 16-month interval as were young adults, even though they retained less stimulus-specific information.

TASK DIFFERENCES

Declarative Versus Procedural Knowledge

Healy and her colleagues (e.g., Fendrich, Healy, & Bourne, 1991; Healy et al., 1992) suggested that the degree to which information will be retained across time depends on the class of task. Those tasks that are more procedural in nature (e.g., target detection, mental multiplication, data entry) will show high levels of retention. On the other hand, those tasks that are more declarative (e.g., memory for numerical calculations, memory for vocabulary, memory for course schedules) will show lower levels of retention across time.

Although there is some evidence to support the theory of superior retention of procedural learning (Cooke, Durso, & Schvaneveldt, 1994; Druckman & Bjork, 1991; Fisk & Hodge, 1992), the statement that procedural tasks do not decline must be interpreted with some caution. First, the tasks must be proceduralized for such benefits in retention to accrue (i.e., rather than undertaken as step-by-step recipe following, the task components are encapsulated; Anderson, 1982). For example, Mengelkoch, Adams, and Gainer (1971) found that discrete procedural responses did decline, but they were training a very complex flight simulator skill, and their subjects were clearly not asymptotic at the end of training. Thus, the procedural skill decline may have been because the skill had not yet been proceduralized. Druckman and Bjork (1991) have argued that procedural tasks do show decline, especially if they have a number of steps that are not cued either by the equipment or by preceding steps. Adams (1987) suggested that procedural responses are forgotten after a year but relearning is very rapid due to savings.

Thus there are two issues to be considered regarding the retention of procedural skills for older adults. First, researchers must make certain that the older adults are capable of first proceduralizing the task of interest. This may vary depending on the task (Fisk & Rogers, 1991). Second, retention of procedural tasks may be enhanced by cues or through environmental support. That is, age differences in retention should be reduced for procedural tasks that reinstate the original learning context (Craik & Jennings, 1992).

Charness and Campbell (1988) studied the acquisition and 1-month retention of the proceduralized ability to mentally square two numbers. They discovered generally similar acquisition functions for young (mean age 24), middle-aged (mean age 41), and older (mean age 67) adults. Moreover, the decline after 1 month was minimal (11%) and did not differ with age. Thus, the Charness and Campbell data support the idea that proceduralized tasks are well retained and that the amount of retention does not diminish with old age. The mental squaring algorithm learned by the subjects has several components, each of which may serve as cues for the remainder of the solution process.

The aforementioned superiority of proceduralization was concerned with tasks that can be compiled in the sense of Anderson (1982, 1983). However, procedural memory (e.g., priming) has also been reported to be superior when compared with episodic memory (e.g., recognition) over long-term retention intervals (for a review see Mitchell, Brown, & Murphy, 1990). Although the results are somewhat mixed, "the general picture is that procedural performance declines most rapidly with short intervals ranging from minutes to hours and then stabilizes over longer intervals (days, weeks, and months)" (Mitchell et al., 1990, p. 265). In terms of age-related effects, Mitchell et al. demonstrated that priming effects were similar for young and older adults across retention intervals up to 21 days.

Thus from a lower level of analysis of procedural memory (e.g., priming) to more complex procedural skills (e.g., mental multiplication), long-term retention is quite good. In addition, the minimal loss that does occur does not differ for young and older adults. Proceduralization of skills may prove to be insurance against loss due to intervals of disuse for both young and older adults.

Memory Search Versus Visual Search

Even within the domain of search–detection tasks, there are differences in the processes underlying skill acquisition. For example, Fisk, Corso, and Hodge (1992) demonstrated that there are fundamental differences between memory search and visual search such that training on one task does not transfer to the other, even when the same stimuli are used. Moreover, Fisk and Rogers (1991) demonstrated that the pattern of age-related differences in skill acquisition varies across memory search tasks (wherein age differences are small) and visual search tasks (wherein age differences are substantial).

The importance of distinguishing between memory and visual search tasks is also evident in the retention literature. Fisk and Hodge (1992) found no decline of memory search skills for young adults after

30 days and significant, although minimal, decline in visual search (8%). In a hybrid task with both memory and visual search components, a decline of 15% was observed after 30 days. Thus, not only does skill acquisition vary across task types, so does skill retention.

From an age-related perspective, it appears that age differences in retention do not differ across search detection tasks. That is, for both memory search (Fisk, Cooper, Hertzog, & Anderson-Garlach, 1995; Rogers, Gilbert, & Fisk, 1994) and visual search (Fisk et al., 1994) the age differences are larger for the retention of stimulus-specific information and small, or nonexistent, for the retention of task-specific information. It is difficult to compare absolute levels of retention across search domains because Fisk et al. (1995) and Rogers, Gilbert, and Fisk (1994) used 3- and 6-month retention intervals whereas Fisk et al. (1994) used a 16-month retention interval. However, the patterns of age-related differences and similarities in retention are comparable across the memory search and the visual search tasks assessed in those two experiments. This is particularly important because older adults acquire similar levels of skill in memory search tasks but not in visual search tasks (Fisk & Rogers, 1991). Thus, irrespective of original level of skill acquisition, older adults show more decline for the stimulus-specific aspects of search skills.

SPACING OF RETENTION INTERVALS

Age-related comparisons of retention across various intervals show a diverse pattern; sometimes there are age differences in forgetting, other times there are not. Salthouse (1991) lamented that "it appears impossible at the current time to reach any firm conclusions concerning possible age differences in the effectiveness of retaining information across intervals extending beyond a few hours" (p. 235).

However, whether age differences in retention are observed seems to depend on the length of the retention interval (for a review see Fisk et al., 1994). For example, in the domain of memory for pictorial stimuli, age differences are not found at immediate testing or after 48 hours (Park, Royal, Dudley, & Morrell, 1988; Rybarczyk, Hart, & Harkins, 1987); however, age differences are observed at 1-week (Park et al., 1988) and 4-week intervals (Park, Puglisi, & Smith, 1986). Thus, studies that investigate retention after only hours or days may not accurately reflect true age differences in long term retention. Such studies are informative about age differences for shorter retention intervals, but it would be unwise to extrapolate the results to encompass longer intervals for two reasons: (a) young and older adults may show similar levels of retention at short intervals but diverge after longer intervals, or (b) older adults may show more initial forgetting but the two age groups may converge at longer intervals (e.g., Hultsch & Dixon, 1983).

INTERVENING ACTIVITIES

The period between the acquisition of a skill and its subsequent implementation, may contain many activities, both related and unrelated to the skill. Such activities might improve skill retention, harm it, or have no discernible effect on it. For example, similar tasks that require contradictory responses will interfere with retention (reviewed in Annett, 1979). To illustrate, consider learning to use a spreadsheet that is required for paying monthly bills. If an alternative spreadsheet is used during the interim, interference is likely to occur, especially if the function keys are not compatible across the two systems. Alternatively, if the programs are highly compatible, retention for the original program will be facilitated.

Older adults may be more susceptible to the potentially deleterious effects of intervening activities. Fisk et al. (1995) demonstrated that the 3-month retention of memory search performance was disrupted when an incompatible search task was performed during the retention interval. Young adults showed 8% more loss, and older adults showed 30% more stimulus-specific loss, in the interfering condition relative to a retention interval without interference. Thus, the Fisk et al. data indicate that older adults may be more susceptible to retention loss due to interfering activities. It would be of interest to determine whether older adults also show more benefits of facilitative intervening activities (e.g., refresher training). The Willis and Nesselroade (1990) data discussed earlier are suggestive that refresher training is beneficial for older adults, although they had no comparison to benefits for young adults.

INDIVIDUAL DIFFERENCES

The importance of individual differences in retention has been discussed for more than 70 years. For example, Luh (1922) suggested that individual variability would increase with the time interval, would increase inversely with degree of original learning, and would increase with the difficulty of the task. These variables remain issues of importance in current studies of retention.

More recent investigations have focused on the influence of individual differences in rate of skill acquisition on the rate of decline of skills over time. For example, Kyllonen and Tirre (1988) assessed skill acquisition and retention of a paired associates task for 710 young adults (U.S. Air Force recruits). Using retention intervals of less than 20 minutes, they found that faster learners retained more information, even though their faster learning resulted in fewer original study opportunities. Thus, item-specific learning speed predicted retention. They also observed that general learning speed, as measured by general associative learning tests, predicted stimulus-specific learning speed.

Contrary to Kyllonen and Tirre (1988), others have argued that, if original learning levels are equated, retention functions are equivalent for fast and slow learners (Gentile, Monaco, Iheozor-Ejiofor, Ndu, & Ogbonaya, 1982; Hagman & Rose, 1983). Kyllonen and Tirre argued that the discrepancy between their results and others' stems from different means of equating initial levels of learning. Without my reiterating their entire argument, their conclusion is presented here: "If fast and slow learners are equated by performance on one (e.g., an immediate) retention test, then there should be no differences in performance between the two groups on a later retention test. But if learners are equated . . . by the number of successive successes experienced, then fast learners will retain more . . . [Thus] the equating method used . . . is a critical determinant [of retention differences]" (pp. 416–417). This distinction must be considered when making comparisons between the retention of younger and older adults.

Although the effects of within-group differences in abilities have not been addressed in studies of age differences in skill retention, this is an important issue for future investigations. A particular sample of older individuals may be more likely to have a high number of slower learners relative to a sample of younger adults. Thus a comparison of the two age groups would yield significant differences in retention performance. However, such differences might not indicate an age difference in retention; instead they might indicate that a larger percentage of the older adults are slower learners. The focus of interest, then, is on why older adults are slower learners, not why older adults retain information more poorly. (A related issue is the importance of including larger numbers of subjects in studies of long-term retention.)

One potentially viable area of investigating age differences in skill acquisition would be understanding the individual differences in abilities that predict individual differences in learning, and hence, individual differences in retention. For example, Kyllonen and Tirre (1988) found that general learning speed and general knowledge were important predictors of task performance and retention. Whether similar abilities predict learning and retention for older adults is an empirical question. However, there is some evidence to suggest that the abilities that are predictive of skill acquisition vary across age groups as a function of task type (e.g., Hertzog, Cooper, & Fisk, in press; Rogers, Fisk, & Hertzog, 1994). Consequently, the degree to which rate of learning (and other variables) predict level of retention must be directly assessed for older adults.

DIRECTIONS FOR FUTURE RESEARCH

There are some situations in which older adults appear to retain information and skills as well as younger adults. When retention intervals are short, when task-specific (vs. stimulus-specific) retention is assessed, or when the information to be retained has been proceduralized, age differences are minimal. One avenue of research is to determine how best to capitalize on these intact abilities.

In other cases, there is documented evidence of age-related declines in retention across time. Stimulus-specific information, for example, is better retained by young adults than older adults. Moreover, longer retention intervals sometimes lead to age differences in retention. The evidence of age differences in retention leads to two research questions. First, what is the cause of such age-related declines, and, second, can these declines be overcome through training (e.g., overtraining, augmented feedback, refresher training, etc.). One of the practical reasons for studying the retention of skills is that a precise understanding of skill loss (and the degree to which it changes with age) can serve as a basis for determining when refresher training will be needed (Goldberg & O'Rourke, 1989). Thus, if the goal is for an older adult to acquire a skill and have that skill level of performance available at all times, refresher training might be critical. Only if we understand retention functions will we be able to understand when best to schedule refresher training. An important consideration will be whether retention functions and training benefits differ across task domains.

Many of the variables discussed revealed effects on retention for young adults that have not yet been investigated for older adults (e.g., overlearning, feedback). Those variables that have been studied from an age-related perspective are still not well understood (e.g., instructional manipulations, task differences). Understanding the effects of these variables on the skill retention of older adults will be valuable in resolving the two research questions posed above. Of course, understanding the retention of laboratory-based skills will not be sufficient for a complete understanding of general retention (Annett, 1979; Fisk & Kirlik, this volume). We may learn which variables are important, and perhaps some general principles about age-related differences in skill retention will emerge. However, parallel efforts conducted outside the laboratory will be necessary to test the generality of these principles for real-world tasks.

ACKNOWLEDGMENTS

The author was supported in part by a grant from the National Institutes of Health (National Institute on Aging) Grant No. P50 AG11715 under the auspices of the Center for Applied Cognitive Research on Aging (one of the Edward R. Roybal Centers for Research on Applied Gerontology). This chapter is based on a presentation given at the Aging and Skills Conference in Destin, FL (February, 1995). Thanks to the attendees at the conference for their input and Mary Cregger, Dan Fisk, and Darlene Howard for constructive criticism on a draft of the chapter.

REFERENCES

Adams, J. A. (1987). Historical review and appraisal of research on the learning, retention, and transfer of human motor skills. *Psychological Bulletin, 101*, 41–74.

Anderson, J. R. (1982). Acquisition of cognitive skill. *Psychological Review, 89*, 369–406.

Anderson, J. R. (1983). *The architecture of cognition*. Cambridge, MA: Harvard University Press.

Annett, J. (1979). Memory for skill. In M. M. Gruneberg & P. E. Morris (Eds.), *Applied problems in memory* (pp. 215–247). London: Academic Press.

Bosman, E. A. (1993). Age-related differences in motoric aspects of transcription typing skill. *Psychology and Aging, 8*, 87–102.

Brainerd, C. J., Kingma, J., & Howe, M .L. (1985). On the development of forgetting. *Child Development, 56*, 1103–1119.

Charness, N., & Bosman, E. A. (1990). Expertise and aging: Life in the lab. In T. H. Hess (Ed.), *Aging and cognition: Knowledge organization and utilization* (pp. 343–385). Amsterdam: Elsevier.

Charness, N., & Campell, J. I. D. (1988). Acquiring skill at mental calculation in adulthood: A task decomposition. *Journal of Experimental Psychology: General, 117*, 115–129.

Cooke, N. J., Durso, F. T., & Schvaneveldt, R. W. (1994). Retention of skilled search after nine years. *Human Factors, 36*, 597–605.

Craik, F. I. M., & Jennings, J. M. (1992). Human memory. In F. I. M. Craik & T. A. Salthouse (Eds.), *The handbook of aging and cognition* (pp. 51–110). Hillsdale, NJ: Erlbaum.

Druckman, D., & Bjork, R. A. (1991). *In the mind's eye: Enhancing human performance*. Washington, DC: National Academy Press.

Ebbinghaus, H. (1964). *Memory: A contribution to experimental psychology*. (H. A. Rugers & C. E. Bussenius, Trans.). New York: Dover. (Original work published 1885)

Ericsson, K. A., & Charness, N. (1994). Expert performance: Its structure and acquisition. *American Psychologist, 49,* 725–747.

Fendrich, D. W., Healy, A. F., & Bourne, L. E. (1991). Long-term repetition effects for motoric and perceptual procedures. *Journal of Experimental Psychology: Learning, Memory, and Cognition, 17,* 137–151.

Fisk, A. D., Cooper, B. P., Hertzog, C., & Anderson-Garlach, M. M. (1995). Age-related retention of skilled memory search: Examination of associative learning, interference, and task-specific skills. *Journals of Gerontology: Psychological Sciences, 50B,* P150–161.

Fisk, A. D., Corso, G. M., & Hodge, K. A. (1992, November). *On the nature of learning in consistent search-detection tasks.* Paper presented at the annual meeting of the Psychonomic Society, St. Louis, MO.

Fisk, A. D., Hertzog, C., Lee, M. D., Rogers, W. A., & Anderson-Garlach, M. M. (1994). Long-term retention of skilled visual search: Do young adults retain more than old adults? *Psychology and Aging, 9,* 206-215.

Fisk, A. D., & Hodge, K. A. (1992). Retention of trained performance in consistent mapping search after extended delay. *Human Factors, 34,* 147–164.

Fisk, A. D., & Rogers, W. A. (1991). Toward an understanding of age-related memory and visual search effects. *Journal of Experimental Psychology: General, 120,* 131–149.

Gentile, J. R., Monaco, N., Iheozor-Ejiofor, I. E., Ndu, A. N., & Ogbonaya, P. K. (1982). Retention by "fast" and "slow" learners. *Intelligence, 6,* 125–138.

Goldberg, J. H., & O'Rourke, S. A. (1989). Prediction of skill retention and retraining from initial training. *Perceptual and Motor Skills, 69,* 535–546.

Hagman, J. D., & Rose, A. M. (1983). Retention of military tasks: A review. *Human Factors, 25,* 199–213.

Healy, A. F., Fendrich, D. W., Crutcher, R. J., Wittman, W. T., Gesi, A. T., Ericcson, K. A., & Bourne, Jr., L. E., (1992). The long-term retention of skills. In A. F. Healy, S. M. Kosslyn, & R. M. Shiffrin (Eds.), *From learning processes to cognitive processes: Essays in honor of William K. Estes* (pp. 87–118). Hillsdale, NJ: Lawrence Erlbaum Associates.

Hertzog, C., Cooper, B. P., & Fisk, A. D. (1994). Aging and individual differences in the development of skilled memory search performance. *Psychology and Aging.*

Howe, M. L. & Hunter, M. A. (1986). Long-term memory in adulthood: An examination of the development of storage and retrieval processes at acquisition and retrieval. *Developmental Review, 6,* 334–364.

Hultsch, D. F., & Dixon, R. A. (1983). The role of preexperimental knowledge in text processing in adulthood. *Experimental Aging Research, 9,* 17–22.

Jagacinski, R. J., Greenberg, N., Liao, M., & Wang, J. (1993). Manual performance of a repeated pattern by older and younger adults with supplementary auditory cues. *Psychology and Aging, 8,* 429–439.

Jamieson, G. H. (1971). Learning and retention: A comparison between programmed and discovery learning at two age levels. *Programmed Learning, 8,* 34–40.

Jones, M. B. (1989). Individual differences in skill retention. *American Journal of Psychology, 102,* 183–196.

Kausler, D. H. (1991). *Experimental psychology, cognition, and human aging.* New York: Springer-Verlag.

Kyllonen, P. C., & Tirre, W. C. (1988). Individual differences in associative learning and forgetting. *Intelligence, 12,* 393–421.

Luh, C. W. (1922). The conditions of retention. *Psychological Monographs, 31* (No. 3), Whole (No. 142).

Masson, M. E. J., & McDaniel, M. A. (1981). The role of organizational processes in long-term retention. *Journal of Experimental Psychology: Human Learning and Memory, 7,* 100–110.

McDaniel, M. A., & Kerwin, M. L. E. (1987). Long-term prose retention: Is an organizational schema sufficient. *Discourse Processes, 10,* 237–252.

Mengelkoch, R. F., Adams, J. A., & Gainer. C. A. (1971). The forgetting of instrument flying skills. *Human Factors, 13,* 397–405.

Mitchell, D. B., Brown, A. S., & Murphy, D. R. (1990). Dissociations between procedural and episodic memory: Effects of time and aging. *Psychology and Aging, 5,* 264–276.

Nelson, T. O., & Vining, S. K. (1978). Effects of semantic versus structural processing on long-term retention. *Journal of Experimental Psychology: Human Learning and Memory, 4,* 198–209.

Park, D. C., Puglisi, J. T., & Smith, A, D. (1986). Memory for pictures: Does an age-related decline exist? *Psychology and Aging, 1,* 11–17.

Park, D. C., Royal, D., Dudley, W., & Morrell, R. (1988). Forgetting of pictures over a long retention interval in young and older adults. *Psychology and Aging, 3,* 94–95.

Rogers, W. A. (in press). Individual differences, aging, and human factors: An overview. In A. D. Fisk and W. A. Rogers (Eds.), *Handbook of human factors and the older adult.* San Diego: Academic Press.

Rogers, W. A., Fisk, A. D., & Hertzog, C. (1994). Do ability–performance relationships differentiate age and practice effects in visual search? *Journal of Experimental Psychology: Learning, Memory, and Cognition, 20,* 710–738.

Rogers, W. A., Gilbert, D. K., & Fisk, A. D. (1994, April). *Long-term retention of general skill and stimulus-specific abilities in associative learning: Age-related differences.* Paper presented at the fifth Cognitive Aging Conference, Atlanta, GA.

Rybarczyk, D. D., Hart, R. P., & Harkins, S. W. (1987). Age and forgetting rate with pictorial stimuli. *Psychology and Aging, 2,* 404–406.

Salthouse, T. A. (1984). Effects of age and skill in typing. *Journal of Experimental Psychology: General, 13,* 345–371.

Salthouse, T. A. (1991). *Theoretical perspectives on cognitive aging.* Hillsdale, NJ: Lawrence Erlbaum Associates.

Schendel, J. D., & Hagman, J. D. (1991). Long-term retention of motor skills. In J. E. Morrison (Ed.), *Training for performance: Principles of applied human learning* (pp. 53–92). New York: Wiley and Sons.

Schneider, W. (1985). Training high performance skills: Fallacies and guidelines. *Human Factors, 27,* 285–300.

Willis, S. L., & Nesselroade, C. S. (1990). Long-term effects of fluid ability training in old-old age. *Developmental Psychology, 26,* 905–910.

Wortman, P. M. (1975). Long-term retention of information as a function of its organization. *Journal of Experimental Psychology: Human Learning and Memory, 1,* 576–583.

CHAPTER 10

Aging and the Acquisition of Computer Skills

Sara J. Czaja
University of Miami

By the year 2025, the global population of people aged 65 and older will increase threefold. Forecasts for the United States project that there will be 58.6 million older people by 2025 with the greatest growth occurring among people aged 75 and older (Office of Technology Assessment, 1985). At the same time as the population is aging, rapid technological developments are changing the nature of work, the form and scope of personal communication, education and leisure activities, and health care delivery. Computers are now commonplace in most public places and are becoming commonplace in home environments. Many routine activities such as shopping and banking involve the use of some form of computer technology. An important question is how well an aging society will adjust to these technological developments. The critical issue is whether technological change will enhance or impede the ability of older adults to live and work with greater independence. This issue is especially relevant for the current cohort of older adults, as a large percentage of them are unlikely to have had exposure to technology. This problem may be exacerbated by the fact that many system designers assume older people will have limited interactions with technology and thus fail to consider them as a potential user group in the design process. To ensure that older people are able to successfully use computer technology and to maximize the benefits of this technology for older adults we need to conceptualize older adults as active users of technology and understand the implications of age-related changes in abilities for the design and implementation of technological systems.

This chapter examines issues relevant to aging and the design of computer technology. The first section discusses settings in which older adults are likely to interact with computer technology. The next section reviews age-related changes in cognitive abilities which may have relevance to the performance of computer tasks. This is followed by a discussion of the available literature on the use of computers by older adults and the implications for training and interface design. The overall goal of the chapter is to synthesize our knowledge of aging and cognition which has relevance to the performance of computer tasks in order to outline areas of needed research and also to provide systematic guidelines for the design of future technological systems.

APPLICATIONS OF COMPUTER TECHNOLOGY

There are a variety of settings in which older people are likely to use computer technology including the work environment, the home environment, and health care settings. The following discussion presents an overview of the use of technology within these settings in order to illustrate that technology has become a part of most routine tasks and activities.

Employment

During the past decade, new computer and communication technologies have been and continue to be rapidly introduced into most occupational settings. Consequently most workers, including older workers, now need to interact successfully with computer technology simply to perform their jobs. It is estimated that within the current decade computer technology will affect approximately 7 million factory jobs and 38 million office jobs (Sauter, Murphy, & Hurrel, 1990). In office environments the personal computer is becoming the most dominant piece of office equipment, second only to the telephone. For example, secretaries and office personnel now need to use word processing, electronic mail, and data base management packages to perform standard office tasks. Managers, bank tellers, sales clerks, and cashiers are also using computers on a regular basis to carry out routine tasks such as sales transactions, inventory management, and decision making. Computer-interactive tasks are also becoming prevalent in the general manufacturing, chemical, manufacturing, and nuclear power industries.

Given that the use of computers is prevalent in the workplace and that the number of older workers is likely to increase in the future, use of computers by older workers is a significant issue that must be addressed by employers and system designers. This issue must be considered from two perspectives: maintaining currently employed elderly in the labor force and promoting employment opportunities for the those who are unemployed. With respect to the first issue, computers may threaten the job security of older workers. Computers change the nature of work, causing workers to learn and use different skills. This may create problems of skill obsolescence and job displacement among older workers as computers were not in widespread use when today's older workers entered the work force. In order to keep pace with changes in job demands workers need retraining to acquire the necessary technical skills to successfully interact with computer hardware and software. This may be problematic for older workers, as the literature suggests that older people acquire new skills less readily than younger adults. As noted by Gist, Rosen, and Schwoerer (1988), older workers are especially vulnerable to problems with skill obsolescence given that they have a longer work history over which skills and abilities can erode, and they may not have opportunities to learn the skills required by changing job requirements.

In terms of employment opportunities, computers may enhance the likelihood of employment opportunities for older people as computers make work at home a more likely alternative. Older people who find it difficult to leave home because of health or transportation problems may benefit from such arrangements. Also, computer tasks are more amenable to part time work and research has shown that part-time work is often preferred by older people (Robinson, Coberly, & Paul, 1985). Technology also reduces the physical demands of tasks, which is beneficial for older people, as there are age-related decrements in strength and endurance (Stones & Kozma, 1985). However, computer tasks involve cognitive skills that may be problematic for older people because of age-related changes in cognitive abilities. Further, older people have limited opportunities to offset these declines in abilities with experience. Currently, knowledge regarding the impact of technology on an aging workforce is limited. There is a need for more research in this area to insure that older workers can successfully interact with technology in a safe and comfortable manner.

Home Environments

Computers and communication technologies are also being used with increased frequency in home settings. The use of these technologies in the home can enhance the quality of life for older people. Computers can provide people with mobility limitations easier access to information and services. For example, computer-based communication systems can be used to facilitate grocery shopping and banking. Older people commonly report problems with these tasks because of restricted mobility, inconvenience, difficulty transporting grocery items, and fear of crime (Nair, 1989).

Home computers can also be used to expand educational, recreational, and social opportunities. Older people have more leisure time and spend the majority of their discretionary time at home (Moss & Lawton, 1982). They often report problems with social isolation, loneliness, and boredom (Neugarten, 1977). Computers can help alleviate these problems by providing opportunities for hobbies and educational activities within home settings. Software is available for instruction in a wide variety of topics such as nutrition, foreign languages, art, history, and science. Electronic links can be also be established with universities for participation in continuing education courses.

Electronic networks can also make it easier for older people to maintain ties to family and friends and to form new friendships. Furlong (1989) found substantial use of e-mail, conferencing, news, and bulletin boards among users of SeniorNet. Eilers (1989) found that older people who used home computers reported the following benefits: social interaction, mental stimulation, and memory enhancement. In a study (Czaja, Guerrier, Nair, & Landauer, 1993) that examined the feasibility of older people using an electronic text message system, the participants reported that they liked using the system and that it was valuable in terms of providing a means for social interaction and mental stimulation.

Computers and other forms of communication technology also offer the potential for augmenting memory functioning by serving as a real time memory aid. An individual can create a personal database that contains prompting for meetings, important dates, nutrition, and medication schedules. Telecommunication devices are also being developed that provide home safety and security services. Systems can be programmed to monitor home appliances, electrical and ventilation systems and be linked to emergency networks and services. Overall, these devices can enhance the ability of older people to live independently at home.

Health Care

Home computers can also increase the ability of older people to participate directly in disease prevention and health care management. For example, computers may be used for computer-assisted health instruction. They may also be used to provide individuals with reminders of medication schedules or instructions on diet and rehabilitation practices. Leirer, Morrow, Tanke, and Pariante (1991) demonstrated that computerized voice mail is an effective means of reducing medical noncompliance among elderly people. Electronic links may also be established between older adults and care givers and medical personnel. For example, a care giver can send a daily e-mail message to older clients inquiring about their needs or health status. Conversely, older clients can use e-mail to contact medical personnel if they have questions or general concerns. Galienne, Moore, and Brennan (1993) found that the use of a computer-based communication system, ComputerLink, was valuable to family care givers of Alzheimer's patients, as the system facilitated interaction between the care givers and nurses. The majority of care givers were older adults; the average age of the sample was 60 years. ComputerLink is a subnetwork on the Cleveland public access computer network, FreeNet. The care givers accessed the network via personal computers in their home.

Clearly, the success of these potential applications is dependent on the willingness and ability of the elderly to use computer-based technologies. A number of studies (Ansley & Erber, 1988; Czaja, Hammond, Blascovich, & Swede, 1989; Krauss & Hoyer, 1985) showed that older people are receptive to the use of technology and willing to learn to interact with computer systems. The more important issue concerns the design of user interfaces that promote use of technology by a broad spectrum of older adults. Further, older people must be provided with adequate training and support. The following sections addresses these issues. The emphasis is on the implications of age-related changes in cognition for system design.

ISSUES SURROUNDING THE USE OF TECHNOLOGY BY OLDER ADULTS

Age-Related Changes in Cognitive Abilities

Examination of the data regarding aging and cognition suggests that older adults may have difficulty acquiring the skills necessary for successful interaction with computers. In general, the skill acquisition literature indicates that older people have more difficulty than younger people in acquiring new skills and that they achieve lower levels of performance (Charness & Bosman, 1990) This is largely because of age-related changes in cognitive processes.

There is substantial evidence that there are age-related declines in most component processes of cognition. As summarized by Park (1992), processes that decline include attentional processes, working memory capabilities, discourse comprehension, inference formation, and interpretation, encoding and retrieval processes in memory, and information processing speed. Decrements in these components abilities could place older people at a disadvantage with respect to computer-interactive tasks, as these tasks are primarily characterized by cognitive demands.

For example, age-related reductions in processing speed may impact negatively on the ability of older people to acquire computer skills. Declines in processing speed not only limit the speed at which older people are able to respond but also the performance of other cognitive operations. A recent study by Salthouse (1993) suggests that age-related reductions in working memory are mediated by the slowing of processing speed. Age differences in learning, attention, and reading comprehension have also been linked to slower rates of processing.

Older adults need more time to receive and process information especially if the task is complex. Generally age differences in response speed increase as the complexity of the task increases (Salthouse, 1985). Further, older people often trade speed for accuracy. Thus, allowing sufficient time for older adults to process information is important for learning, especially learning complex tasks such as computer tasks. A number of studies (e.g., Witte, 1975) showed that older adults perform better in learning or recall situations in which extended or self-paced schedules are employed. However, allowing more time is unlikely to completely eliminate age differences in performance. Generally, the data indicate that providing more time improves the performance of older adults and reduces but does not eliminate age differences on measures of learning.

Age decrements in memory could also contribute to difficulties in the acquisition of computer skills. As discussed by Hockey, Briner, Tattersall, and Wiethoff (1989), one of the primary characteristics of computer tasks is the high demand placed on working memory. Users must learn new concepts or how to attach new meaning to familiar concepts (e.g., *file*) and to some extent learn a new lexicon. Research has shown that older people are less efficient at encoding information and less likely to use elaborate rehearsal strategies (Craik & Simon, 1980), organize information, and use mediators (Hulicka & Grossman, 1967). Age-related difficulties in learning and recall are especially pronounced if the learning problem is in an unfamiliar cognitive domain and requires building new schemata (Welford, 1985). It is likely that computers represent an unfamiliar cognitive domain for most older people and require learning new schemata. For example, concepts related to window and mouse operation are unlikely to be familiar and fit into already existing schemata.

The processing resource theory of aging and cognition (see Park,

1992) also asserts that older adults will have difficulty acquiring skills that involve the formation of new schemata. This theory maintains that age differences in the performance of cognitive tasks become manifest when tasks require a substantial amount of processing as is the case when the learning task represents an unfamiliar cognitive domain and there is little contextual support.

Findings regarding aging and automatic processes also have relevance to the issue of aging and the acquisition of computer skills given the importance of automatic processing to the performance of skilled activities. A number of studies (e.g., Fisk, McGee, & Giambra, 1988; Fisk, Rogers, & Giambra, 1990; Rogers & Fisk, 1991), examining visual search, showed attenuated ability on the part of older adults to develop new automatic processes. It is hypothesize that this attenuated ability is due to a disrupted learning mechanism, *priority learning*, whereby older adults are unable to inhibit irrelevant, distracting information and focus on important target information as learning progresses. There is evidence (Rabbit, 1965; Plude & Hoyer, 1985) that older adults may not select the most relevant information for processing and that this may inhibit performance. Thus, it is important that learning environments are as free from disruptions and distractions as possible and that important information in training materials is highlighted. Further training and learning materials should only focus on information relevant to the task.

The foregoing discussion highlights some aspects of cognitive processing which may have relevance to the ability of older adults to acquire computer skills. The tone of the discussion suggests that older people are likely to have difficulty when attempting to learn computer skills. However, the work of Willis (1987, 1989) and others regarding cognitive training is encouraging. The findings from this research indicate considerable plasticity in the elderly's cognitive functioning. As is demonstrated in the next section, whereas there may be age differences on measures of learning in the acquisition of computer skills, older people are able to learn to use computer technology. It may be that existing interfaces or traditional training methods create problems for older people. The next sections summarizes current findings regarding aging and the use of computers. The discussion is organized according to training and learning studies and those examining interface design. Within each section the design implications of the research findings for system design are discussed.

Aging and Computer Training

A number of studies have been conducted that have examined the issue of aging and the acquisition of computer skills. Most of these studies focused on text editing and were concerned with identifying factors that influence learning success or compare the effectiveness of various training techniques. Although these studies showed that older people can learn to use computer technology, they also suggest that older people have more difficulty than younger people in acquiring computer skills.

Egan and Gomez (1985) conducted a series of experiments concerned with identifying and isolating individual differences in learning a text editing task. They found that age was a significant predictor of learning difficulty. Age was related to number of first-try errors and execution time per successful text change such that errors and execution time increased with age. The participants in their studies ranged in age from 28 to 62 years. In terms of isolating the components of text-editing that account for learning difficulty, they found that age was associated with difficulty producing the correct sequence of symbols and patterns to accomplish the desired editing change. This finding supports the conjecture that age-related decrements in memory may contribute to learning difficulties. The text editor was command based and necessitated remembering a command language and producing a complicated command syntax. In fact, they found that when a display editor was used, in which changes were made by positioning a cursor at the location of change and using labeled functions keys rather than a command language, the predictive power of age, with respect to the difficulty of learning, was greatly reduced.

Elias, Elias, Robbins, and Gage (1987) also examined age differences in the acquisition of text editing skills and attempted to identify sources of difficulty encountered by older persons. The participants in their study ranged in age from 18 to 67 years. They were trained to use a widely available word processing program using audiotape and a training manual. The training was self-paced and a trainer was available to assist the subjects.

Their results indicated that all participants, regardless of age, were able to learn the fundamentals of word processing. However, the older participants took longer to complete the training and evaluation protocol. They also required more trainer interventions and performed more poorly on the review examination. The older participants did not retain as much of the information as the younger people. Further, the type of difficulties encountered by the older adults during training suggested that they had difficulty suppressing knowledge that was inappropriate for text editing, such as knowledge related to the operation of a typewriter. This finding is consistent with our findings (Czaja, Hammond, Blascovich, & Swede, 1989) regarding inappropriate typewriter analogies. In our studies of text editing, we found that older people had difficulty grasping the concept of *computer file* and also had problems with the use of the *enter* key. It may be that they were unable to modify previously well learned concepts relating to typewriters. Halasz and Moran (1982), in their study of text editing, found that many of the errors made by the study participants could be explained by inappropriate use of their knowledge about typewriters. Elias et al. (1987) pointed out that when teaching older people text editing it is important to point out differences between using a typewriter and using a computer for document preparation.

Gist et al. (1988) examined the influence of age and training method on mastery of a spreadsheet program. Training consisted of either a tutorial or a behavioral modeling approach. The results indicated that the modeling approach was superior to the tutorial approach for both younger and older subjects. They also found that the older people performed more poorly on a training postest.

Garfein, Schaie, and Willis (1988) also examined the ability of older adults to learn a spread sheet package (Lotus 1-2-3). In addition they examined abilities that are predictive of acquiring computer skills. Their results indicated that all participants were able to operate a computer and use the spreadsheet package after only two brief training sessions. Training consisted of two 90-minute sessions. There were no significant age effects for the performance measures. However, it should be pointed out that the age range of the participants was 49 to 67 years; there was no younger control group. With respect to abilities the data indicated that measures of fluid intelligence (abstract reasoning) predicted microcomputer proficiency.

Zandri and Charness (1989) examined the influence of training method (learning alone or with a peer, with and without preliminary information about computers) on learning to use a calendar and notepad system. The sample consisted of younger (20–39 years) and older (58–64 years) subjects with no prior software experience. They found that the older adults took twice the amount of time to proceed through the self-paced tutorials than the younger adults and required more assistance during training. However, the older people achieved nearly equal levels of performance as the younger participants. These results support the conjecture that self paced training is beneficial for older people. Providing preliminary information about computers did not consistently improve the performance of the older subjects and resulted in lower performance for the younger participants. The authors suggested that this finding may reflect the way in which the information was provided. The preliminary information was given on jargon sheets and did not include examples directly related to the task.

In a more recent study, Charness and colleagues investigated how training techniques and computer anxiety affected the acquisition of word processing skills by younger and older adult trainees (Charness, Schumann, & Boritz, 1992). Half of the subjects received an advanced organizer prior to training. As before, the results indicated that the older adults took longer to complete the lessons and required more frequent help. They also performed more poorly on a review quiz than did the younger subjects. Further, the advanced organizer did not improve performance of either younger or older adults. Amount of computer anxiety did not affect performance. There were no age differences in computer anxiety.

In a separate study, the investigators examined whether a self-paced active training condition versus a fixed-paced passive learning condition would be better for older adults. As before, the older adults performed more poorly than the younger adults. The self-paced training was found to be superior for all participants. As discussed by the authors, this finding could be interpreted in a positive light, as it implies that employers need not devise specialized training programs for older workers.

Our findings regarding text editing are consistent with those of other investigators. In our initial study of text editing (Czaja, Hammond, Blascovich, & Swede, 1989) we examined the ability of different age groups to learn text editing. In addition, the training method was varied to compare the effectiveness of various training strategies. The training methods included online instruction, instructor based training, and manual based training. The results indicated that the younger participants were more successful at learning text editing than the older participants. The older people took longer to complete the posttraining tasks and also made more errors. Examination of the error data indicated that the older adults made more formatting errors that were related to the design of the printed page, for example, line spacing.

With respect to training strategy, online instruction was found to be inferior to instructor and manual based training for all participants. The online package used in the study created a passive learning experience in that the learners made prescribed responses to prompts on the screen. Belbin (1970) has shown that active, discovery learning is superior for older adults.

In a more recent study (Czaja, Hammond, & Joyce, 1989) we attempted to identify training strategies which would be effective in teaching older adults to learn text editing. We designed a goal-oriented training method and compared it with a more traditional approach—use of a manual and lecture. As shown in Figs. 10.1 and 10.2, the

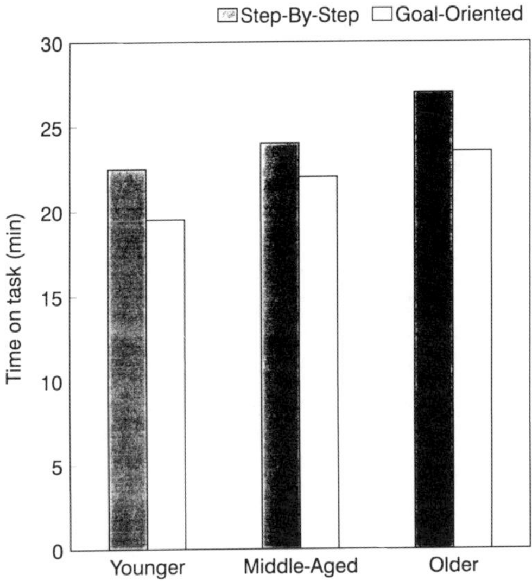

FIG. 10.1 Average time on a text editing task as a function of age and training condition.

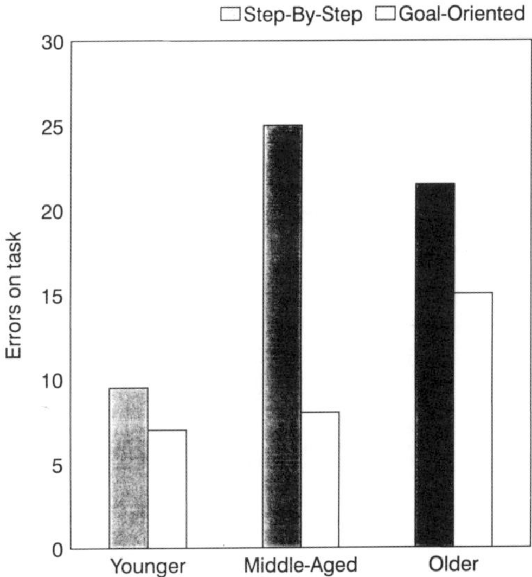

FIG. 10.2 Average number of errors committed on a text editing task as a function of age and training condition.

goal-oriented approach resulted in improved performance for all participants. People receiving goal-oriented training took less time per task and made fewer errors. Overall, the results did demonstrate that the learning performance of older people can be improved by the manipulation of training strategies. Further, these manipulations resulted in performance improvements for all participants.

The goal oriented approach involved introducing the elements of text editing in an incremental fashion, moving from the simple to the more complex. It also involved structuring the training into a series of problem solving tasks such that the learners were given a number of text editing tasks and had to use a specifically designed manual to achieve the goal of completing the tasks. Thus, the training involved active discovery on the part of the learner, a system that was proven to be effective with older adults (Belbin & Belbin, 1972). The manual was written as a series of goal-oriented units. The language was simplified and, wherever possible, analogies were drawn between computer concepts and familiar concepts (e.g., *file*). However, differences between using a typewriter and using a computer were stressed. Finally, the manual was designed in a streamlined fashion minimizing the amount of necessary reading. Another important finding of the study was that, even though there were age differences on the performance of the criterion tasks, the older adults were able to master the basic concepts of text editing.

Morrell, Park, Mayhorn, and Echt (1995) recently completed a study that examined how age-related changes in cognition and instructional format affected performance on the ELDERCOMM bulletin board system. Groups of young-old (M = 68.60) and old-old (M = 79.9) adults were presented with procedural instructional materials or a combination of conceptual information and procedural instructions for the operation the bulletin board system. They found age differences in performance such that the young-old adults were better able to perform the tasks on the bulletin board system; the old-old adults made more performance errors. They also found that the procedural instructions were superior for all participants. The authors concluded that conceptual training may not be beneficial for older adults; instead, clearly written, concise, and illustrated instructions may be more appropriate for this age group.

We recently completed a study (Czaja & Sharit, 1993) that examined whether there were age differences in the performance of three simulated real-world computer tasks—a data entry task, a file modification task, and an inventory management task. These particular tasks were chosen because they vary in skill demands and are representative of computer tasks in a wide variety of work settings. Although the study was not concerned with training, it is worth mentioning because it presents data regarding the performance of older people on computer-tasks other than text editing. As shown in Figs. 10.3 and 10.4, for all three tasks, the older people took longer to complete the task problems and committed a greater number of errors than younger people. The longest response times were found for the most complex task, thein-ventory management task. The older people also reported the tasks to be more stress-inducing and difficult. These differences were found even when differences in prior experience with computers were controlled. However, it should be pointed out that, despite the age differences, the older people were able to learn to perform the tasks after a relatively brief amount of training (90 min). Perhaps if they were provided with more practice and task experience the age differences in performance would have been reduced.

Overall, the results from these studies indicate that older people are able to learn to use computers. However, they have more difficulty than younger people. The findings also indicate that training manip-ulations can improve the performance of the elderly. More research is needed to identify training strategies which are beneficial to older learners.

On the basis of the current findings we can draw the following

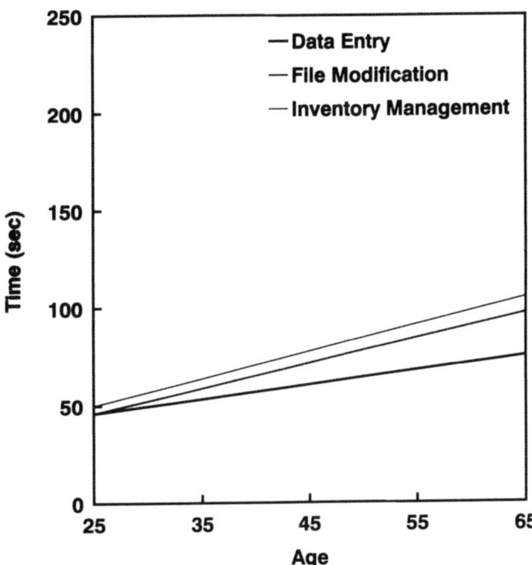

FIG. 10.3 Average time per task problem for three computer tasks as a function of age.

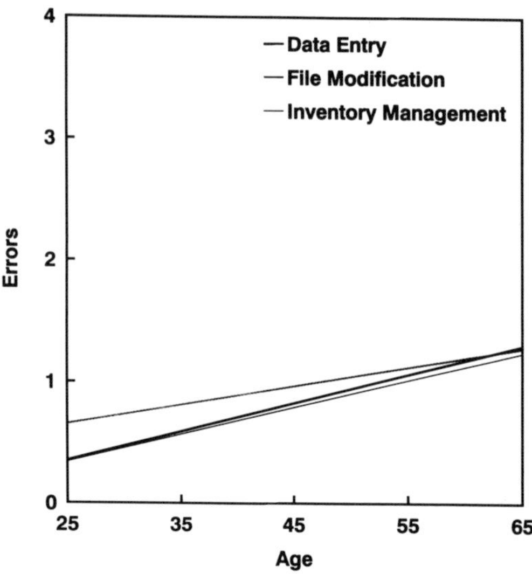

FIG. 10.4 Average number of errors per task problem for three computer tasks as a function of age.

conclusions with respect to designing training programs to facilitate the ability of older people to successfully acquire computer skills:

- It is important to familiarize the learner with basic concepts regarding hardware and software and use of the equipment so that the learner can build an appropriate mental model of the system. However, this information should not be too detailed.
- It is important to address any concerns the learner has about using the equipment (e.g., when text scrolls it is not lost) so that they are comfortable using the system.
- Familiar concepts should be used in training so that the learner can build on existing knowledge. However, distinctions between computers and typewriters should be highlighted.
- Feedback and instructor support should be given to the learner. Several studies have shown that older people need more assistance during the learning process.
- The learner should be given sufficient time to process and integrate the information. It appears that self-paced learning schedules may be appropriate for older adults.
- The training environment must be free from distractions.
- Training materials should be well organized, streamlined, and important information should be highlighted. Illustrations should be used where possible to compliment information provided in the text.

- The training program should involve active participation on the part of the learner.
- The learner should be provided with sufficient practice and errors should be corrected immediately so that they do not become "learned."

Interface Design

The design of the computer interface is also a critical issue when considering the ability of older people to acquire computer skills. The flexibility of today's computer systems offers enormous potential for designing systems which are suitable for older people. However, the design of such systems requires an understanding of how age-related changes in abilities impact on the performance of computer tasks ("what do older people find difficult"), and the identification of design alternatives that facilitate the performance of older people. Unfortunately, work in this area has been minimal. Thus, the following discussion can only offer speculative suggestions with respect to software design.

The aging and cognitive ability literature suggests that systems that place minimal demands on working memory are more suitable for older people. Generally, the results from the computer studies support this conjecture. For example, in our study of computer communication we found that the study participants sometimes had difficulty remembering the address name (e.g., "mail," "weather") needed to access a particular application. We also needed to add some on-screen reminders regarding the procedures for sending mail. Similarly, in our research on text editing, we found that older adults had more difficulty recalling operating procedures than younger adults. As noted, Egan and Gomez (1985) found that a display editor was less difficult for older people to use than a line editor was. The line editor required the users to recall complex commands and a command language.

In general, these findings suggest that menu-based systems might be beneficial for older people because they reduce the memory demands placed on users. Menus involve recognition of options, minimizing the need for recall. Joyce (1989) found that older people were better able to use a text editor with pull-down menus than one using a command language. Charness and colleagues (Charness, Kelley, Bosman, & Mottram, in press) compared a keystroke command interface, menu, and menu-plus-icon-based interface on word processing skill acquisition for a sample adults. They predicted an age by interface interaction such that the keystroke condition (the more difficult condition) would be more difficult for older adults, as it provided the least amount of environmental support. They found a significant main effect of interface such that performance was worse for the keystroke condition; however, they failed to find an age-by-interface interaction. They also found main effects for age such that the performance of the older adults was lower than that of the younger adults (see Charness et al., chapter 11, this volume, for a discussion of these results).

Although menu-based systems may be beneficial for older people the design of the system needs to be carefully evaluated. For example, the number of levels of the menus is an important issue as it affects the ease with which users can locate menus items. It would appear that, given age-related declines in working memory, the number of levels of the menu should be kept to a minimum so that users do not get lost and thus do not have difficulty locating commands. Also, the name of the menu should reflect the contents, and the items in a menu should have some logical association. These recommendations should reduce memory demands.

The use of icons might also prove beneficial for older people, as icons also provide environmental support and reduce memory load. Again, this issue needs to be carefully evaluated, as the use of icons can add to the complexity of the system. For example, if there is a large number of icons, or the meaning of the icon is not readily apparent, the user has to learn a new set of associations. The size of the icons is also important. Icons that are small in size are likely to be difficult for older people to see or access with a mouse.

The motor demands associated with menus and icons also need to be considered. In most systems, the user interacts with a mouse to click on a menu or an icon. Use of the mouse requires fine positioning and coordination (translation) of movements between the desk space and the screen space. In our study of text editing (Czaja, Hammond, Blascovich, & Swede, 1989) we found that older people had difficulty with cursor movement and with positioning text on the screen. Charness et al. (in press) found that novice older learners committed far more mouse-related errors than younger adults. They found that the older adults had particular difficulty acquiring smaller targets. They speculated that part of the problem was learning to control the fine positioning aspects of the movement. In a follow-up study (Charness, 1995) they compared the use of a light pen versus use of a mouse for target selection between a sample of younger and older adults. They found that the use of the light pen resulted in faster movement times for both the younger and older subjects and that age differences were greater with the mouse than with the light pen. They also found that small targets were especially problematic for the older people. Charness (1995) suggested that light pens might be preferable for older people. However, he cautioned that only a limited array of activities was tested and that the mouse speed was set at the slowest possible setting. Further, the sample included only novices. In general, the design of input devices is an area that needs research attention. This is especially true for people who are frail or have some type of hand or finger disability as they are likely to have different requirements with respect to input devices.

Another issue that needs to be addressed is the effect of experience on performance. It may be that age differences on the performance of computer tasks are reduced or eliminated with extensive practice. Salthouse (1984) has shown that experience on a task can compensate for age-related declines in abilities. Attention to this issue is especially important with respect to computer tasks, as older people are much less likely than younger people to have had experience with these types of tasks.

CONCLUSIONS

The intent of this chapter was to outline some of the issues relevant to the use of computer technology by older adults. The information presented suggests that unless careful attention is given to the design of the user interface and the design of training strategies successful use of computers may prove difficult for older people. This is not to suggest that older people will not be able to use this technology. Clearly, existing data indicate that older people are willing and able to use computers. However, there is a need for more research in this area so that we can optimize their interactions with these types of systems. In this regard we need to translate theory regarding aging and cognition into guidelines for system design and test these designs with both younger and older user populations. Vast opportunities exist for more research in the area of aging and human–computer interaction.

REFERENCES

Ansley, J., & Erber, J. T. (1988). Computer interaction: Effects on attitudes and performance in older adults. *Educational Gerontology, 14*, 107–119.

Belbin, R. M. (1970). The discovery method in training older workers. In H. L. Sheppard (Ed.), *Toward an industrial gerontology* (pp. 56–60). Cambridge, MA: Schenkman.

Belbin, E., & Belbin, R. M. (1972). *Problems in adult retraining*. London: Heinman.

Charness, N., & Bosman, E. A. (1990). Human factors and design for older adults. In J. E. Birren & K. W. Schaie (Eds.), *Handbook of the psychology of aging* (3rd ed., pp. 446–460). New York: Academic.

Charness, N., Schumann, C. E., & Boritz, G. A. (1992). Training older adults in word processing: Effects of age, training technique and computer anxiety. *International Journal of Aging and Technology*, 5, 79–106.

Charness, N. (1995, August). *Senior-friendly input devices: Is the pen mightier than the mouse?* Paper presented at the 103rd annual meeting of the American Psychological Association, New York, NY.

Charness, N., Kelley, C., Bosman, E., & Mottram, M. (in press). Cognitive theory and word processing training: When prediction fails. In W. A. Rogers, A. D. Fisk, & N. Walker (Eds.), *Aging and skilled performance: Advances in theory and application*. Mahwah, NJ: Lawrence Erlbaum Associates.

Craik, F. I. M., & Simon, E. (1980). Age differences in memory: The roles of attention and depth of processing. In L. W. Poon, J. L. Fozard, L. S. Cermack, D. Arenberg, & L. W. Thompson (Eds.), *New directions in memory and aging: Proceedings of the George A. Talland Memorial Conference* (pp. 95–112). Hillsdale, NJ: Lawrence Erlbaum Associates.

Czaja, S. J., Hammond, K., & Joyce, J. B. (1989). *Word processing training for older adults.* (Final report submitted to the National Institute on Aging; Grant # 5 R4 AGO4647-03).

Czaja, S. J., Hammond, K., Blascovich, J. J., & Swede, H. (1989). Age related differences in learning to use a text-editing system. *Behavior and Information Technology*, 8, 309–319.

Czaja, S. J., Guerrier, J., Nair, S. N., Landauer, T. K. (1993). Computer communication as an aid to independence for older adults. *Behavior and Information Technology*, 12, 197–207.

Czaja, S. J., & Sharit, J. (1993). Age differences in the performance of computer-based work. *Psychology and Aging*, 1, 1–9.

Egan, D. E., & Gomez, L. M. (1985). Assaying, isolating, and accommodating individual differences in learning a complex skill. *Individual Differences in Cognition*, 2, 174–217.

Eilers, M. L. (1989). Older adults and computer education: "Not to have the world a closed door." *International Journal of Technology and Aging*, 2, 56–76.

Elias, P. K., Elias, M. F., Robbins, M. A., & Gage, P. (1987). Acquisition of word-processing skills by younger, middle-aged, and older adults. *Psychology and Aging*, 2, 340–348.

Fisk, A. D., McGee, N. D., & Giambra, L. M. (1988). The influence of age on consistent and varied semantic category search performance. *Psychology and Aging*, 3, 323–333.

Fisk, A. D., Rogers, W. A., & Giambra, L. M. (1990). Consistent and varied memory/visual search: Is there an interaction between age and response set effects? *Journal of Gerontology: Psychological Sciences*, 45, P81–P87.

Furlong, M. S. (1989). An electronic community for older adults: The SeniorNet network. *Journal of Communication*, 39, 145–153.

Gallienne, R. L., Moore, S. M., & Brennan, P. L. (1993). Alzheimer's care givers: Psychological support via computer networks. *Journal of Gerontological Nursing, December*, 15–22.

Garfein, A. J., Schaie, K. W., & Willis, S. L. (1988). Microcomputer proficiency in later-middle-aged adults and older adults: Teaching old dogs new tricks. *Social Behavior*, 3, 131–148.

Gist, M., Rosen, B., & Schwoerer, C. (1988). The influence of training method and trainee age on the acquisition of computer skills. *Personnel Psychology*, 41, 255–265.

Halasz, F., & Moran, T. P. (1982). Analogy considered harmful. *Proceedings of Human Factors of Computing Systems* (pp. 383–386). Gaithersberg, MD: Association of Computing Machinery.

Hockey, G. R., Briner, R. B., Tattersell, A. J., & Wietoff, M. (1989). Assessing the impact of computer workload on operator stress: The role of system controllability. *Ergonomics, 32,*, 1401–1418.

Hulicka, I. M., & Grossman, J. L. (1967). Age-group comparisons for the use of mediators in paired-associate learning. *Journal of Gerontology, 22,* 46–51.

Joyce, B. J. (1989). *Identifying differences in learning to use a text-editor: The role of menu structure and learner characteristics.* Unpublished master's thesis, State University of New York at Buffalo.

Krauss, I. K., & Hoyer, W. J. (1985). Technology and the older person: Age, sex, and experience as moderators of attitudes towards computers. In P. K. Robinson, J. Livingston, & J. E. Birren (Eds.), *Aging and technological advances* (pp. 349–350). New York: Plenum.

Leirer, V. O., Morrow, D. G., Tanke, E. D., & Pariante, G. M. (1991). Elder's nonadherence: Its assessment and medication reminding by voice mail. *The Gerontologist, 31,* 515–520.

Morrell, R. W., Park, D. C., Mayhorn, C. B., & Echt, K. V. (1995, August). *Older adults and electronic communication networks: Learning to use ELDERCOMM.* Paper presented at the 103rd annual meeting of the American Psychological Association, New York.

Moss, M., & Lawton, M. P. (1982). Time budgets of older people: a window on four lifestyles. *Journal of Gerontology, 37,* 115–123.

Nair, S. (1989). *A capability-demand analysis of grocery shopping problems encountered by older adults.* Unpublished master's thesis, State University of New York at Buffalo.

Neugarten, B. L. (1977). Personality and aging. In J. E. Birren, & K. W. Schaie (Eds.), *Handbook of the psychology of aging* (pp. 626–649). New York: Van Nostrand Reinhold.

Office of Technology Assessment (1985, June). *Technology and aging in America* (OTA-BA-264). Washington, DC: U.S. Congress, Office of Technology Assessment.

Park, D. C. (1992). Applied cognitive aging research. In F. I. M. Craik & T. A. Salthouse (Eds.), *Handbook of aging and cognition* (pp. 449–494). Hillsdale, NJ: Lawrence Erlbaum Associates.

Plude, D. J., & Hoyer, W. J. (1985). Attention and performance: identifying and localizing age deficits. In N. Charness (Ed.), *Aging and human performance* (pp. 47–99). New York: Wiley.

Rabbit, P. A. (1965). An age decrement in the ability to ignore irrelevant information. *Journal of Gerontology, 20,* 233–238.

Robinson, P. K., Coberly, S., & Paul, C. E. (1985). Work and retirement. In R. H. Binstock and E. Shanas (Eds.), *Handbook of aging and the social sciences* (2nd ed., pp. 503–527). New York: Van Nostrand Reinhold.

Rogers, W. A., & Fisk, A. D. (1991). Age-related differences in the maintenance and modification of automatic processes: Arithmetic stroop interference. *Human Factors, 33,* 45–56.

Salthouse, T. A. (1984). Effects of age and skill in typing. *Journal of Experimental Aging Psychology: General, 113,* 345–371.

Salthouse, T. A. (1985). Speed of behavior and its implication for cognition. In J. E. Birren, & K. W. Schaie (Eds.), *Handbook of psychology of aging* (pp. 400–426). New York: Van Nostrand Reinhold.

Salthouse, T. A. (1993). Speed and knowledge as determinants of adult age differences in verbal tasks. *Journal of Gerontology, 48,* 29–36.

Sauter, S. L., Murphy, L. R., & Hurrell, J. T. (1990). Prevention of work related psychological disorders: A national strategy proposed by the National Institute for

Occupational Safety and Health. *American Psychologist, 45*, 1146–1158.

Stones, M. J., & Kozma, A. (1985). Physical performance. In N. Charness (Ed.), *Aging and human performance*, (pp. 261–292). New York: Wiley.

Welford, A. T. (1985). Changes of performance with age: An overview. In N. Charness (Ed.), *Aging and human performance* (pp. 333–365). New York: Wiley.

Willis, S. L. (1987). Cognitive training and everyday competence. In K. W. Schaie & C. Eisdorfer (Eds.), *Annual review of gerontology and geriatrics* (pp. 159–188). New York: Springer.

Willis, S. L. (1989). Improvement with cognitive training: Which old dogs learn what tricks? In L. W. Poon, D. C. Rubin, & B. A. Wilson (Eds.), *Everyday cognition in adulthood and late life* (pp. 545–572). Cambridge, MA: Cambridge University Press.

Witte, K. L. (1975). Paired-associate learning in young and elderly adults as related to presentation. *Psychological Bulletin, 82*, 975–985.

Zandri E., & Charness, A. (1989). Training older and younger adults to use software. *Educational Gerontology, 15*, 615–631.

CHAPTER 11

Cognitive Theory and Word Processing Training: When Prediction Fails

Neil Charness
Florida State University

Elizabeth Bosman
Baycrest Centre for Geriatric Care

Catherine Kelley
University of Waterloo

Melvin Mottram
Alberta Safety Council

One way to judge the progress of a field is to see whether we can predict accurately from principles discovered in the laboratory to real-world situations. If we cannot, then it may be time to go back to the laboratory and re-examine our experimental paradigms and our theories. A parallel can be seen with biological research, comparing in vitro with in vivo testing. The effect should not disappear as you scale up from cell cultures to laboratory animals to human populations, and there should be no unintended side effects, such as was the case for the drug thalidomide.

One of the major problems in scaling up laboratory results in social sciences such as psychology is that we usually deal with people who can change the method of doing nearly any task, and they typically perform a given task in a vast range of environmental settings. To circumvent this problem, we typically attempt to hold constant as many variables as possible that might be involved in performance, manipulating just the few we feel are critical to the process we are investigating. We can often constrain task strategy with such controls. Unfortunately, we usually do not have this level of control in the field where strategies can and do vary freely to fit the environmental constraints.

Also, in aging research in particular, given the difficulty in locating participants for our experiments, and the heterogeneity of older adults, we rely heavily on repeated measurements with the same people: within-subject experimental designs. Such experiments usually involve many (10–1000) massed trials of similar or identical experimental materials. Such extensive replication of basic trial types is often necessary to achieve reliable estimates of mental processing times. Repeated-measures designs also allow the participant to act as his or her own control, thereby minimizing the effects of individual differences.

These techniques provide our laboratory experiments with high internal validity, but leave the question of external validity (or ecological validity) open in two respects. First, we do not usually encounter an hour or two of intense repetitive mental or physical activities in our daily lives. (Exceptions do come to mind, such as assembly-line work.) Second, the variables we choose to hold constant usually vary enormously in range in the real world. We usually do not know, or fail to check, the range over which they vary. (Luminance levels in the environment versus the laboratory is one example. The probability of consistent versus varied mapping for learning in the classroom is another.) We also do not usually know whether the variables we choose to hold constant interact with the variables we do manipulate. So, a critical step on the road to a robust science is to check whether an intervention based on our hard-won principles of behavior works as planned. Such checking usually requires a field study, first to observe what ranges of variables typically exist, and second to see whether our chosen experimental variables are the most powerful ones operating in the multivariate world. A schematic of our ideal scientific method (e.g., patterned loosely after Kerlinger, 1973) is offered in Fig. 11.1.

In psychology generally, and in cognitive aging research in particular, we tend to be weakest in evaluating that part of the scientific cycle that deals with testing our predictions in the world and bringing those results back into the lab for reexamination.

Recently, our research group had the opportunity to participate in a project that required an applied approach. This project was part of a

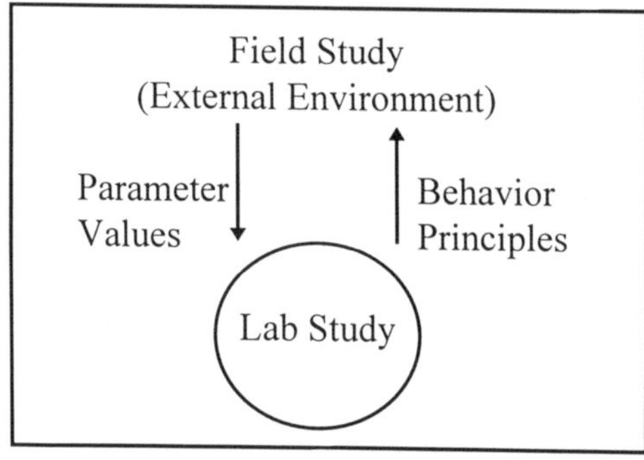

FIG. 11.1 The lab-life feedback loop.

human factors project for CARNET, the Canadian Aging Research Network. One of the aims of this national network of centres of excellence was to find ways to improve the productivity of an aging population. We chose to focus on the tool of the day, the modern microcomputer. Great claims have been made for how the service sector is to be transformed by modern computer hardware and software. However, some research showed that older adults are at a disadvantage when learning to use computers (see Kelley & Charness, 1995, for a review). We felt that middle-aged and older workers were in some danger of being left behind by the computer revolution. A second concern was that much of the prior research was done using computer systems with interaction styles very different from those used in modern, graphical user interface systems. One of our goals was to determine effective training conditions for older workers, primarily via different styles of computer interface, in the hope of finding one that would be particularly beneficial to older adults.

In this research we trained adults to use a real word processing package, Microsoft Word for Windows 1.1a, in order to ensure high generalizability for our conclusions. Our main focus was on age and interface effects. To ensure some degree of rigor, we attempted to turn the task into a laboratory task by creating three parallel interface conditions (keystrokes, menus, menus plus icons) using a tutorial procedure and predefined learning experiences and tests.

ENVIRONMENTAL SUPPORT

In our first study with novices we were particularly enthusiastic about exploring the newer graphical user interfaces (GUIs) that have begun to replace the old keystroke command interfaces that dominated computing from its inception. In a keystroke-based command entry system, the user instructs the computer to carry out actions by pressing keys, such as the SHIFT key simultaneously with the F12 key to save a file. With GUIs, the user manipulates an input device such as a mouse or a trackball to click on a menu or a picture (icon) to do the same task. While it may require clicking through several layers of menus to find some commands, the principle is that there is a visual cue in the environment that guides action selection. There is quite a lot of theorizing about memory and aging that leads to the prediction that GUIs ought to be particularly helpful to novice older users since they present command learning as a form of cued recall (menus) or recognition (icons). The older keystroke-based techniques are classic examples of learning for which the cue for the action sequence is nowhere to be seen in the environment (a form of free recall).

There have been surprisingly few studies conducted in which keystroke-entry interfaces have been compared to graphical or menu-based interfaces, and these yielded mixed results (e.g., Antin, 1988; Davies, Lambert, & Findlay, 1989; Hauptmann & Green, 1983; Sengupta & Te'eni, 1991; Tombaugh, Paynter, & Dillon, 1989; Whiteside, Jones, Levy, & Wixon, 1985; Wolf, 1992). One problem with comparing different interfaces is that real interfaces vary along many dimensions other than command entry style (Whiteside et al., 1985). To overcome this problem, we used the same word processor in all three conditions of our study. We simply varied the method that was used to select commands. In the Word for Windows word processor, formatting changes require three basic steps. A user first must find the text to change, then select it, and then choose a command. The actions that were required to execute the first two steps were entirely identical across the three interfaces. We only altered the method used to select the command. For instance, to bold a word, in the keystrokes condition the person pressed the *control* key simultaneously with the *b* key. In the menus condition, the person was required to click the *bold* option in a dialog box. In the menus plus icons condition, the person could use the latter procedure or click a *bold* icon. The displays facing participants in the three conditions were identical, except for the presence of an icon bar in the menus plus icons condition and the fact that the visible menu in the keystrokes condition was disabled. An example of the menus plus icons screen appears in Fig. 11.2.

In order to determine *a priori* which of our three conditions was the most difficult, we looked at some theoretical frameworks for making predictions about interface that provided fairly complete formal models of task difficulty.

One of the earliest and most specific models, based on a model human information processor (Card, Moran, & Newell, 1983), proposes to model behavior with the GOMS technique, using formal descriptions of Goals, Operators, Methods, and Selection rules. GOMS was developed initially in a text editing environment, which is similar to our task domain of word processing (Card, Moran, & Newell, 1980). An important constraint is that GOMS is meant to apply to experienced users only. On the other hand, GOMS-type models have been used to predict the difficulty of learning to use a text editing system (Bovair, Kieras, & Polson, 1990; Kieras & Polson, 1985), and therefore have some relevance to our work.

However, GOMS analysis was not suitable for making predictions in our study. This is because the GOMS model and the similar complexity

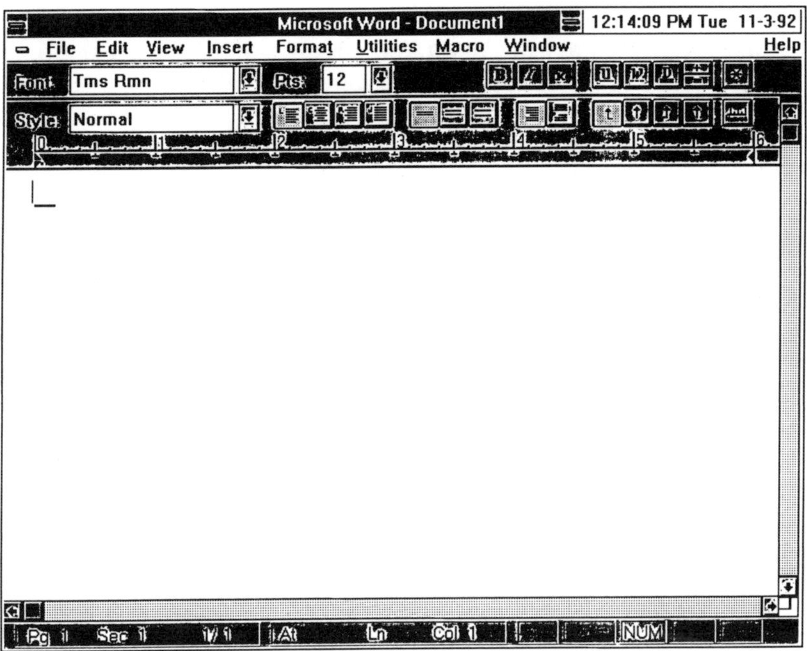

FIG. 11.2 The menus plus icons word screen.

model developed by Kieras and Polson (1985) pertain to the structure of command execution rather than the mechanics of command execution. As mentioned before, the structure of command execution was identical across conditions. This parallelism was verified by a thorough task analysis, conducted at the unit task structure level of analysis (Card et al., 1983). Although identical command structures were found for each of the three conditions, we did not believe that identical predictions would be made for each condition, due to the working memory demands imposed by the keystrokes-only interface. While the Kieras and Polson (1985) model explicitly states that the ability to learn to use a computer system is a function of the demands placed on working memory while learning, assessment of working memory demands is done by counting the number of productions that a user must hold in memory at any one time. No provision is made for the different working memory demands imposed by using free recall (command line or control key) interfaces versus cued recall (menus or icons) interfaces. A more complete simulation architecture in which working memory demands are fully specified at this level would be required to make strong predictions in our study.

Finally, there are competence models of command system difficulty that would apply to the case of novices, such as the task action grammar (TAG) model of Payne and Green (1986). TAG attempts to unpack command structure via metarules and instantiations of those rules as feature-value to action rules. Command languages that can be described with fewer metarules should be easier to learn and use. If metarules are equal between languages, the one with fewer total rules should be easier. Unfortunately, attempts to replicate basic TAG predictions have not always succeeded (Cramer, 1994; Cramer, Charness, Tompa, & Bennett, 1994), perhaps due to the larger command set utilized in these studies or perhaps because structure and mnemonics are somewhat confounded in the original TAG analysis. Because we are using a commercial word processor with a command set that is an order of magnitude larger than that investigated in Cramer et al. (1994), TAG analysis was rejected as unworkable.

Thus, rather than try for a precise model of novice behavior we instead fell back on general principles from human–computer interaction and from aging research that we felt made predictions about the expected relative positions of interfaces and people. Our feeling was that if these principles could be effective predictors then we could move ahead to more precise task models.

In putting together the variable set we manipulated (age, interface) we drew on theory in a loose way. We knew that, generally speaking, older adults would learn more slowly than younger ones (e.g., Craik & Jennings, 1992; Hultsch & Dixon, 1990). However, age differences are often, but not always, reduced when environmental support is high (Craik, 1986). That is, if people have to use self-initiated cues to access memory (e.g., free recall), they do much worse than when they can capitalize on cues in the environment (cued recall, recognition). Despite the mixed results in the human–computer interaction literature, we also suspected that modern direct manipulation interfaces, as seen in the GUIs appearing in the Apple Macintosh and Windows environments, ought to be easier to learn than old-style command line interfaces. Similarly, the age–complexity hypothesis (e.g., Cerella, Poon, & Williams, 1980) argues that the more difficult the task, the greater the expected gap in performance between young and old. Juxtaposing these observations led to our first prediction.

Prediction 1: A keystrokes-based interface ought to be much more difficult for older adults to learn than a menu-based or menu plus icon-based interface. That is, there should be an age by interface interaction, given the greater reliance of older adults on environmental support to aid memory performance.

FANNING THE FLAMES OF FAILURE

We also were intrigued by the possibility that modern software packages may be suffering from a surfeit of methods in the options that they present to a user. Take word processing software as an example. In the package we use, Microsoft Word for Windows, there are often three ways to carry out the same action. If the user wants to apply italic formatting to a selected word, he or she can use the format/font menu and click italics in the dialog box (menu), or can click a button on an icon bar that shows a slanted I (icon), or can press the *control* and *i* keys on the keyboard simultaneously. If the user forgets one way (e.g., the keystrokes), he or she may remember one of the others or find them by searching for cues at the top of the screen.

Although providing multiple methods would seem to be a good thing, potentially it runs up against a classic memory retrieval phenomenon known as the *fan effect* (Anderson, 1974). If there are multiple links to a proposition, people are slower to access any one of those links relative to the case where there is only one link. If someone learns that "the hippie is in the park," and "the lawyer is in the station," and "the hippie is in the bank," verifying either of the two sentences about the hippie takes significantly longer than verifying the one sentence about the lawyer. To quote the famous architect, Miese van der Rohe, "less is more" when it comes to acting quickly on facts. Theoretically, there is a time penalty associated with spreading activation in a multiply-related concept structure compared to one in which the links are one to one.

There is evidence in the human-computer interaction field consistent with this interpretation too. Carroll and Carrithers (1984) showed that eliminating unnecessary complexity by removing options from menu systems improves performance for novices. This may be due to narrowing the search space for commands, or reducing the command–action links.

So a second prediction is that if we train people to do actions two ways, versus one way, those learning one way ought to perform more efficiently.

Prediction 2: When there are multiple links to the same concept, response time should be slowed to access any one of them relative to a 1:1 linking (e.g., the fan effect; Anderson, 1974). Thus, a menus plus icons interface that links the same outcome to two different action routes ought to lead to slower or more error-prone performance than a menus-only interface for those multiply-linked commands.

A similar prediction arises from modern attention theory: a consistent command context, one to one mapping (menus-only), ought to lead more quickly to automatic responding than a variable context, two to one mapping (menus plus icons).

SLOW GOING?

Finally, we wondered how successfully the ubiquitous finding of slowing in response time by older adults, relative to younger ones, would scale up to the case of self-paced training time. Brinley plots (Brinley, 1965) of young response time (RT) versus old RT have led to what we can call cognitive aging's first law:

$$\text{Old RT} = 1.7\ (\pm .3) \times \text{Young RT}. \tag{1}$$

This relationship is seen as reflecting generalized mental slowing (e.g., Cerella, 1990; Hale & Meyerson, 1995; Meyerson, Hale, Wagstaff, Poon, & Smith, 1990; Salthouse, 1991). Thus, there should be little problem scaling up this law from milliseconds to minutes or hours. Nonetheless, the empirical time band for this law is extremely narrow. Most response time studies fall in the range of 250 ms to 1 s. Much human design, for instance for highways, plans for human response times in the range of 2.5 s for responding to critical events (e.g., Olson & Sivak, 1986). Verifying the value of this parameter for self-paced learning is critical for those who design training programs. Thus, our third prediction was:

Prediction 3: Time to complete training in a self-paced protocol ought to yield the relationship that Old group training time should be in the range of 1.4 to 2.0 times longer than young group training time.

THE ENVELOPE, PLEASE

(The reader should make his or her prediction now about which predictions were confirmed.) In the research we are presenting, we do very well for a baseball batter or an oil-prospecting company, but not very well for scientists. Only one of three predictions holds. We hope to focus attention on why theory failed us and how we can go about improving our chances that predictions from the laboratory will scale up to the real world.

First, we highlight the major results from the study. For more details, see Charness, Kelley, Bosman, and Mottram (in preparation). In the novice study, we tested 72 adults assigned to a 3 × 3 design, with both age (young: $M = 27$; middle: $M = 46$; and old: $M = 63$) and interface (keystrokes, menus, menus plus icons) between-subjects factors. Our sample was well educated, with education levels not varying by age group. We defined *novices* to be those who reported that they had never taken any computer course; had never or rarely used a computer for any reason, and had never used a word processor, text editor, spreadsheet, or other office automation software. All participants reported that they could type.

The first study used three variants of Microsoft Word for Windows 1.1, as was described. We also developed three parallel tutorial manuals that were identical except for the instructions for choosing commands. One test procedure, the multiple choice test, also asked for knowledge about this formatting procedure in parallel ways, by presenting the correct alternative as a keystroke variant (ctrl-b) for keystrokes, a menus alternative for the menus condition, and as an icon alternative for the menus plus icons condition.

In this study we left many degrees of freedom to the participant by allowing people to work through the three parallel tutorial manuals at their own pace. We used a multisession training procedure (much like that of a training course), but allowed only 3 days of training.

The study was carried out over a 4-day span. Each of the first three days the participant worked in a self-paced fashion through a carefully prepared tutorial specific to the assigned interface. At the end of the day there was a review test for the material. On Day 4 there were two performance tests. One was a multiple choice test, the other an online editing performance test. Interfaces, tutorials, and performance tests were kept as parallel as possible.

MAJOR RESULTS

Given that we videotaped word processing performance in both tutorial, review, and final performance test stages, we had a wealth of measures. Time-based measures included the time taken for each day's tutorial and review test, and the time to complete the final performance quiz. Accuracy measures included scores for the reviews, multiple choice test performance, and the final performance tests, including detailed analyses of types of errors. Principal components factor analysis shows, however, that the time-based measures load on a single factor (accounting for about 71% of the variance in measures).

Similarly, the accuracy measures can be collapsed onto a single factor score for the purpose of providing a reasonably powerful test of age by interface effects. Note that we computed factor scores over both novice and experienced users for these analyses (Studies 1 and 2), so particularly for the performance composite, most of the means for novices are quite low. Correspondingly, for the time composite, the means tend to be high. We collapsed measures partly because we felt that there would be greater power to detect interactions that we expected, but failed to find, with the individual measures.

Time-Based Measures

An analysis of variance (ANOVA) using the time factor score (combining measures taken in sessions 1–3, for tutorial training times and review quiz times, and final performance test time) shows a main effect of age, $F(2, 63) = 41.5$, $MSE = .426$, $p < .001$, but no effect of interface nor an age by interface interaction (both F's < 1). The young group's mean factor score of $-.405$ is lower than the middle-age group's score of .318, which in turn is lower than that for the older group, 1.304. Because age was distributed fairly continuously, we show a plot of the factor scores as a function of age in Fig. 11.3. The older the person, the longer it took to work through the tutorials and tests. The regression equation shows that the time factor score increases about .5 for each decade increase in age.

Accuracy-Based Measures

We collapsed the final performance test scores (score, error-free score, help requests, efficiency) and the score on the multiple choice test to a

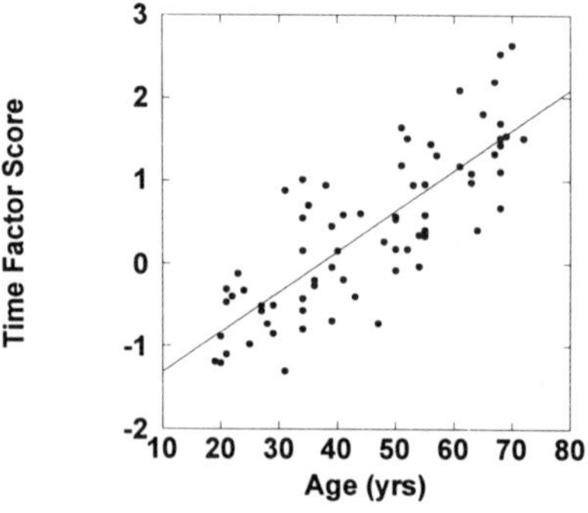

FIG. 11.3 Time factor score by age for novices, r = .81.

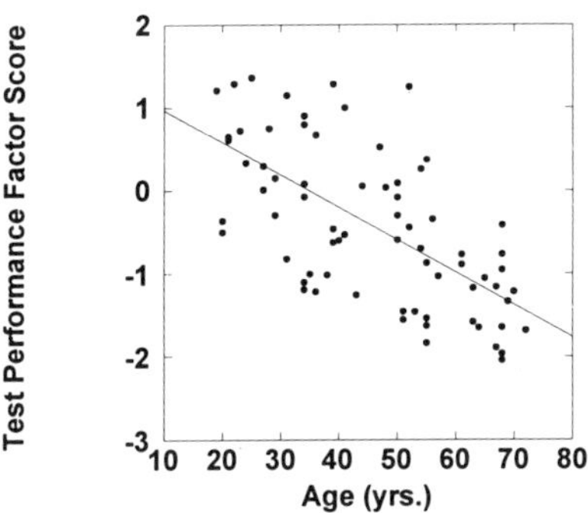

FIG. 11.4 Age by performance factor score for novices, r = .66.

single factor score (again accounting for 70% of the variance in these measures). An ANOVA with this composite yielded a main effect of age, $F(2, 63) = 24.03$, $MSE = .533$, $p < .001$, as well as a main effect of interface, $F(2, 63) = 3.28$, $p < .05$, but no evidence of an interaction effect ($F < 1$). The factor scores were higher for young ($M = .239$) than middle-age ($M = -.289$) than for old ($M = -1.204$) adults. The keystrokes condition yielded worse performance ($M = -.720$) than the menus ($M = -.202$) or the menus plus icons ($M = -.331$) conditions, though the latter two did not differ. Again, because age is reasonably continuous, we plot age versus test performance factor score in Fig. 11.4.

Finally, it is fair to ask about the extent to which the two factors correlate for novice computer users. If generalized slowing underlies most behavior, it may ultimately be reflected in accuracy as well as in time to carry out activities. For instance, people could "give up" on a task if they exceed a self-imposed deadline for solving the task, yielding lower accuracy scores. Next we show a plot of the time factor against the performance factor in Fig. 11.5. Indeed, the time factor and the performance accuracy factor are showing parallel pictures of word processing performance (possibly reflecting generalized slowing that is age-associated).

WHY THEORY FAILED

Prediction of an Age-by-Interface Effect for Word Processing Performance

Age by Interface interactions were nowhere to be seen for our main dependent variables, or for the factor scores discussed previously. One

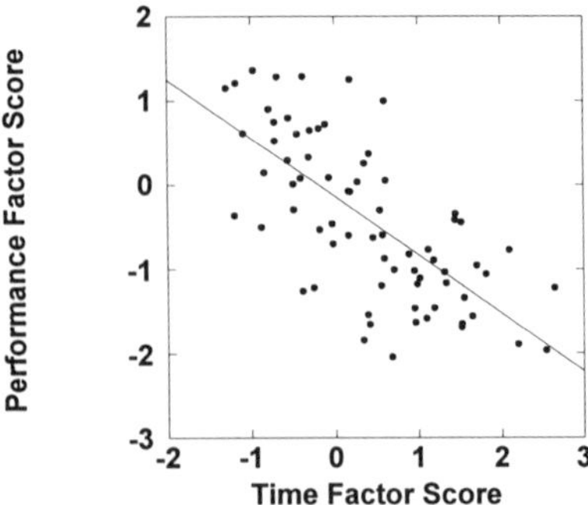

FIG. 11.5 Time factor score by performance factor score for novices, r = −.70.

could first fault power in the design. After all, we had only eight people in each cell in a between-subjects design. Still, the design was powerful enough to show both age and interface main effects (the latter only for the performance factor score). We are tempted to argue that if this sample size is not sufficient to show an effect, it probably means that most companies will also not show a significant effect with their more age-homogeneous employee groups. Our sample contained a very broad range of ages, with many retired adults in the older group. Interactions of age with interface are at best a second-order performance factor in our study. It is also of some solace to note that virtually all prior studies have also failed to find significant age by interface or training interactions (see Kelley & Charness, 1995, for a review).

One potential explanation for our failure to find an interaction is that the task we presented was sufficiently difficult and complex that people learned to operate the word processor only at a surface level, doing the commands mechanically without ever building up a schema or mental model of the word processing task. People may have been rote-memorizing procedures in all interface conditions. That is, in terms of the age-complexity hypothesis, all the conditions were equally difficult. Still, the significant main effect of interface showed that final performance on the keystrokes variant was much worse than either of the other two interfaces. The age-complexity hypothesis predicts that the more difficult condition, keystrokes, should have been even worse for older adults compared to younger ones.

Another hedge for our failure to predict accurately would be to argue that because the sessions were self-paced, young and old adjusted their time on task in a way that equalized their information extraction. If we had forced both groups through the tutorial at the same pace, we might have obtained the sought-for interaction. Although the older group took considerably longer than the middle-aged and young groups to traverse the tutorial materials, they still scored less well on the performance test. That is, they did not allocate sufficient time to eliminate the age-related performance differences. If they were not well calibrated with respect to learning time generally (e.g., Bieman-Copland & Charness, 1994; Murphy, Sanders, Gabriesheski, & Schmitt, 1981), they should have been particularly hurt by the more difficult keystrokes interface.

Nonetheless, one of the most robust theories from cognitive psychology, chunking theory (Miller, 1956; Simon, 1974), predicts interaction effects. Simon (1974) suggested that it takes 5 to 10 s to fixate a new rote chunk in long-term memory for young adults. Superimposing generalized slowing (by a factor of 1.7), we predict that it takes between 9 and 17 s for old adults to acquire a new chunk. It should take longer to build up a keystroke-based pairing, because the stimulus condition offers less environmental support. That is, people need to build up specific internal representations of both the desired action and the method. Assume that easy-to-learn chunks (menus condition) take 5 s and that difficult-to-learn ones (keystrokes) take 10 s for young adults. The corresponding times for older adults should be 9 and 17 s, and a graph would show this to represent a strong interaction. There are the same number of chunks (commands) to be learned in each tutorial across interfaces. So, given the lack of time difference main effects or interactions across interfaces, it is obvious that much time was spent on learning other than just the specific commands (and recall that older adults were less successful at the end). Perhaps if we had trained to a criterion the interaction would have emerged. Still the ratio of old learning time to young learning time for the tutorials was 1.8.

Once a chunk is encoded, it is used as a unit. Thus a keystroke-based chunk is no different than a menu-based one or an icon-based one. The time to apply the chunk to match new situations, however, is still subject to the same generalized slowing process, and older adults should be slower to apply their knowledge (chunks) than younger adults. Again, by happy coincidence, the ratio of old to young time to do the final performance test was 1.75.

Prediction of a Fan Effect

We find it easier to explain away the failure to find a fan effect. Investigations showed that if you can generate integrated representations for facts, there is a reduced fan effect (Moeser, 1979), or it can even be reversed (Myers, O'Brien, Balota, & Toyofuku, 1984). There are also asymmetries possible in terms of object location mappings. If many objects are associated with the same spatial location, there is no fan effect, but the slowing in response time appears if many locations are associated with a single object (Radvansky & Zacks, 1991). In short, the way in which mappings are achieved is critical to the appearance of a fan effect. In our studies, we do not have access to the representational structures that participants assembled as they learned how to carry out word processing commands.

Further, the fan effect is typically a moderate response time effect, 300 to 400 ms, something that we could not easily expect to show given the nature of our dependent variables and accuracy of measurement (1–10 s for high reliability of coding event occurrences). Also, only a subset of commands were open to fan effects (the formatting ones) so we obviously have a fairly weak test. We attempted to segregate out just the formatting commands but still cannot find significant interface effects.

Also, in typical fan experiments, participants are trained to the point where there is perfect recall of the fan items before being given a speeded recognition task. We suspect that some of our people would not meet the criterion of knowing all the commands. As well, they were not under instructions to respond as quickly as possible during the test of command knowledge. Thus, we were probably overly optimistic to expect to observe fan effects in our study. It is also possible that fan effects have minimal influence for complex cognition that takes place in time bands beyond a second or two and for tasks that do not involve time stress.

If we leave aside the case of novices and move toward expert word processors, the instantiation of editing operations is likely to be sufficiently over-practiced and routine (Card et al., 1980) that fan effects disappear. People may differentiate the internal representation of the command structure in ways that escape a fan effect. For instance, the print icon in Word for Windows 6.0 lets you print one copy of the current document, as does the File/Print menu route. The latter menu route is more specialized, however, so that if you want to print just the current page, or a selection of pages, or make multiple copies, you can do that too. So, you may associate the print icon with printing the document, and the File/Print dialog box may become associated only with special printing situations. Inevitably, for skilled performers, typing speed and degree of experience with a software package are likely to be the more important predictors of performance than any fan considerations.

SUGGESTIONS FOR MAKING PROGRESS

Generalized slowing does an excellent job of predicting the time taken to complete both the tutorials and the final performance test. What are we to do with a principle such as *environmental support* (Craik, 1986)? First, environmental support theory needs elaboration. Otherwise it may suffer the same fate as depth of processing, demise due to circular definition, because high environmental support seems to be defined in terms of minimal young-old performance differences. Such elaboration requires either: (a) finding a way to scale environments for support a priori, or (b) defining a process model for memory functioning that makes clear predictions about how a given configuration of retrieval cues ought to function. Although the latter is probably a more difficult task, it is probably the preferred route for translating lab principles to applied settings. We believe that environmental support, writ large, has strong utility for making the lives of older adults safer and more comfortable (e.g., Charness & Bosman, 1995). We also see utility in further research on the role of environmental features in supporting memory functioning, particularly with respect to training (e.g., Camp et al., 1993).

Returning to our opening theme, we started out looking for some predictions based on general principles of age and interface, hoping to move on to quantitative predictions following the demonstration of their efficacy. The initial results from a realistic word processing training exercise brought us up short. We need to go back and re-examine the general principles.

Prediction success comes from strong theories. We generally have only weak theories in cognitive aging (see Salthouse, 1991, chapter 1). Our greatest success in prediction arose primarily from an empirical relation between young and old response time. There are no deep models available that yield the parameter for that relation from simpler principles (such as, for instance, measured differences in neural conduction times, or at a more fundamental levels of neural functioning, age-related declines in calcium ion pump efficiency, or quantity and quality of cell vesicles releasing neurotransmitters).

We can foresee two paths to progress. The first is to continue on our present path, which consists primarily of measurement of age differences across a broad range of tasks using limited sets of manipulated factors to derive empirical predictions about performance. The analytical technique adopted is either an ANOVA or a multivariate regression model of cognitive aging, with dependent variables being predicted from experimental factors. Unfortunately, the hypothesis-testing mind set of most researchers leads them to believe that the most important generalization taken from a study is whether a factor is significant or not. We think that attending to the size of the effect (e.g., by examining the regression equation parameters, or the mean differences in ANOVA) rather than solely to its significance may be quite important for deciding what factors to pursue in future studies. We don't mean to disparage normal science in cognitive aging. Hunting for critical parameters parallels the state that many sciences faced early in their existence, for instance, astronomy when compiling reliable measurements about the positions and movements of the planets and stars. We do want to encourage people to use these parameters to build predictive models.

The second path to progress is to derive strong theories about performance differences using mathematical and computer simulation models (e.g., Kieras & Polson, 1985; Richman, Staszewski, & Simon, 1995). Needless to say, reliable measurements are a necessary condition for this path, but obviously not a sufficient one. It will take a great deal of effort to formalize the learning of a commercial word processor by translating this process into production system models. Perhaps large-scale simulation architectures such as SOAR (e.g., Newell, 1990) can be tried. One challenge is that modern commercial word processors are very complex; for example, the Word for Windows 6.0 word processor includes over 500 commands. Modeling performance would require very detailed task analyses, which might take so much time that the word processor would be obsolete by the time that the research was completed.

We also believe that getting feedback on our theories from occasional forays into applied research is a necessary step on either road to progress. We can all benefit from attempting to scale up our favorite laboratory effects, and discovering the inevitable mismatches between lab-generated theory and applied data. Such failures can spur us on to identify missing factors and to propose more inclusive theories about cognitive aging.

ACKNOWLEDGMENTS

This work was supported by grants from the Natural Sciences and Engineering Research Council of Canada, NSERC A0790, and by the Canadian Aging Research Network (CARNET), one of 15 Networks of Centres of Excellence supported by the Government of Canada.

REFERENCES

Anderson, J. R. (1974). Retrieval of propositional information from long-term memory. *Cognitive Psychology, 6,* 451–474.

Antin, J. F. (1988). An empirical comparison of menu selection, command entry and combined modes of computer interaction. *Behaviour and Information Technology, 7,* 173–182.

Bovair, S., Kieras, D. E., & Polson, P. G. (1990). The acquisition and performance of text-editing skill: A cognitive complexity analysis. *Human-Computer Interaction, 5,* 1–48.

Bieman-Copland, S., & Charness, N. (1994). Memory knowledge and memory monitoring in adulthood. *Psychology and Aging, 9,* 287–302.

Brinley, J. F. (1965). Cognitive sets, speed and accuracy of performance in the elderly. In A. T. Welford & J. E. Birren (Eds.), *Behavior, aging and the nervous system* (pp. 114–149). Springfield, IL: Charles C. Thomas.

Camp, C. J., Foss, J. W., Stevens, A. B., Reichard, C. C., McKitrick, L. A., & O'Hanlan, A. M. (1993). Memory training in normal and demented elderly populations: the E-I-E-I-O model. *Experimental Aging Research, 19,* 277–290.

Card, S. K., Moran, T. P., & Newell, A. (1980). Computer text-editing: An information-processing analysis of a routine cognitive skill. *Cognitive Psychology, 12,* 32–74.

Card, S. K., Moran, T. P., & Newell, A. (1983). *The psychology of human-computer interaction.* Hillsdale, NJ: Lawrence Erlbaum Associates.

Carroll, J. M., & Carrithers, C. (1984). Blocking learner error states in a training-wheels system. *Human Factors, 26,* 377–389.

Cerella, J. (1990). Aging and information-processing rate. In J. E. Birren & K. W. Schaie (Eds.), *Handbook of the psychology of aging* (3rd ed., pp. 201–221). San Diego: Academic Press.

Cerella, J., Poon, L. W., & Williams, D. M. (1980). Age and the complexity hypothesis. In L. W. Poon (Ed.), *Aging in the 1980s. Psychological issues* (pp. 332–340). Washington, DC: American Psychological Association.

Charness, N., & Bosman, E. A. (1995). Compensation through environmental modification. In R. A. Dixon & L. Bäckman (Eds.), *Compensating for psychological deficits and declines: Managing losses and promoting gains* (pp. 147–168). Mahwah, NJ: Lawrence Erlbaum Associates.

Charness, N., Kelley, C. L., Bosman, E. A., & Mottram, M. (in preparation). *Training novice adults in word processing: Effects of age and interface.*

Craik, F. I. M. (1986). A functional account of age differences in memory. In F. Klix & H. Hagendorf (Eds.), *Human memory and cognitive capabilities: Mechanisms and performances* (pp. 409–422). Amsterdam: North-Holland.

Craik, F. I. M., & Jennings, J. M. (1992). Human memory. In F. I. M. Craik & T. A. Salthouse (Eds.), *The handbook of aging and cognition* (pp. 51–110). Hillsdale, NJ: Lawrence Erlbaum Associates.

Cramer, M. (1994). *Effects of structure, other mnemonics and descriptive text on command language usability.* Doctoral dissertation, Computer Science Department, University of Waterloo, Ontario, Canada.

Cramer, M., Charness, N., Tompa, F., & Bennett, G. (1994). The influence of structure and other mnemonics on command language usability. In R. Oppermann, S. Bagnara, & D. Benyon (Eds.), Human–computer interaction: From individuals to groups in word, leisure and everyday life. *Conference Proceedings from the ECCE7 Seventh*

European Conference on Cognitive Ergonomics. GMD-Studien Nr. 233 Gesellschaft fur Mathematik und Dataverarbeitung mbH D-53754 Sankt Augustin (ISBN 3-88457-233-4).

Davies, S. P., Lambert, A. J., & Findlay, J. M. (1989). The effects of the availability of menu information during command learning in a word processing application. *Behaviour and Information Technology, 8,* 135–144.

Hale, S., & Myerson, J. (1995). Fifty years older, fifty percent slower? Meta-analytic regression models and semantic context effects. *Aging and Cognition, 2,* 132–145.

Hauptmann, A. G., & Green, B. F. (1983). A comparison of command, menu-selection and natural-language computer programs. *Behaviour and Information Technology, 2,* 163–178.

Hultsch, D. F., & Dixon, R. A. (1990). Memory and learning and aging. In J. E. Birren & K. W. Schaie (Eds.), *Handbook of the psychology of aging* (3rd ed., pp. 258—274). San Diego: Academic Press.

Kelley, C. L., & Charness, N. (1995). Issues in training older adults to use computers. *Behaviour and Information Technology, 14*(2), 107–120.

Kerlinger, F. N. (1973). *Foundations of behavioral research.* New York: Holt, Rinehart & Winston.

Kieras, D. E., & Polson, P. G. (1985). An approach to the formal analysis of user complexity. *International Journal of Man-Machine Studies, 22,* 365–394.

Meyerson, J., Hale, S., Wagstaff, D., Poon, L. W., & Smith, G. A. (1990). The information-loss model: A mathematical theory of age-related cognitive slowing. *Psychological Review, 97,* 475–487.

Miller, G. A. (1956). The magical number seven, plus or minus two: Some limits on our capacity for processing information. *Psychological Review, 63,* 81–97.

Moeser, S. D. (1979). The role of experimental design in investigations of the fan effect. *Journal of Experimental Psychology: Human Learning and Memory, 5,* 125–134.

Murphy, M. D., Sanders, R. E., Gabriesheski, A. S., & Schmitt, F. A. (1981). Metamemory in the aged. *Journal of Gerontology, 36,* 185–193.

Myers, J. L., O'Brien, E. J., Balota, D. A., & Toyofuku, M. L. (1984). Memory search with interference: The role of integration. *Cognitive Psychology, 16,* 217–242.

Newell, A. (1990). *Unified theories of cognition.* Cambridge, MA: Harvard University Press.

Olson, P. L., & Sivak, M. (1986). Perception-response time to unexpected roadway hazards. *Human Factors, 28,* 91–96.

Payne, S. J., & Green, T. R. G. (1986). Task action grammars: A model of the mental representation of task languages. *Human Computer Interaction, 2,* 93–134.

Radvansky, G. A., & Zacks, R. T. (1991). Mental models and the fan effect. *Journal of Experimental Psychology: Human Learning and Memory, 17,* 940–953.

Richman, H. B., Staszewski, J. J., & Simon, H. A. (1995). Simulation of expert memory using EPAM IV. *Psychological Review, 102,* 305–330.

Salthouse, T. A. (1991). *Theoretical perspectives on cognitive aging.* Hillsdale, NJ: Lawrence Erlbaum Associates.

Sengupta, K., & Te'eni, D. (1991). Direct manipulation and command language interfaces: A comparison of users' mental models. In H.-J. Bullinger (Ed.), *Human aspects in computing: Design and use of interactive systems and work with terminals* (pp. 429–434). North Holland: Elsevier Science.

Simon, H. A. (1974). How big is a chunk? *Science, 183,* 482–488.

Tombaugh, J. W., Paynter, B., & Dillon, R. F. (1989). Command and graphic interfaces: User performance and satisfaction. In G. Salvendy & M. J. Smith (Eds.), *Designing and using human-computer interfaces and knowledge based systems* (pp. 369–375). North Holland: Elsevier Science.

Whiteside, J., Jones, S., Levy, P. S., & Wixon, D. (1985). User performance with command, menu, and iconic interfaces. In L. Borman & B. Curtis (Eds.), *Proceedings of the ACM / SIGChi Conference on Human Factors in Computing*. North-Holland: Elsevier Science.

Wolf, C. G. (1992). A comparative study of gestural, keyboard, and mouse interfaces. *Behaviour and Information Technology, 11,* 13–23.

CHAPTER 12

Instructional Design for Older Computer Users: The Influence of Cognitive Factors

Roger W. Morrell
Institute of Gerontology, University of Michigan

Katharina V. Echt
University of Georgia

Personal computers are an integral part of the 1990s. They are used for a variety of purposes, from controlling inventories to balancing checkbooks to writing book chapters such as this one. Although recent advances in electronic technology have resulted in the widespread use of computers by children and teenagers in educational and recreational settings and by young and middle-aged adults in business environments, it appears that the information highway has bypassed a majority of older adults. Results from several surveys reveal that adults over the age of 65 report using electronic devices less often and have less experience with personal computers than younger adults (Brickfield, 1984; Kerschner & Hart, 1984; Rogers, Walker, Gilbert, Fraser, & Fisk 1994; Schwartz, 1988), thus allowing them fewer opportunities than younger individuals to participate in contemporary culture (Furlong, 1989).

There are several reasons for the discrepancy between younger and older individuals' use of computers. The first reason is that, historically, the cohort of individuals over the age of 65 matured during a time when electronic technology was being conceived. Throughout most of these adults' lives, many of the electronic innovations in communication that are available today had not been realized. It is only within the last decade that electronic technology has become exceedingly pervasive in our society. Thus, opportunities were not available for today's older adults to learn how to utilize many of these types of products. Furthermore, the instructional manuals that accompanied most early personal computers were generally time intensive and/or difficult to understand because the directions often failed to describe adequately how basic procedures could be generalized to more complex operations. In many cases, some degree of programming expertise was also required for operation of the machines. Consequently, instructional sets were geared toward the younger learner in classroom situations.

A second reason older adults may use electronic technology less than younger adults is that computer hardware and software manufacturers have focused their marketing attention primarily on younger populations or on business applications, because these potential clients are assumed to have more uses for this technology (Hoot & Hayslip, 1983). Current advertising for electronic products often omits the older adult population as possible consumers, depicts older adults as unaware of the benefits of electronic devices or opposed to learning how to use them. This is surprising, because there are numerous potential uses of computer technology in the everyday lives of older adults (Ramm & Gianturco, 1973). Results from several studies also do not support the notion that older individuals are more resistant to computer technology than are young adults or that they experience insurmountable amounts of difficulty in using computers or other forms of electronic technology for simple or complex tasks (Ansley & Erber, 1988; Garfein, Schaie, & Willis, 1988; Hartley, Hartley, & Johnson, 1984; Krauss & Hoyer, 1984; McNeely, 1991).

Another possible reason that older adults report using computers and electronic technology less often than younger people is that little systematic applied research has been conducted on how age-related changes in cognition might affect acquisition of the skills needed for older adults to utilize these types of devices. Thus, there is little evidence to guide the development of these products for the older population. There are numerous published studies available on the variables that may influence success in teaching children and young adults to use computer technology, but the body of literature on older adults and computer use is relatively small, as is the range of topics investigated and the types of computer tasks employed. Although much of the current research is methodologically sound and may be used to form a solid basis for further study, most results cannot be extended to practical situations as solutions which may be utilized to enhance the acquisition of computer skills in the older adults.

Therefore, the purpose of this chapter is to suggest not only an extension of this body of research but also an alternative way to design and conduct studies on this topic. First, the past research on computers and older adults is examined with careful attention directed toward the training studies that have been conducted. We suggest that researchers may have been premature in comparing training techniques (such as individual or paired learning conditions), as the current focus of this type of research is on how to present instructional material and not on the material itself. We recommend that the instructional materials (manuals or tutorial software) must be examined initially in order to determine how aging affects the comprehension and learning process in order to design instructional materials for older adults. Second, because instructional materials for these adults must be designed with their (cognitive) needs in mind, we discuss how basic cognitive research may serve as a basis for the development of training materials and software that are specifically designed to facilitate the acquisition of computer skills in older adults. We focus on the development of instructional materials for computer use as a practical example of how our recommendations may be utilized. Our suggestions may well transfer to other domains where the design of instructional materials for older adults are an issue. Third, we provide two specific examples of how to expand the subject matter that has been traditionally investigated in this area. Finally, it is important to note that although we focus on older adults specifically, it is likely that the suggestions that we provide for instructional design may impact on the design of instructions for individuals of all ages.

PRIOR RESEARCH ON COMPUTERS AND THE ELDERLY

What do we know about older adults and their use of computers? Most research efforts that have focused on the effects of aging on acquiring computer skills have been concentrated in two areas: how attitudes or anxiety affect computer task performance in young and older adults, and how age and training methods affect the acquisition of computer skills. Typically, these cross sectional studies compared computer performance (in terms of error rates and time required to perform computer tasks) or responses to questionnaires on the topic by groups of young adults to performance and responses by groups of older adults. The findings on the effects of attitudes and anxiety on computer performance are briefly reviewed while the results from the studies on the effects of age and training techniques on skill acquisition are outlined in detail in this section of the chapter.

Attitudes and Anxiety

A number of investigations were conducted on how experience may modify older adults' attitudes toward computers, as there is a concern that poor attitudes in older adults toward using computers might hamper training efforts in the workplace (Charness & Bosman, 1992). This research is based on the premise that attitudes are acquired and altered through experience, and this experience can be direct or indirect (McGuire, 1985). The methodology of these studies was based on the rationale that attitudes toward using computers may be changed whenever new information in the form of training sessions about computers is encountered (Jay & Willis, 1992).

In general, the results from these studies suggest that attitudes toward computers may be modified under certain conditions. Danowski and Sacks (1980) reported that favorability in post treatment responses to a short attitude questionnaire was significantly higher than pretreatment responses after a three-week period of computer use by older residents of an urban retirement hotel. The exposure of the older adults to computers for recreation and messaging resulted in increased levels of self-confidence, desire to interact with the computers, and positive feelings toward the extent to which computers can aid older adults, as well as lower levels of loneliness in the elderly sample. Jay and Willis (1992) utilized a multidimensional computer attitude measure to determine the effect of experience on attitudes toward using computers with their sample of well educated older adults. Their findings suggested that a 2-week training program on desktop publishing resulted in attitude change on two attitude dimensions: computer efficacy and comfort. Maintenance of attitude change was established for at least two weeks following training. Zandri and Charness (1989) also noted that training strategy appears to affect attitudes toward computers after four sessions (of approximately 3 hours each) of training on notepad and calendar functions. They suggest that attitudes toward computers were bolstered by the "social support provided by partnering and confidence fostered by a jargon sheet" (Zandri & Charness, 1989, p. 628). Attitude change, however was not reported after a 10-minute computer interaction opportunity (Ansley & Erber, 1988) or following one day of training on a Wordstar program (Czaja, Hammond, Blascovich, & Swede, 1986). In summary, interaction with computers does appear to bring about changes in attitudes toward the use of computers in some instances. Change would appear to be dependent on the amount of exposure to the information (with longer amounts of time producing change), the content of the training (with change associated with material that was interesting and personally relevant to the older adults), and the attitude measure administered (with multidimensional measures being capable of capturing change to a greater extent than unidimensional instruments; Jay & Willis, 1992).

Related research investigated the effects of attitude and anxiety on the performance of computer tasks. These studies are founded on the conjecture that older adults may have less favorable attitudes toward computers than younger adults do, which might ultimately undermine their performance of computer tasks. It has also been surmised that because older adults are less familiar with electronic technology, their level of anxiety might interfere with their acquisition of computer skills during training to a greater degree than younger adults' might. Interestingly, most researchers did not find significant age differences in attitudes toward computers (Ansley & Erber, 1988; Krauss & Hoyer, 1984). Furthermore, several researchers failed to show significant relationships between attitude and computer performance (Czaja et al., 1986; Zandri & Charness, 1989). Similarly, general level of anxiety was not shown to predict correct performance on computer exercises, the number of error types or errors made, the time required to complete either the training manual or the actual exercise, or the number of requests for assistance (Kurzman & Arbuckle, 1994). Findings from work by Charness, Schumann, and Boritz (1992, Experiment 1) also suggest that pretraining anxiety has little influence over the amount of knowledge acquired during training although they did show that computer anxiety generally diminished across training sessions.

Taken together, these findings suggest that the concern of older computers users' performance on computer tasks being affected by negative attitudes and high anxiety is possibly unwarranted, as pretraining attitudes and anxiety were shown to have little effect on skill acquisition and subsequent performance of computer tasks by the older adults. Rather, experience with computers appears to affect attitudes and anxiety levels. It was noted, however, that the volunteers in these studies may have a more positive attitude toward computers, and this may have contributed to the failure to find a relationship between initial attitude and performance which may ultimately reduce the generalizability of these findings (Charness & Bosman, 1992).

Age and Training Method

Several trends in the performance of computer tasks by individuals of different age groups are apparent from the results of computer training studies with young and older adults and related research. Older adults were shown to be slower than younger adults in acquiring computer skills, with speeds ranging from 1.2 or 1.5 to 2.5 times slower than younger adults on word processing tasks (Charness et al., 1992; Elias, Elias, Robbins, & Gage, 1987; Zandri & Charness, 1989, respectively). Older adults also usually make more mistakes and require more assistance than younger adults when performing computer tasks (Charness & Bosman, 1992). Some researchers, however showed minimal age differences in the performance of computer tasks, or no age differences at all (e.g., Hartley et al., 1984, with young and older adults, and Garfein et al., 1988, with middle-aged and older adults) Finally, learners of all ages appear to gain more knowledge when paired with a partner or when they are taught in small groups, compared with being taught through individual instruction (Danowski & Sacks, 1980; Zandri & Charness, 1989). Conclusions from studies on the differential effect of training methods on young and old adults, however, are not as clear.

As noted earlier, older adults may not have had as much access to computer training opportunities as younger adults, which may account for the older adults' reporting less usage of computers than younger individuals report. In order to reduce this gap, a few investigations were conducted on how to teach older adults to use computers. Because it is reasonable to assume that different computer training approaches might be more effective for skill acquisition for different age groups, various training approaches have been manipulated with the hope of isolating the optimal technique that might facilitate skill acquisition in older adults. Gist, Rosen, and Schwoerer (1988) compared the effects of different training techniques (video modeling versus a computer-based tutorial condition) on younger and older workers (defined as age 45 and above) for learning how to use a spreadsheet program. The modeling condition was found to increase performance relative to the tutorial condition for both age groups. Similarly, Czaja et al. (1986) investigated using a standard manual, online instruction, and instructor-based training for teaching older adults to perform text-editing tasks. Although they found that the online instruction was inferior to the other conditions and that the other conditions did not differ, they readily admitted that the computer-based instruction was probably not comparable to the other conditions because (a) it did not simulate real task conditions, (b) it produced a passive learning experience, and (c) it introduced complex functions before introducing more simple functions. Moreover, none of the methods tested by Czaja and her colleagues was considered effective in teaching people word processing.

In related research, Charness et al. (1992, Experiment 2) attempted to control the nature of the training session by manipulating whether the learner was actively (self-paced condition) or passively (fixed-paced condition) involved in a training tutorial on acquiring word processing skills. Findings revealed a significant main effect for training approach with trainees registering average quiz scores of 12.8 in the self-paced condition compared to 10.4 in the fixed-paced condition (Charness et al., 1992, Experiment 2). Finally, two studies examined the effect of advance organizers on the acquisition of computer skills in young and old adults. Although Zandri and Charness (1989) reported an interaction on one dependent variable between training technique and age (learning alone or with a peer, and with and without preliminary information about computers) in their investigation on teaching young and older adults to use keypad and calendar functions, they concluded that the advance organizer did not consistently facilitate performance for older adults because "having the jargon sheet in advance resulted in better performance for individuals but did not make any difference for partners" (Zandri & Charness, 1989, p. 623). In a follow-up study, the use of an advance organizer did not improve performance levels on a word processing quiz for either young or old adults (Charness et al., 1992, Experiment 1).

Finally, one study is available that examined the effect of different types of instructional material on learning how to perform computer tasks in both young and old adutls. Kelley, Charness, Mottram, and Bosman (1994) compared a keystrokes-only condition, in which computer commands were accessed by pressing combinations of keys, and a menus condition for teaching young and older adults to perform word processing tasks. Learners in the menus condition were required to recognize the desired command from a list of possible commands or from groups of pictures that appeared on the screen, which was considered to reduce memory demands by the researchers. All subjects did better when using a menus interface (which was suggested to be similar to a cued recall paradigm). Interestingly, in this study, prior experience was also shown to enable older adults to learn to use new software, with results comparable to those achieved for younger computer users.

In summary, all of these investigations (outlined in Table 12.1) failed to demonstrate an age group by training method interaction, which suggests that none of the training methods can be considered optimal for teaching computer skills to older adults or for learners of any age. These findings do, however provide important clues as to how instructions may be designed to enhance computer skill acquisition in the elderly (and other age groups). More specifically, two groups of researchers reported that one training method produced better computer task performance than another in both young and old adults (i.e., Gist et al., 1988; Kelley et al., 1994) We argue that the reason for these findings is that the "superior" method in some way substantially reduced the cognitive demands of the computer tasks above and beyond the inferior method, thus facilitating performance. For example, in one instance, Gist and colleagues (1988) suggested that the

TABLE 12.1
Computer Training Studies With Young and Old Adults

Authors	*Task*	*Instructional Materials and Results*
Zandri & Charness, 1989	Notepad and calendar, functions	Written, self-paced instructions with cue cards and help sheets available to reduce memory demands in one condition; advance organizer did not consistently facilitate performance for older adults
Charness, Schumann, & Boritz, 1992 Experiment 1	Word processing	Computer-based self-paced instruction with advance organizers provided in one condition; advance organizer did not improve performance levels for either young or old adults
Charness, Schumann, & Boritz, 1992 Experiment 2	Word processing	Computer-based self-paced instruction with active and passive learning opportunities available in two conditions; participants performed better in the self-paced condition relative to fixed-paced condition
Kelley, Charness, Mottram, & Bosman, 1994*	Word Processing	Tutorial manual with Menus condition that required participants to recognize words or pictures to assess commands; Superiority for Menus condition
Gist, Rosen, & Schwoerer, 1988*	Operation of a Spreadsheet program	Computer-based interactive tutorial and a modeling condition which integrated the procedures; Superiority for modeling condition
Czaja et al., 1986	Word Processing	Interactive computer-based, edited manual, and instructor-based instructions: No method considered effective

*Indicates that the superior technique reduced cognitive demands.

reason for better performance associated with the modeling technique compared to tutorial training was that "trainees developed more realistic expectations of what action was required for each step in the program" (Gist et al., 1988, p. 263). In other words, the modeling sequence demonstrated the steps of the procedure. Therefore, a possible alternative explanation for the modeling superiority effect, in cognitive terms, is that the model's demonstration integrated the procedures by showing how the step-by-step instructions were actually performed, which ultimately reduced demands on working memory and thus enhanced performance. In the other study, by Kelley et al. (1994), a menus condition was found to be superior to a keystrokes-only condition. In this instance, the authors likened the superior format to a cued recall paradigm, which is considered by researchers in cognition to reduce memory demands relative to a recall condition.

Theoretically, the provision of environmental support in the form of command menus facilitated performance for both old and young adults (Kelley et al., 1994). Brief cognitive interventions, however, did not facilitate performance, as was shown in the two studies that examined the effects of advance organizers on performance (i.e., Charness et al., 1992, Experiment 1; Zandri & Charness, 1989).

The implications of these findings on the design of instructional materials for teaching computer skills to older adults are threefold. First, from the small amount of data that is available, it is possible to conclude that instructions or training methods that extensively reduce cognitive demands are likely to enhance performance of computer tasks for older adults and subsequently for younger adults. Second, instructions that facilitate performance for older adults are also likely to enhance performance for younger adults (but not vice versa). Therefore, the lack of an age by training method interaction being observed is not such bad news, except that the data do not substantiate the researchers' original hypotheses. One possible reason for the lack of this finding is that the older volunteers in these samples probably have high levels of cognitive functioning; therefore there is little cognitive decline to mediate. The elusive age by training method interaction might surface with a more impaired older group such as a sample of old-old (ages over 75) individuals. Finally, we would argue that certain underlying cognitive mechanisms that have been shown to evidence age-related decrements are likely to be influential in the acquisition of computer skills in older adults: Among these are text comprehension, working memory, spatial ability, and perceptual speed. Therefore, instructions that are designed to reduce demands on these mechanisms may be able to facilitate performance in older (and younger) adults. Each of these factors will be discussed in the next section of this chapter.

INFLUENTIAL COGNITIVE ASPECTS OF AGING

There is a large body of evidence available that documents that most component processes of cognition decline with advanced age. We do not propose to relate exhaustively the findings of the cognitive aging literature in this portion of the chapter. Extensive reviews of systematic research are available elsewhere (i.e., Craik & Salthouse, 1992; Salthouse, 1991), as well as pertinent examples of how age-related declines in cognition may affect functioning in the everyday world (i.e., Park, 1992; Poon, Rubin, & Wilson, 1989). We also agree that age-related changes in vision and audition may impede many types of training efforts with older adults. Therefore, we refer you to Charness and Bosman (1992) for an in-depth elaboration of this topic. Instead, we have chosen to briefly emphasize four underlying cognitive processes (among others) that undergo age-related changes that are likely to be influential in the acquisition of computer skills in older adults: text comprehension, working memory, spatial ability, and perceptual speed.

Text Comprehension

A number of findings suggest that text comprehension may present particular problems with increasing age. This is especially germane to the present topic because the most common method of presenting instructions for using computer hardware or software and most types of electronic technology is in the form of poorly worded pamphlets or large manuals composed of massive amounts of text. The use of such instructional formats may prove to be unsuccessful for the older learner because the majority of results from research that compares young and old adults on measures of immediate comprehension of verbal material consistently shows that older adults are less able to report information from recently presented material than are young adults (Botwinick & Storandt, 1974; Hartley, 1988). This finding appears to be reliable across investigations with written text (Dixon, Hultsch, Simon, & von Eye, 1984) and spoken text (Cohen, 1979) and with comprehension measures based on recall (Gordon & Clark, 1974) or recognition (Gordon, 1975; Taub, 1976). Additionally, in studies for which the primary manipulation has been to determine whether information probed in the comprehension test was either implicit or explicit in the presented material, it was demonstrated that older adults have more difficulty than younger adults with implicit inferences than with explicit inferences (Cohen, 1979; Till & Walsh, 1980; Zacks, Hasher, Doren, Hamm, & Attig, 1987). Furthermore, some findings suggest that older adults are less accurate than young adults at recalling gist information, relative to supporting detail information from text (Dixon, Simon, Nowak, & Hultsch, 1982; Meyer & Rice, 1981).

With respect to teaching older adults to use computers with written instructions, these findings suggest that it is likely that there will be age differences in subsequent tests of skill acquisition and that older adults will be disadvantaged relative to younger adults. It is important, however to recognize that there are probably many more underlying factors associated with the age-related differences expected in acquiring computer skills compared to those responsible for text comprehension in general, as using instructional materials to learn to perform actions is more complicated than just simply recalling or recognizing textual information, as in traditional laboratory studies. There are also probably many contributing variables involved in the age-related deficits in text comprehension that were reported. One viable reason for the observed age differences is that working memory constraints are responsible at least in part for the discrepancies in the comprehension of discourse between young and older adults (Gathercole & Baddeley, 1993).

Working Memory

Baddeley (1986) described working memory as a cognitive system that consists of a central executive (or processor) capable of attention, selection, and manipulation. The central executive is assumed to have a limited amount of processing capacity, some portion of which may be devoted to the short-term storage of information. Other storage demands may be divided to two subsidiary slave systems: the articulatory loop, which is able to maintain verbal information by subvocal rehearsal (verbal working memory), and the visuospatial scratch pad, which performs a similar function through the visualization of spatial material (spatial working memory; Baddeley, 1986). Other researchers suggested that working memory is not a unitary concept and that it is domain-specific (see Daneman & Tardif, 1987, for a detailed discussion). That is, there may be two separate processors (or multiprocessors) for representing and manipulating verbal–symbolic information and spatial information (Daneman & Tardif, 1987). Working memory was also conceptualized as consisting of some type of general-purpose processing resource that is drawn upon by cognitive tasks that require the simultaneous storage of recently presented material and processing of additional information (Salthouse, 1985). Currently, however there is little agreement among researchers on this issue (Salthouse, 1985).

Despite the theoretical debate just outlined, there is general agreement that working memory evidences substantial age-related decrements (Baddeley, 1986; Craik & Jennings, 1993; Hultsch & Dixon, 1990), which could be due to deficits in storage (Foos, 1989; Light, Zelinski, & Moore, 1982), processing (Cohen, 1981; Craik, Morris, & Gick, 1990; Wright, 1981), or both (Foos & Sabol, 1981; Babcock & Salthouse, 1990). Most evidence also indicates that older adults are inordinately affected by increases in task complexity, as it was shown that older adults have exhibited greater impairments of performance than have younger adults when the complexity of both verbal and spatial working memory tasks has increased (Light & Anderson, 1985; Salthouse, Mitchell, Skovronek, & Babcock, 1989; Wright, 1981).

Taken together, these findings have several important implications on older adults' acquiring computer skills. Older adults could be expected to follow simple clear stepwise instructions just about as well as younger adults for the performance of certain types of basic computer tasks. The demands of performing computer tasks, however, may exacerbate any existing problems with working memory exponentially as they strive to increase their computer expertise or as the tasks become more complex. Because of these increased requirements on working memory, older adults would be expected to have greater amounts of trouble performing more complex computer procedures than younger adults.

Spatial Ability

As the complexity of the personal computer has increased, so has the efforts of manufacturers to develop ways to make the machines more user friendly. One solution to the original keyboard driven personal computer is the creation of menu driven products that are operated primarily by mouse procedures. In most recent models of personal computers, software is supplied that requires users to simply click or double-click with their mice on the desired icon, box, or word to perform an intended operation. As more menu driven software packages are introduced that require intricate mouse skills, it is likely that greater amounts of spatial ability must also be utilized.

Charness (1995) noted that a computer mouse operates in a plane that is different from the plane of the computer screen. This aspect may pose particular problems for older adults compared to younger adults, because the consensus from the literature in this area is that spatial abilities increase during adolescence, reach their peak during the second or third decade of life, and decrease steadily thereafter (Salthouse, 1982). In general, increased age was found to be associated with lower levels of performance on tests of spatial visualization ability, tasks requiring the integration of spatial information, and performance tests that require a high degree of working memory operations or ongoing information processing (Salthouse, 1991).

It is important to recognize that older adults do appear to be able to use visual–spatial characteristics because memory performance for such attributes was shown to be well above chance in work by Smith and Park (1990). But higher accuracy for young adults than for older adults was reported in measures of memory for spatial location (e.g., Park, Cherry, Smith, & Lafronza, 1990), and older adults in general do not remember visual–spatial characteristics of presented items as well as younger adults (see Salthouse, 1991, for a discussion). Therefore, some decrements in spatial ability must exist. It is probable, then, that performance on computer procedures will reflect age differencesbecause of the dependence of such tasks on spatial ability. Therefore, younger adults should outperform older adults on these types of tasks.

Perceptual Speed

The slowing of most behavioral activities and mental operations with increased age has been extremely well documented in the aging literature. Older adults generally take more time than younger adults to perform most motor and cognitive tasks. For example, a number of findings have suggested that simple reaction time, which requires the programming of a single movement, can be maintained well into old age, but with more complex movements, older adults may take as long to make a unilateral response as it takes younger individuals to make a bilateral response (see Spriduso & MacRae, 1988). Furthermore, the ability for older adults to program responses may be more sensitive to small changes in response complexity and less consistent than that of younger adults (Light & Anderson, 1989). Age differences have also been evidenced in perceptual speed (the rate at which mental operations are performed) and appear to widen as the complexity of cognitive tasks, which require ever larger amounts of mental processing to perform, increases (Hale, Myerson, & Wagstaff, 1987; Salthouse, 1993).

Perceptual speed in particular, has been conceptualized as a component ability for higher order cognitive processing and was demonstrated to predict performance on a wide variety of cognitive tasks (Park et al., in press). Earles and Coon (1994) showed that perceptual speed may be associated with 70% of the age differences in memory for performed activities. Most important, when statistical control procedures are used to adjust for differences in perceptual speed, age differences in various measures of cognitive functioning (including paired-associate and free recall memory, reasoning, memory for activities, and spatial abilities) are found to be mediated by age differences in speed (Lindenberger, Mayr, & Kliegl, 1993; Salthouse, 1993, 1994). Results from two studies by Salthouse and Babcock (1991) also suggest that age-related differences in processing of very simple operations contributes to the age-related deficits in working memory that have been observed.

Summary

All of these findings suggest that younger adults should acquire computer skills more quickly than older adults and make fewer errors than older adults because of age-related deficits in underlying cognitive mechanisms in the older age group. This prediction appears to be substantiated by the results from the training studies presented in an earlier portion of this chapter that demonstrated in all instances that the older adults took longer and made more errors than the younger adults when performing the computer tasks under investigation. Our intent is to use this discussion as background to propose how findings from the mainstream cognitive aging literature might be applied in practical settings to design instructions that can be used to teach older adults to use computers. We suggest that in some cases, age-related declines in text comprehension, working memory, spatial ability, and perceptual speed might be mediated by the manner in which instructional materials are constructed. Designing instructional materials that take into consideration such age-related declines should subsequently enhance the acquisition of computer skills in older adults and reduce the age-related differences in performance observed.

DESIGNING INSTRUCTIONS FOR OLDER ADULTS

In the preceding section of this chapter we suggested that four underlying cognitive processes that undergo age-related changes might be influential in the acquisition of computer skills in older adults: text comprehension, working memory, spatial ability, and perceptual speed. How can we design instructional materials for teaching older adults to use computers that take into consideration age-related declines in these cognitive factors? To answer this question, we surveyed the cognitive aging literature. We located few applied studies that generally addressed this question and no studies were found that specifically took into account age-related deficits in cognitive factors when designing instructions (or training methods) for teaching older adults how to use computers (with the possible exception of Kelley et al., 1994). Therefore, we are relying on results from work in the fields of educational psychology and instructional technology, primarily concerned with younger adults, to form the basis for two possible solutions that are presented in this section of the chapter. Because instructions for using computers may be presented in two distinctive formats, we suggest that the addition of illustrations to written text may facilitate comprehension for instructions presented in manual form and the addition of animation to instructional software may improve the understandablity of on-line tutorials for older adults. Both of these design components may act to mediate age-related declines in text comprehension, working memory, and spatial abilities. Designing instructions that take speed factors into account will be discussed separately.

The Addition of Illustrations to Text

Learning to use a computer may be considered analogous to learning how to perform a series of procedural tasks. That is, specific steps (keys presses or mouse operations) must be performed in a strict sequential manner for the desired outcome to occur. At a very basic level, a number of single computer operations must be understood to use a computer. Because most instructions for using computers are presented in written form, this comprehension process requires the learner to translate written instructions (in working memory) into representation of one or more physical actions and then to actually perform the physical action(s). For example, to make a word bold in a document, one must select the word, and press COMMAND+B in one type of word processing package. After reading the instructions, the learner must realize that he or she should move the cursor to the word that is to be selected by using the mouse and click the mouse two times at the beginning of the word to select or highlight it. Then the learner must physically reach to the keyboard, locate the COMMAND and "B" keys and then press them simultaneously to change the formatting of the word to bold. This example is a somewhat simple computer task with probably small working memory demands.

Most of us know from experience, however that the actual operation of a personal computer is rarely that simple or easy. Using a personal computer effectively requires that we understand and be able to perform a large number of simple procedures. We must also remember how to perform these simple actions because effective usage demands that we combine a number of simple operations in a strict procedural manner in order to accomplish more complex computer tasks. This may become especially difficult for older adults.

Several researchers suggest that one way to facilitate the comprehension of written information for older adults in an everyday situation is by organizing the material in a standard format (usually in relatively small discrete segments), writing the text in simple language, avoiding negatives and inferences, and writing in the active rather than the passive voice (Hartley, 1994; Morrow, Leirer, & Sheikh, 1988; Park, 1992). Implicit in this set of guidelines is the belief that, by following these directives, the working memory demands of the text would be reduced because text written in this manner would require less organization and integration of the concepts on the part of the reader. Following these suggestions, Morrell, Park, and Poon (1989) compared instructions for taking medication as they were originally presented on a prescription signature from a pharmacy to revised versions of the same material in which the instructions were explicitly stated in a standard format. Their findings demonstrated that both young and old adults understood and remembered more of the information in the revised format than in its original form.

Furthermore, many recent computer applications require users to move a mouse so that the cursor reaches a predetermined destination on the screen for an operation to be successful. Another possible way, in addition to the guidelines above, to reduce the working memory demands of procedural text and demands on spatial ability when using a mouse is to add realistic text-relevant illustrations to the text. Hartley (1994) noted that words are important for conveying ideas that must be treated sequentially (such as following a set of instructions) but that illustrations are useful for conveying visual concepts, spatial concepts, and ideas that have to be considered simultaneously. That is, illustrations may serve to translate or organize and integrate the information included in the written instructions, thus reducing working memory and spatial demands and enhancing comprehension. Illustrations also appear to aid the recall of the textual material that they illustrate (Hartley, 1994).

Because no studies are available that have focused on the effect of illustrations on the performance of procedural computer tasks, we reviewed results from studies with other kinds of tasks of this nature. In all instances the addition of illustrations to written instructions have been shown to be facilitative of performance relative to other instructional formats. For example, pictorial information was shown to improve children's performance on a pyramid construction task relative to an exclusively oral condition (Murphy & Wood, 1981). Similarly, picture prompts were used successfully to train developmentally disabled adolescents on a variety of procedural tasks (Frank, Wacker, Berg, & McMahon, 1985; Wacker & Berg, 1983). Other results with young adults (ages 17–31) have demonstrated that the operation of a mechanical device was most efficient with pictorial-related or pictorial-redundant written instructional formats (Booher, 1975). Furthermore, findings by Kieras and Bovair (1984) revealed that a block diagram of the device model that described the internal mechanisms of a simple control panel was more helpful in aiding learners to understand how the panel worked than simple rote learning or a set of operating procedures for the panel without the pictorial aid. In another more recent study, high school students were supplied with one of six versions of a procedural text (literal written, analogic written, illustrated literal, illustrated analogic, literal written combined with matched illustrations, or analogic written combined with matchedillustrations) that explained how to tie a bowline knot (Hayes & Henk, 1986). Results revealed that illustrations were helpful for both immediate and delayed performance of the task. Research by Stone and Glock (1981) using college students revealed a similar pattern of findings. In their study, the immediate assembly of a model cart was found to be significantly more accurate with illustrated text instructions than with instructions composed of either illustrations or text alone.

Only one study of this type has included a group of older adults. Morrell and Park (1993) provided groups of young adults (aged 18–30) and older adults (aged 60–75) with instruction booklets for building figures of different difficulty out of Lego blocks. The instructions were composed of either text only, illustrations only, or text and illustrations. They hypothesized that adding illustrations to instructional text may lessen age-related performance differences by minimizing processing demands on working memory and spatial ability for older adults. Results indicated that although younger adults outperformed the older adults in all instructional conditions, instructions composed of text and illustrations (as shown in Fig. 12.1) significantly reduced errors in construction for both age groups relative to the other formats. Measures of spatial and verbal working memory and text comprehension ability were also found to account for substantial age-related variance across the different format conditions.

Taken together, the results from this research suggest that the addition of realistic text-relevant illustrations to written procedural instructions for computer usage may be a way to enhance skill acquisition in older adults because the illustrations may act to reduce the processing demands inherent in textual instructions.

The Addition of Animation to On-Line Tutorials

Over the last several years computer hardware and software manufacturers seem to have become aware that many people find learning how to use a computer a difficult process. Probably for this reason, efforts have been made to develop instructional materials that will make their products appear easier to use. One recent advance has been the addition of tutorial software to the system disks provided for setting up the machines that guides new users through basic operations and some of the more complicated procedures. Animated demonstrations are believed to be effective in teaching interface methods (Palmiter,

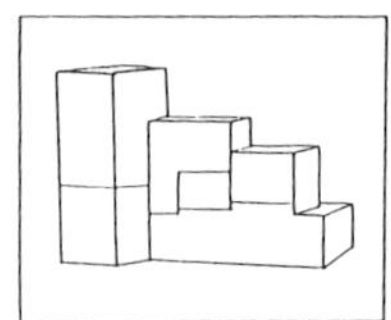

FIGURE D

Step 1.
Using unit D1 as a base, attach unit D2 to the top of unit D1 by lining up the green dot on unit D2 with a green dot on unit D1.
(see Illustration 1)

Step 2.
Attach unit D4 above unit D3 by lining up all of the squares on unit D4 with squares on unit D3. (see Illustration 2)

Step 3.
Attach units D3 and D4 along side units D2 and D1 by lining up the points of three of the arrows on units D3 and D4 with the points of arrows on units D1 and D2.
(see illustration 3)

Step 4.
Attach unit D7 to the top of unit D1 by lining up the diamond on unit D7 with a diamond on unit D1.
(see Illustration 4)

Step 5.
Attach unit D6 to the tops of units D3 and D4 by lining up all of the green dots on unit D6 with green dots on unit D3.
(see Illustration 5)

When you have completed Figure D, place it in the tray in front of you. Turn the page and proceed to the next assembly.

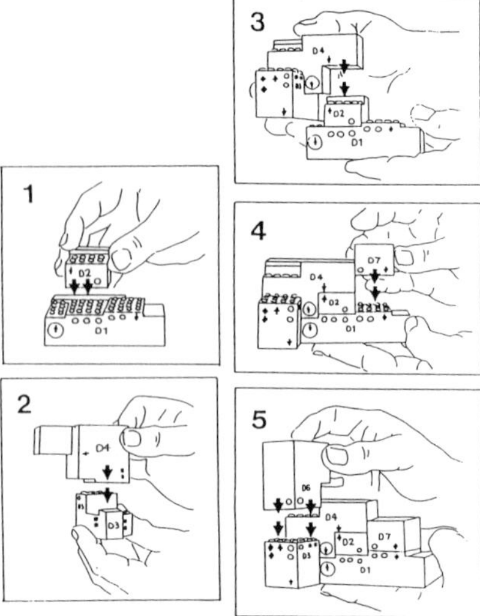

FIG. 12.1 Example of text and illustrated procedural instructions. From "The effects of age, illustrations, and task variables on the performance of procedural assembly tasks," by R. W. Morrell and D. C. Park, 1993, *Psychology and Aging, 8,* pp. 389–399. Copyright © 1993 by the American Psychological Association. Reprinted by permission.

Elkerton, & Baggett, 1991). Computer-based instruction which uses animated demonstrations has also become extremely popular in the classroom for teaching a variety of concepts.

Despite the promise of this instructional format, little empirical evidence has been collected on the use of animated demonstrations in computer-based instruction, and almost none of the of the studies that are available in this area consider the relationship between underlying cognitive mechanisms and the effect of animated demonstrations on learning or skill acquisition. Most of the research is focused on classroom activities other than computer use and some of the results do not favor the use of animation as a presentation variable relative to other instructional formats, possibly because of procedural flaws that may limit the generalizability of the outcomes (Rieber, 1994). Several findings, however suggested that animated material produces superior performance relative to other types of instructions. For example, it was shown that elementary school students who received animated graphic presentations learned more about Newton's laws of motion than students receiving static graphics or no graphics when some level of practice was incorporated in the learning experience (Rieber, 1990). When this study was conducted with a sample of university students, however, no differences were found between the instructional conditions although the young adults' response times on the posttest indicated that those who received the animated presentations took significantly less time to answer the follow-up questions than participants in the other format conditions (Rieber, Boyce, & Assad, 1990). Findings from Park and Gittelman (1992) demonstrated that college students in an animated visual display condition needed significantly fewer trials than those in the static visual display condition for the acquisition of electronic troubleshooting skills. It has also been demonstrated that significant effects for animations emerged when lesson materials on learning a mathematical rule were carefully designed to direct high school students' attention to pertinent details and when students' animated science lesson frames were presented in groups or "chunks" of textual and visual sequences (Baek & Layne,1988; Rieber, 1991, respectively). In related work concerning the effect of motion on procedural learning with young adults, video instructions that include motion were found to be superior relative to still illustrations for performance of procedural tasks (Spangenberg, 1973). Similarly, animated demonstrations presented simultaneously with text were also shown to yield superior skill acquisition and subsequent performance on procedural computer tasks and also on problem solving tasks in young participants when compared to other methods of instruction at immediate testing but not on delayed assessments (Mayer & Anderson, 1991; Mayer & Sims, 1994; Palmiter & Elkerton, 1993).

It was suggested that animated sequences may facilitate learning because they better communicate ideas involving changes over time, which may ultimately reduce the level of abstraction from many temporal concepts, than instructions composed of text alone (Rieber, 1994). It is also possible that when animation is combined with text, the combination of ingredients may act to integrate procedural information above and beyond what can be accomplished by the addition of static graphics to text in computer-based instruction. For example, animated instructions are able to show the complete fluid process of a procedure, whereas the viewer must infer this process from a series of illustrations. In this case, demands on working memory would be reduced to a greater extent with animation than with static illustrations because fewer inferences would be required from the learner.

Furthermore, animated instructions are capable of eliminating many of the constraints of depicting spatial relationships usually encountered by illustrations. Thus, the combination of animation and text may be able to reduce some of the spatial requirements of some types of procedural tasks relative to the combination of illustrations and text. It is possible then, that the use of animated demonstrations might be more efficient for teaching older adults to use computers relative to text-based or illustrated textual instructions. No research of this type has been conducted with older adults at the present to add credence to our argument.

Taking Speed Into Account

How can we design sets of instructions to take into account age-related slowing? Obviously, a manual that contains instructions for performing computer procedures can be read and followed at one's own pace. The bulk of the computer training literature also recommends that self-paced training be utilized to enhance learning for all age groups, and it is important to note that all of the training studies with older adults that were reviewed in this chapter utilized self-paced techniques. Therefore, we will simply recommend a few additional aspects to take into consideration when designing on-line tutorials for older adults. Although there is little research to guide our discussion on this topic, we offer three suggestions. First, there must be sufficient time built into the software for the processing of operations by older adults. We present text screens at an 8- to 10-second rate for older adults in our own laboratory. The presentation time of animations should also be slowed so that older adults will have time to watch the instructional material. Finally, interactive elements and changes between screens included in the software should be programmed more slowly for older adults. One way to accomplish this is to utilize screens and graphics that fade instead of features that abruptly disappear from view. Substantial control of the software should also be given to the learner to allow movement from concept to concept, to start and stop particular sections, or review materials (rewind) previously covered (such as in the form of ''Click Here to Continue'' or ''Click Here to See Again'' screens).

CONCLUSIONS

In this chapter, we have focused on the design of instructional material for computer use by the elderly as a example of how to design instructions to solve a practical problem in the everyday lives of the elderly. In doing so, we have attempted to provide an alternative way of conducting research on aging and computer use with the basic premise of concentrating first on the training materials and then on the training technique. We have suggested that several theoretical cognitive mechanisms might be influential in the acquisition of computer skills in older adults. We argue that instructional materials can be designed to mediate such age-related declines so as to reduce the differences in computer skill acquisition that have been observed between young and older adults. When instructions are designed in this manner it is likely that they may also be beneficial for young adults and other special user populations. Furthermore, this method may be applied to design of instructional materials for other purposes as well. To illustrate our argument, we have provided two specific examples of how to expand the subject matter that has been traditionally investigated in this area. Most importantly, we have tried to demonstrate that it is necessary to integrate findings from a number of different disciplines (education, instructional technology, human factors, and cognitive psychology) in order to isolate efficient training materials and methods for older computer users so that older adults may more readily take advantage of the exciting world of electronic technology that is quickly developing around them.

ACKNOWLEDGMENTS

This chapter was supported by Grant P50 AG11715 from the National Institute on Aging of the National Institutes of Health to Roger W. Morrell as Director of a research project conducted through the Center for Applied Cognitive Research on Aging, one of the Edward R. Roybal Centers for Research in Applied Gerontology. We thank Denise C. Park for her theoretical consultation. We also thank Lisa A. Howard for her assistance in acquiring the reference materials that were used in preparation of this work.

REFERENCES

Ansley, J., & Erber, J. T. (1988). Computer interaction: Effect on attitudes and performance in older adults. *Educational Gerontology*, 14, 107–119.

Babcock, R. L., & Salthouse, T. A. (1990). Effects of increased processing demands on age differences in working memory. *Psychology and Aging*, 5, 421–428.

Baddeley, A. D. (1986). *Working memory*. Oxford: Clarendon.

Baek, Y. K., & Layne, B. H. (1988). Color, graphics, and animation in a computer-assisted learning tutorial lesson. *Journal of Computer-Based Instruction*, 15, 131–135.

Booher, H. R. (1975). Relative comprehensibility of pictorial information and printed words in proceduralized instructions. *Human Factors*, 17, 266–277.

Botwinick, J., & Storandt, M. (1974). *Memory, related functions and age*. Springfield, IL: Charles C. Thomas.

Brickfield, C. F. (1984). Attitudes and perceptions of older people toward technology. In P. K. Robinson, J. Livingston, & J. E. Birren (Eds.), *Aging and technological advances* (pp. 31–38). New York: Plenum.

Charness, N. (1995, August). *Is the mouse mightier than the pen?* Paper presented at the annual meeting of the American Psychological Association, New York, New York.

Charness, N., & Bosman, E. A. (1992). Human factors and aging. In F. I. M. Craik & T. A. Salthouse (Eds.), *Handbook of aging and cognition* (pp. 495–545). Hillsdale, NJ: Lawrence Erlbaum Associates.

Charness, N., Schumann, C., & Boritz, G. (1992). Training older adults in word processing: Effects of age, training technique, and computer anxiety. *International Journal of Technology and Aging, 5*, 79–105.

Cohen, G. (1979). Language comprehension in old age. *Cognitive Psychology, 11*, 412–429.

Cohen, G. (1981). Inferential reasoning in old age. *Cognition, 9*, 59–72.

Craik, F. I. M., & Jennings, J. M. (1992). Human memory. In F. I. M. Craik & T. A. Salthouse (Eds.), *The handbook of aging and cognition* (pp. 51–110). Hillsdale, NJ: Lawrence Erlbaum Associates.

Craik, F. I. M., Morris, R. G., & Gick, M. L. (1990). Adult age differences in working memory. In G. Vallar & ST. Shallice (Eds.), *Neuropsychological impairments of short-term memory* (pp. 247–267). Cambridge, England: Cambridge University Press.

Craik, F. I. M., & Salthouse, T. A. (1992). *Handbook of aging and cognition*. Hillsdale, NJ: Lawrence Erlbaum Associates.

Czaja, S. J., Hammond, K., Blascovich, J. J., & Swede, H. (1986). Learning to use a word-processing system as a function of training strategy. *Behaviour and Information Technology, 5*, 203–216.

Daneman, M., & Tardif, T. (1987). Working memory and reading skill re-examined. In M. Coltheart (Ed.), *Attention and performance XII* (pp. 491–508). HIllsdale, NJ: Lawrence Erlbaum Associates.

Danowski, J. A., & Sacks, W. (1980). Computer communication and the elderly. *Experimental Aging Research, 6*, 125–135.

Dixon, R. A., Hultsch, D. F., Simon, E. W., & von Eye, F. (1984). Verbal ability and text structure effects of adult age differences in text recall. *Journal of Verbal Learning and Verbal Behavior, 23*, 569–578.

Dixon, R. A., Simon, E., W., Nowak, C. A., & Hultsch, D. F. (1982). Text recall in adulthood as a function of level of information, input modality, and delay interval. *Journal of Gerontology, 37*, 358–364.

Earles, J. L., & Coon, V. E. (1994). Adult age differences in long-term memory for performed activities. *Journal of Gerontology: Psychological Sciences, 49*, 32–34.

Elias, P. K., Elias, M. F., Robbins, M. A., & Gage, P. (1987). Acquisition of word-processing skills by younger, middle-age, and older adults. *Psychology and Aging, 2*, 340–348.

Foos, P. W., & Sabol, M. A. (1981). The role of memory in the construction of linear orderings. *Memory & Cognition, 9*, 371–377.

Foos, P. W. (1989). Adult age differences in working memory. *Psychology and Aging, 4*, 269–275.

Frank, A. R., Wacker, D. P., Berg, W. K., & McMahon, C. M. (1985). Teaching selected microprocessor skills to retarded students via picture prompts. *Journal of Applied Behavior Analysis, 18*, 179–185.

Furlong, M. S. (1989). An electronic community for older adults: The SeniorNet network. *Journal of Communication, 39*, 145–153.

Garfein, A. J., Schaie, K. W., & Willis, S. L. (1988). Microcomputer proficiency in later-middle-aged and older adults: Teaching old dogs new tricks. *Social Behaviour, 3*, 131–148.

Gathercole, S. E., & Baddeley, A. D. (1993). *Working memory and language*. Hillsdale, NJ: Lawrence Erlbaum Associates.

Gist, M., Rosen, B., & Schwoerer, C. (1988). The influence of training method and trainee age on the acquisition of computer skills. *Personnel Psychology, 41*, 255–265.

Gordon, S. K. (1975). Organization and recall of related sentences by elderly and young adults. *Experimental Aging Research, 1*, 71–80.

Gordon, S. K., & Clark, W. C. (1974). Application of signal detection theory to prose recall and recognition in elderly and young adults. *Journal of Gerontology, 29*, 64–72.

Hale, S., Myerson, J., & Wagstaff, D. (1987). General slowing of nonverbal information processing: Evidence for a power law. *Journal of Gerontology, 42*, 131–136.

Hartley, J. (1994). *Designing instructional text.* East Brunswick, NJ: Nichols Publishing Company.

Hartley, J. T. (1988). Aging and individual differences in discourse memory. In L. L. Light and D. M. Burke, (Eds.), *Language, memory and aging* (pp. 36–57). New York: Cambridge University Press.

Hartley, A. A., Hartley, J. T., & Johnson, S. A. (1984). The older adult as computer user. In P. K. Robinson, J. Livingston, & J. E. Birren (Eds.), *Aging and technological advances* (pp. 347–348). New York: Plenum.

Hayes, D. A., & Henk, W. A. (1986). Understanding and remembering complex prose augmented by analogic and pictorial illustrations. *Journal of Reading Behavior, 18*, 63–78.

Hoot, J. L., & Hayslip, B. (1983). Microcomputers and the elderly: New directions for self-sufficiency and life-long learning. *Educational Gerontology, 9*, 493–499.

Hultsch, D. F., & Dixon, R. A. (1990). Learning and memory in aging. In J. E. Birren & K. W. Schaie (Eds.), *Handbook of the psychology of aging* (pp. 259–274). San Diego, CA: Academic Press.

Jay, G. M., & Willis, S. L. (1992). Influence of direct computer experience on older adults' attitudes toward computers. *Journal of Gerontology: Psychological Sciences, 47*, 250–257.

Kelley, C. L., Charness, N., Mottram, M., & Bosman, E. (1994, April). *The effects of cognitive aging and prior computer experience on learning to use a word processor.* Paper presented at the Cognitive Aging Conference, Atlanta, GA.

Kerschner, P. A., & Hart, K. C. (1984). The aged user and technology. In R. E. Dunkle, M. R. Haug, & M. Rosenberg (Eds.), *Communications technology and the elderly: Issues and forecasts* (pp. 135–144). New York: Springer.

Kieras, D. E., & Bovair, S. (1984). The role of a mental model in learning to operate a device. *Cognitive Science, 8*, 255–273.

Krauss, I. K., & Hoyer, W. J. (1984). Technology and the older person: age, sex and experience as moderators of attitudes towards computers. In P. K. Robinson, J. Livingston, & J. E. Birren (Eds.), *Aging and technological advances* (pp. 349–350). New York: Plenum.

Kurzman D., & Arbuckle, T. (1994, April). *Computers and older adults: Does anxiety have an effect on performance?* Paper presented at the Cognitive Aging Conference, Atlanta, GA.

Light, L. L., & Anderson, P. A. (1985). Working memory capacity, age, and memory for discourse. *Journal of Gerontoloty, 40*, 737–747.

Light L. L., Zelinski, E. M., & Moore, M. (1982). Adult age differences in reasoning from new information. *Journal of Experimental Psychology: Learning, Memory, and Cognition, 10*, 46–60.

Lindenberger, U., Mayr, U., & Kliegl, R. (1993). Speed and intelligence in old age. *Psychology and Aging, 8*, 207–220.

Mayer, R. E., & Anderson, R. B. (1994). The instructive animation: Helping students build connections between words and pictures in multimedia learning. *Journal of Educational Psychology, 84*, 444–452.

Mayer, R. E., & Sims, V. K. (1994). For whom is a picture worth a thousand words? Extensions of a dual-coding theory of multimedia learning. *Journal of Educational*

Psychology, 86, 389–401.

McGuire, W. J. (1985). Attitudes and attitude change. In G. Lindzey & E. Aronson (Eds.), *Handbook of social psychology* (Vol. III, pp. 131–176). New York: Addison-Wesley.

McNeely, E. (1991). Computer-assisted instruction and the older-adult learner. *Educational Gerontology, 17*, 229–237.

Meyer, B. J. F., & Rice G. E. (1981). Information recalled from prose by young, middle, and old adult readers. *Experimental Aging Research, 7*, 253–268.

Morrell, R. W., & Park, D. C. (1993). The effects of age, illustrations, and task variables on the performance of procedural assembly tasks. *Psychology and Aging, 8*, 389–399.

Morrell, R. W., Park, D. C., & Poon, L. W. (1989). Quality of instructions on prescription drug labels: Effects on memory and comprehension in young and old adults. *The Gerontologist, 29*, 345–354.

Morrow, D., Leirer, V., & Sheikh, J. (1988). Adherence and medication instructions: Review and recommendations. *Journal of the American Geriatric Society, 36*, 1147–1160.

Murphy, C. M., & Wood, D. J. (1981). *Journal of Experimental Child Psychology, 32*, 279–297.

Palmiter, S., & Elkerton, J. (1993). Animated demonstrations for learning procedural computer-based tasks. *Human–Computer Interaction, 8*, 193–216.

Palmiter, S., Elkerton, J., & Baggett, P. (1991). Animated demonstrations vs written instructions for learning procedural tasks: A preliminary investigation. *International Journal of Man-Machine Studies, 34*, 687–701.

Park, D. C. (1992). Applied cognitive aging research. In F. I. M. Craik & T. A. Salthouse (Eds.), *Handbook of aging and cognition* (pp. 449–494). Hillsdale, NJ: Lawrence Erlbaum Associates.

Park, D. C., Cherry, K. E., Smith, A. D., & Lafronza, V. (1990). Effects of distinctive context on memory for objects and their locations in young and older adults. *Psychology and Aging, 5*, 250–255.

Park, O., & Gittelman, S. S. (1992). Selective use of animation and feedback in computer-based instruction. *Educational Technology Research and Development, 40*, 27–38.

Park, D. C., Smith, A. D., Lautenschlager, G. L., Earles, J., Frieske, D. A., Zwahr, M. D., & Gaines, C. (in press). The contributions of speed, working memory, and inhibitory function to long-term memory performance across the life span. *Psychology and Aging*.

Poon, L. W., Rubin, D. C., & Wilson, B. A. (1989). *Everyday cognition in adulthood and late life*. New York: Cambridge University Press.

Ramm, D., & Gianturco, D. (1973). Computers and technology: Aiding tomorrow's aged. *Gerontologist, 13*, 322–325.

Rieber, L. P. (1990). Using animation in sceince instruction with young children. *Journal of Educational Psychology, 82*, 135–140.

Rieber, L. P. (1991). Effects of visual grouping strategies of computer-animated presentations on selective attention in sceince. *Educational Technology Research and Development, 39*, 5–15.

Rieber, L. P. (1994). *Computers, graphics, and learning*. Madison, WI: Brown & Benchmark.

Rieber, L. P., Boyce, M., & Assad, C. (1990). The effects of computer animation on adult learning and retrieval tasks. *Journal of Computer-Based Instruction, 17*, 46–52.

Rogers, W. A., Walker, N., Gilbert, D. K., Fraser, E., & Fisk, A. D. (1994, August). *A questionnaire study of automatic teller machine usage by adults of all ages*. Paper presented at the annual meeting of the American Psychological Association, Los Angeles, CA.

Salthouse, T. A. (1982). *Adult cognition: An experimental psychology of human aging.* New York: Springer-Verlag.

Salthouse, T. A. (1985). Speed of behavior and its implications for cognition. In J. E. Birren, & K. W. Schaie (Eds.), *Handbook of the psychology of aging* (pp. 400–426). New York: Van Nostrand Reinhold.

Salthouse, T. A. (1991). *Theoretical perspectives on cognitive aging.* Hillsdale, NJ: Lawrence Erlbaum Associates.

Salthouse, T. A. (1993). Speed mediation of adult age differences in cognition. *Developmental Psychology, 29,* 722–738.

Salthouse, T. A. (1994). The nature of the influence of speed on adult age differences in cognition. *Developmental Psychology, 30,* 240–259.

Salthouse, T. A., & Babcock, R. L. (1991). Decomposing adult age differences in working memory. *Developmental Psychology, 27,* 763–776.

Salthouse, T. A., Mitchell, D. R., Skovronek, E., & Babcock, R. L. (1989). Effects of adult age and working memory on reasoning and spatial abilities. *Developmental Psychology, 26,* 845–854.

Schwartz, J. (1988). The computer market. *American Demographics, 10,* 38–41.

Smith, A. D., & Park, D. C. (1990). Adult age differences in memory for pictures and images. In E. A. Lovelace (Ed.), *Aging and cognition: Mental processes, self-awareness, and interventions* (pp. 69–96). Amsterdam: North Holland.

Spangenberg, R. W. (1973). The motion variable in Procedural Learning. *AV Communication Review, 21,* 419–436.

Spirduso, W. W., & MacRae, P. G. (1988). Motor performance and aging. In J. E. Birren & K. W. Schaie (Eds.), *Handbook of the psychology of aging* (pp. 183–200). New York: Academic.

Stone, D. E., & Glock, M. D. (1981). How do young adults read directions with and without pictures? *Journal of Educational Psychology, 73,* 419–426.

Till, R. W., & Walsh, D. A. (1980). Encoding and retrieval factors in adult memory for implicational sentences. *Journal of Verbal Learning and Verbal Behavior, 19,* 1–16.

Taub, H. A. (1976). Method of presentation of meaningful prose to young and old adults. *Experimental Aging Research, 2,* 469–474.

Wacker, D. P., & Berg, W. K. (1983). Effects of picture prompts on the acquisition of complex vocational tasks by mentally retarded adolescents. *Journal of Applied Behavior Analysis, 16,* 417–433.

Wright, R. W. (1981). Aging, divided attention, and processing capacity. *Journal of Gerontology, 36,* 605–614.

Zacks, R. T., Hasher, L., Doren, B., Hamm, V., & Attig, M. (1987). Encoding and memory of explicit and implicit information. *Journal of Gerontology, 42,* 418–422.

Zandri, E., & Charness, N. (1989). Training older younger adults to use software. *Educational Gerontology, 15,* 615–631.

Author Index

Numbers in *italics* indicate pages with complete bibliographic information.

C

H

S

Subject Index